Outlaw History

Revisionist logic

Editor, The Leader:

While reading T. A. Guillory's latest Reflections (Feb. 19 issue of *The Leader*), I was surprised to discover that Prof. Guillory is a revisionist historian.

Discussing propaganda, the professor writes, "By instinct and teaching my generation knew that if it had to be repeated incessantly, it was a lie."

If Prof. Guillory really means this, then one of the many implications is that he knows that the incessantly repeated claim that the Nazis killed six million Jews is a lie.

So, surprise. Surprise. Prof. Guillory is a "Holocaust revisionist."

Welcome to the club, professor.

L. A. ROLLINS
Port Townsend

THE PORTABLE L.A. ROLLINS

Outlaw History

Introduction by
MICHAEL A. HOFFMAN II

*NINE-BANDED BOOKS +
UNDERWORLD AMUSEMENTS*

ISBN: 978-1-943687-27-5
REV: IV.XX.MMXXII

Outlaw History © 2008 L.A. Rollins
"One Honest Man" © 2022 Michael A. Hoffman II
"Prolegomenon" © 2022 Chip Smith

Designed & typeset by Kevin I. Slaughter
Editorial assistance by Daniel Acheampong

All rights reserved. Any work not mentioned above © copyright their respective authors unless noted. No part of this book may be reproduced or transmitted in any form or by any means without written permission of the publishers.

Thanks to:
MRDA
MARK WEBER
GERMAR RUDOLF
RICHARD WIDMANN

This is the third volume in *The Portable L.A. Rollins* series.
See also:
Lucifer's Lexicon ISBN: 978-1-943687-17-6
The Myth of Natural Rights ISBN: 978-1-943687-18-3

Published by:

Nine-Banded Books
Charleston, WV
WWW.NINEBANDEDBOOKS.COM

Underworld Amusements
Baltimore, MD
WWW.UNDERWORLDAMUSEMENTS.COM

Contents

Prolegomenon...............................vii
    Chip Smith
One Honest Man xxvii
    Michael A. Hoffman II

1 **Essays** 35
    The Holocaust as Sacred Cow 37
    Revising Holocaust Revisionism 60

2 **Book Reviews** 97
    Deifying Dogma 99
    Witness to the Holocaust 114
    A Legacy of Hate............................ 135
    Why the Goyim?............................154
    Elie Wiesel: Messenger to All Humanity........177
    The Fateful Triangle 185
    A Trial on Trial 193
    Yehuda Bauer and the "Polemical and Apologetic Bias" of Jewish Historiography 197
    Azriel Eisenberg Presents: The Greatest Sob Story Ever Told 225
    The Terrible Secret 262

PROLEGOMENON
L.A. ROLLINS AND THE
PARLANCE OF OUR TIMES
Chip Smith

IN *LUCIFER'S LEXICON*, L.A. Rollins defined a "Holocaust Revisionist" as "One who denies that he is a denier." That seemed like a pretty good joke a few decades ago. I'm not sure how it plays in the year 2022.

It's not so much that the proverbial "line between satire and reality" has blurred in the intervening years (although that has happened in spades); what I mean to observe is more simply that the *term* "Holocaust denier," which once functioned as a derisive epithet (and perhaps, more generally, as a shibboleth), is no longer clearly recognizable as any such thing. To quote Walter Drake in *The Big Lebowski*,[1] it is now the "preferred nomenclature, dude." It is preferred by historians and magazine editors, by librarians and content curators and, one imagines, by drywall installers and pedicurists. You

---

1 This text is peppered with *Lebowskiisms*. Happy hunting.

see it in book titles, in course syllabi, in the redirected results spat from search engine algorithms, and if you are a person of unsullied reputation who, as a matter of grim professional necessity, is obliged to acknowledge—and, perforce, *condemn*—the peripheral existence of dissident strains of "pseudohistory" regarding events that occurred in the fog of war eight decades ago, you are reflex-bound to call that shit *denial*.

I may be exaggerating, but only a little. Run a search for "Holocaust revisionism" on Wikipedia and see where you land. It's sort of like if you were called "Boogerbreath" in grade school, and the name stuck with you for the rest of your fucking life. There it is in your obituary: *"Boogerbreath died peacefully, surrounded by family and loved ones...."*

Thus has it come to pass that one cleverly contrapuntal twist of wordplay adorning L.A. Rollins' underground adventures as a word-savvy satirist (or, as he would have it, as an "illustrious lexicographer") has essentially been hijacked by the ruling vocabulary. I mean, I'm pretty sure the noun-referent of a joke needs to, you know, *exist*—and the Holocaust *revisionist* now exists only in the fevered imaginings of, one assumes, Holocaust *deniers*.

The shift is stung with irony, of course, and maybe that's funnier. Mindful of Orwell's dictum to observe when "words and meaning have parted company," Rollins saw what was coming. And like Diogenes in his barrel, he had the good sense to be amused.

We can't all be so sanguine, I know. One treads carefully when there are consequences in play, reputations on the line. The presuppositions and suspicions that have long attended the *wrong* kind of freethinking are now readily leveraged against those who trespass, however delicately, only to find themselves censored, deplatformed, disinvited, excommunicated, imprisoned, or otherwise cast to the outer darkness of the latter-day *homo sacer*. Snitches like to insist that "cancel culture" doesn't exist as they freeze your bank account, and I'm sure there's a better joke. It's a shame L.A. Rollins isn't around to tell it.

TO RECKON WITH THE SPECTER of recrudescent illiberalism that has only gathered in intensity since Rollins bit the dust in 2014, I think it is instructive to dwell a bit further on that word—"denier." How, we might ask, did such a punkass pejorative, a catcall that once exuded the shrill, accusatory arrogance of a schoolyard taunt, come to run riot over our better instincts for dispassionate engagement with a controversial subject? I think we can safely ignore the term's Freudian root rot for present purposes, and I'm neither qualified nor inclined to provide a recondite account of the relevant linguistic evolution. But I have been paying attention over the years, and I think I have a sense of what happened.

In essence, it was about damage control.

In his review of Michael Shermer and Alex Grobman's insufferable book *Denying History* (see p. 99), Rollins noted that, after a long run of being ignored or desultorily dismissed in academic circles, Holocaust revisionists—as they were still sometimes referred to back then—had, for a time, begun to receive a certain measure of begrudging aboveground acknowledgment. He was right about this. You could see it at various subtle turns—perhaps beginning with Noam Chomsky's thickly free-speech-qualified support for Robert Faurisson in the early '80s. But the shift in mood and framing became more pronounced in later years, resounding, *inter alia*, in Christopher Hitchens' full-throated defense of David Irving; in Errol Morris' covertly sympathetic documentary portrait of Fred Leuchter; in narrative-violating media appearances by David Cole and Bradley Smith; in the near trespasses of credentialed historians like Norman Finkelstein and Peter Nozick; and, perhaps most provocatively, in the pronouncements of then reigning Holocaust scholar Raul Hilberg, who, choosing his words with lapidary precision, nevertheless counseled that the arguments presented by revisionists should be studied and engaged. Quoth Hilberg:

> If these people want to speak, let them. It only leads those of us who do research to re-examine what we might have considered as obvious. And that's useful for us. I have quoted Eichmann references that come from a neo-Nazi publishing house. I am not for taboos and I am not for repression.[2]

Such cracks in the Overton window were already becoming apparent around the time Deborah Lipstadt traipsed upon the scene with her hysterically intoned 1993 book, *Denying the Holocaust*. And I believe it was

---

2   Christopher Hitchens, "Hitler's Ghost," *Vanity Fair*, June 1996, p. 74.

the event of *that* book's publication, more than anything else, that knocked the bottom out of the creeping perception that "Holocaust revisionism" might constitute a maybe, possibly, qualifiedly, arguably—god forbid—*semi-legitimate* species of historical inquiry. With such sordid business effectively consigned to ignominy, scholars and public intellectuals began to take the cue. They set about the task of redressing their terminology, rehearsing and amplifying a kind of performative outrage that would ultimately prove effective in other contexts. The elevation of the erstwhile watchword "Holocaust denial" to its present exclusionary status as a singularly hostile signifier referring to nothing less than the *ne plus ultra* of morally repugnant irrationalism and irredeemable wrongthink was the central feature of this realignment. It took a few years to fully latch, but the receipts were in.

Now it's the air we breathe. Now you get to say things like, *I mean, he probably denies slavery too. And 9/11. And I heard he's a flat-Earther, and a Q-cultist. Fucking Nazi! Free speech is one thing, BUT....*

Rinse, blather, repeat.

Listen to yourselves, children. A daisy chain of denying deniers in denial disdains and deflects discussion. That's how it works, and it works insidiously well in a variety of domains downstream. With "Holocaust denial" providing the master template, less virulent variants now include "climate denial" and "science denial," to say nothing of the ever-expanding constellation of ostensibly less threatening crankeries espoused by the distant cousins of deniers—the "truthers." Fact-checkers are summoned from the wings. Wear your mask, vector. *Shut the fuck up, Donny.*

It's best not to think too hard about any of this, but if you can get beyond the quasi-tautological verbal misdirection, the revealed presumption inherent in the word "denier"—and its viral variants and inbred cousins—is that some ordained Truth exists to be protected. Under the weight of a Commandment, questions are scandalous.

The social psychologist Jonathan Haidt has memorably declared,

> The fundamental rule of political analysis from the point of psychology is, follow the sacredness, and around it is a ring of motivated ignorance.[3]

I don't for a moment suspect that the Holocaust bugaboo was on Haidt's mind when he developed this insight (although, who knows?), but the shoe fits. Once you descry the nacreous luster of the sacred in a regnant historical narrative, the ring of motivated ignorance comes into focus. It's manifest in penumbras and emanations, as they say, but it is more crudely insinuated in *words*, both spoken and unspoken. The ring is made of language—and the language is shot through with the precepts of holiness.

In the rarefied theater of organized religion, particularly in its Abrahamic or monotheistic guises, prohibitive injunctions blot the scenery like billboard signage, with Shalt Nots from on High functioning as magic show-stoppers that forbid every next question. Under

---

3   Quoted in, *inter alia*, Rod Dreher, "The Ring of Sacredness," *The American Conservative*, April 15, 2021.

the Manichean dichotomy of the Sacred and the Profane, myriad heresies and blasphemies and idolatrous transgressions are readily subsumed, cataloged, annotated, codified, screenshotted, and duly internalized by the devout under the rubric of sin.

Dislocated from its theological idiom, the old-timey language of Commandment and Judgment (which operates in crucial abeyance to the language of Belief) eventually gets smuggled into our secular vernacular. That's the trick, and there needn't be a trickster.

The subterfuge is often thick enough to conceal what has happened, but sometimes—*this* time—the overlay is thuddingly obvious. It's sort of like when you realize that *Barb Wire* is a winky-wink redneck remake of *Casablanca*. Once you see it, there it is. The language of Belief that serves to protect the story of Genesis from critical scrutiny gets tweaked and transfigured to sentinel a story of Genocide. Commandments are recast, in the parlance of our times, as *problematics*; Judgment takes the form of *shame*, then of *prohibition*. As the sinner repents, the denier *recants*. Doubt that is scandalized in one context is *stigmatized* in another. Belief will be rewarded, no matter.

The overlay is fascinating, really. It's like a palimpsest traced over ancient parchment.

FURTHER REMOVED from Lipstadt's pedagogical interdicta, the game is played in subtler moves. The role of language is less concentrated in overt transposition, being more slyly embedded in suggestive sleights and constantly evolving culture-bound associations. But it remains instrumental in policing thought and guarding the bounds of discourse wherever The Sacred is threatened.

There's a lot of useful groundwork here. One thinks of the deflective mood of military euphemism, where, to tag an oft-repeated example, "dead civilians" become "collateral damage"; or, from a different vantage, we might recall the enticing earwormy drift of a De Beers ad campaign as a textbook exemplar of manipulative association. As a guide for the perplexed in essay form, Orwell's "Politics and the English Language" remains nonpareil, and his fictional elaborations of "Newspeak" and crimethink in *1984* are still acutely relevant. If you have the fortitude for more studious disquisition, I think there's value in reading McCluhan, Foucault, Strauss, Schmitt. Just try not to get carried away.[4]

Too much mud in the water? Try this:

When I say, "Diamonds," you say, "Are forever."

When I say, "Conspiracy," you say, "Theory."

When I say, "Transvestite," you say, "Um, no. I think you mean 'trans*person*'?"

And when I say, "No, it's a different thing," you say, "So, first of all, you're *wrong*. Secondly, this is *not OK*. Where have you been *getting* your information? This is really *problematic* and *aggressive*. I'm, like, *literally shaking*...."

---

4   There's no need to get Sapir–Whorfy about such matters, nor do I mean to indulge any shade of obscurantist, Derrida-sifted, ultra-structuralist, logo(de)centric nihilism, paraquat. My armchair understanding is that linguistic relativism is at least mostly wrong and that deconstructionist theory is, for most purposes, "not even wrong." I don't think that language determines reality or that reality "collapses" in language (er, I mean "text"). And yet, Old Bull Lee wasn't wrong when he said, "language is a virus."

Perhaps I will try to apologize, because I meant no offense. Too late. I've been advised that the HR director would like to have a word with me....

This is where you land.

And when you say, "Six Million"? I'll just take that as a prompt to wax nostalgic about Steve Majors' early TV career.

It's weirder and wilier in the rapid churn of online culture. Within the spectacle of crisis-entranced deep-scroll immediacy, festering enmities get dialed up. Linguistic props that embed judgment or feed suspicion or signal tribal allegiance are adrenalized and weaponized in a complexifying array of key-coded shibbolethic winks and hostile memetic fuckeries. Anything you say, or have ever said, even under a pseudonym ten years ago, may be held against you. There are doxxings and rumors of doxxings, and your past or present "association" with whichever newly mob-branded thought pariah—perhaps for whom you "provided a platform," sinner—is often sufficient to trigger an inquest. And if the agenda-driven shitshow masks a deeper Girardian war of all against all, as some have suggested,[5] the final reckoning doesn't matter when they've got your number. Your arguments will be mocked as quaint. *Muh freedom!* Haven't you seen that *xkcd* cartoon? Look at *The Conspiracy Chart*—there's HOLOCAUST DENIAL in the RED ZONE, right up there with ADRENOCHROME.

---

5   Maybe start with: Geoff Shullenberger, "The Scapegoating Machine," *The New Inquiry*, Nov. 30, 2016.

Check your privilege, freethinker! New information has come to light. You've been warned. At critical mass, a house is divided. Struggle sessions come next, but the conversation was corrupted long ago. Holocaust heresy was the canary in the mine, the acid test that we failed.

WHEN YOU SEARCHED for "Holocaust revisionism" in Wikipedia, I'm guessing that you were directed to the entry for "Holocaust denial." That was your prompt. Once internalized, it mostly serves as a subtle reminder—or, to appropriate a recent coinage, as a "nudge"—that can be crassly yet accurately shorthanded as: *Don't go to the no-no place.* By dint of a perversely reconceptualized and now code-encrypted fake "fact-check," the matter is settled (like "the science"), precluded from rational disputation, expunged from our conceptual reach. And to the extent that the canceled term retains any vestige of its descriptive meaning, this is soon overshadowed by the emotive freight of stigma. A pang of enculturated shame—*crimethink*—soon attends both thought and utterance, as if you're giving yourself away.

The authoritarian impulse now reverberates in a congeries of silly rebranded watchwords—*disinformation*, *misinformation*, *fake news*, *hate speech*, etc.—that function as cerebral hazard signs. But whatever shelf-ready term of opprobrium is deployed, we are left to contend with a culturally ensprawled psycholinguistic hegemon that emboldens the political will to censor ideas and punish dissent. Can't you see the signs? Don't go there. Perish the thought, perish the thinker. There oughta be a law. Look! There *are* laws.

When certain ideas come to be bloated with the odium of taboo and are thus assimilated within the normative precepts of a dominant culture, inflection points are inevitable. That which is forbidden assumes, for some, a contradistinctive radiance, a *counter-allure* of its own. Just as the Sacred is, in a sense, defined by the Profane, and just as dogma tempts the heresiarch, a suppressed discourse seduces the would-be transgressor. *You're not thinking of an elephant, are you? Or a blowjob, naughty girl? What's that ringing in your ears?* Prohibitions cultivate lurid fascination, and if sacrosanctity can be momentarily collapsed in the subversive sting of a punchline, the worry is that some of you won't stop there. Suspicion heightens in such an atmosphere, and satanic clubhouses aren't hard to find. Think of the kid who gets mob-nuked for saying it's wrong to punch a Nazi. What does he do next? Epigones abide.

There will always be numskulls who take the bait. If some people seek personal affirmation in their defiant opposition to the sovran egregore, that's already in the script. It is likewise very easy to understand how and why a person who harbors stereotypical animus toward Jewish people might gravitate toward a body of naughty counter-scholarship that tends, at least according to received opinion, to undermine the perceived interests and beliefs of Jewish people. The attraction is easily characterized as revanchist, malicious, racist, anti-Semitic, maybe even evil. You don't have to look very far to find such creatures in the wild either. They flaunt their hatred in crass slogans, and they have been known to appropriate the "denier" label as a badge of counter-signaling pride. They obstreperously proclaim the Holocaust to be a "Jewish lie," and you get to hate them right back as a matter of decorum.

This much is easy. It washes over us like background static. It goes down smooth as a White Russian. It plays to type.

What is far more difficult, against the prevailing cultural mood, is to conjure a fully formed image of a *different* type of person—one who bears no such animosity but who nevertheless finds value in confronting and critically engaging with the same radioactive literature that comic-book villains approach as bias-confirming catnip. That such a *rara avis* might exist at all, much less that they might be motivated by sound rational instincts—say, by the lure of an intellectual challenge, or out of plain curiosity, or just because something seems *interesting*—is nearly inconceivable to many people. As for the possibility that such a person might arrive at the counterintuitive conclusion that a taboo-enshrouded *no-no* claim could be, in whole or part, *true*? Well that's just unconscionable! You might as well try to explain the louche attraction of early John Waters films to someone who never strays from the Hallmark Channel.

It's easier to believe it's Nazis all the way down. There's comfort in that (*at least it's an ethos*). Consult the flowchart, find your way back. Even if a goblin of diabolical logic compels you to admit to some remote technical possibility that even a being most foul might prove to be correct about some surely trifling matter or another, that dread possibility is easy to mark with an asterisk that refers to "Nazi" in a *mise en abyme* of reassuring recursion. Shouting the magic word "denier" from the rooftops is one way of shoring and guarding this comfort. It works talismanically, and it's soon baked into your synapses as a kind of prideful nescience. A spell.

Yet the spell can be broken, at least at the level of the individual. Given such a fragile edifice, it may take nothing more than the quotidian realization that such people—i.e., those who do not conform to the cosseted fairytale role of demonic Nazis—*do* in fact exist.

I say this with confidence because I know myself to be such a person, and I recall how my youthful interest in revisionism quickened in the growing awareness that other such people—*epistemic peers*, in an important sense—shared my oxygen. People like Bradley Smith, David Cole, Samuel Crowell, and of course our Man of the Hour, L.A. Rollins, were notable to *me* for their lack of agenda-driven guile. Contrary to primed expectation, I found they were saying things that seemed, on first and later impression, quite reasonable—and that were, more tellingly, far out of step with the caricature of rank crackpottery and vile mendacity that had been so loudly advertised.

This realization was at once disarming and enlightening (and perhaps a bit naïve), but it left a lasting impression. There's a valuable reorientation that comes with such an experience—a perturbation of one's polarities, as Robert Anton Wilson might have put it, or an adjustment of one's priors, as the "rats" say. The ring of motivated ignorance is easier to pierce when you can't help but see the writhing mass of humanity inside. And it's always there.

ULTIMATELY, IT'S ENOUGH to say that it doesn't matter. If Adolf Hitler had discovered continental drift, it wouldn't be any less true, and if the Dalai Lama were to espouse the virtues of Breatharianism, you would still be well advised to consult with your physician before renouncing nutrients. It gets more complicated when you contemplate the meaning of Prussian blue stains and Wannsee hermeneutics, but the first-ditch presumption of bad faith is still a rut. We don't approach claims from the privileged perspective of objectivity. Perception matters. Beliefs form and root in the company of others and under the shadow of sacred ideals. The playground is dangerous. Play anyway.

TO EMPHASIZE A POINT that I fear is too easily lost in the frequently Asperger's-inflected drift of revisionist (and indeed, anti-revisionist) rhetorical combat, the "Holocaust" is not conveniently reducible to a "claim." Regardless of how matters of dissident contention are to be assessed, it is more useful and accurate to begin with the understanding that the Holocaust is a meta-historical narrative or a *grand récit*, that broadly refers to the ordeal of suffering and catastrophic devastation visited upon European Jewish communities (and some asterisked others) under the yoke of Nazism both before and during the Second World War. As a memorial account of a fraught historical episode when Bad Things happened to Good People, it remains salient. It is one thing to note that such Bad Things might not have included, say, making Good People into lampshades and soap, but if your next move is to reject the Bad Things narrative in its vaulting and nuanced totality, well, I think that's obtuse. It makes about as much sense as rejecting such other historical signifiers as "Manifest Destiny" or "The Trail of Tears" or "The Enlightenment" or even "The Second World War," since mythic elements and falsehoods are inevitably grafted in the grit and grain of all lofty historiography.

Being aware of the reductive and negationist rhetoric to which some revisionists (along with their detractors) are nevertheless prone, I think it is worth emphasizing that historical revisionism has been substantively focused on investigation, interpretation, and the invariably contentious task of separating fact from fiction. With reference to the Holocaust in its historical register, revisionism involves the study of documents, administrative command chains, propaganda, rumor, jurisprudence, site forensics, demographics, cliometrics, and the critical interrogation of eyewitness testimonies. Insofar as theories are advanced from such recherché entanglements, these typically distill to counter-theses concerning *mens rea*, moral equivalence, and the scale or enormity of wartime atrocities. If you're easily distracted by the vagaries of gaschamberology and sixmillionism, or if you're stuck on the notion that the "truth" of the Holocaust is metaphysically contingent on the belief that The Final Solution encoded and served a warrant for instrumental genocide, I will politely suggest that you take a deep breath and think things through.

SANCTIMONIOUS CAVEATS notwithstanding, if you want to dabble in the "other side of genocide," my suggestion—assuming you've cultivated a rudimentary understanding of the canonical history in outline—is to avoid the acrimonious rabbit holes and drive-by debunkeries online and instead read some books that you won't find on Amazon and that never get mentioned during Banned Books Week. I pretty much lost interest in this stuff long ago, but I remember what made an impression.

As a generalist exposition of the "strong" revisionist thesis as it was formed in the 1970s and has been annotated since, Arthur Butz's *The Hoax of the Twentieth Century: The Case Against the Presumed Extermination of European Jewry* remains an essential touchstone. It's a very dense study, and the prose can be a bit turgid, but persevere and you'll come away with a clearer understanding of some core epistemic and conceptual issues (e.g., the problem of dual interpretation; the disjunction between Holocaust literature and World War II history; dogs that didn't bark; precedents from the history of history; etc.) that animate critical appraisal of the standard history. Maybe start there.

My personal favorite is *The Gas Chamber of Sherlock Holmes: And Other Writings on the Holocaust, Revisionism, and Historical Understanding* by the late Samuel Crowell. I'm surely biased as Crowell's publisher, but if you've been groomed to believe that revisionist discourse is steeped in flat Earth-level flummery, an encounter with this subtly developed "literary analysis" of the role of rumor and sociogenic feedback in forming and codifying a master narrative may come as a bracing shock.

If you're a "systemizer" or "on the spectrum," the best deep-dive introduction to the hyper-empirical dimension of Holocaust revisionism is probably Germar Rudolf's anthology *Dissecting the Holocaust*. It's a humdinger.

Those of a more empathic—or romantic—temperament might do well to start with Bradley Smith's singularly captivating intellectual memoirs, *Confessions of a Holocaust Revisionist* and *Break His Bones: The Private Life of a Holocaust Revisionist*. Smith's seemingly effortless, zen-kissed prose style invites comparison to the best stuff by guys like William Saroyan, Kurt Vonnegut, and Richard Brautigan—and his subject isn't revisionism per se but the personal and interpersonal consequences that attend the open expression of doubt about what trusted others believe. I recommend these books to anyone who'll listen.

If you enjoy courtroom drama, there are some jawdropping moments in Michael A. Hoffman II's *The Great Holocaust Trial: The Landmark Battle for the Right to Doubt the West's Most Sacred Relic*, which provides a polemically intoned but fact-filled account of the early Canadian prosecution and trials of Ernst Zündel for the "crime" of "spreading false news" (i.e., distributing revisionist literature). I also recommend Mark Turley's *From Nuremberg to Nineveh*, a juridically incisive study of the postwar Nazi trials and their broader cultural impact.

If you have a taste for gonzo and gossip, go with David Cole's wild ride, *Republican Party Animal: The "Bad Boy of Holocaust History" Blows the Lid off Hollywood's Secret Right-Wing Underground*. David's been through the wringer and has emerged with the damnedest story. An autodidact with an encyclopedic knowledge of World War II history, he is also a born raconteur—and a very funny man.

And speaking of funny men, you *could* just start *here*—with *this* book, L.A. Rollins' *Outlaw History*. Beyond the curious time-capsule fascination that comes in rediscovering texts that might have remained forever obscured in the musty environs of private libraries, an encounter with Rollins' devil-may-care writings on point—many of which date to the 1980s—is likely to provide contemporary readers with a stealthily illuminating glimpse of the lived-in texture of historical revisionism as a site of freewheeling intellectual adventure. The invitation is evergreen.

L.A. ROLLINS WILL BE remembered as a trenchant satirist and a firebrand critic of precious anarcho-libertarian metaphysics. Writing at the distal margins of the libertarian fringe, he exposed the reification of metaphor (in the case of "natural law") and the deification of dogma (in the case of countless secular orthodoxies), and, like it or not, the same contrarian nous resonates in his heterodox interrogations of sacrosanct historiography.

Cobbling essays and book reviews at the periphery of the memory-holed—and curiously *Californian*—milieu of '80s-era revisionism, Lou's role was essentially that of the house cynic. Choosing his words with scrupulous care, he toed no line and held nothing sacred as he checked quotes and double-checked numbers and examined assertions and dates and sources and sources of sources. A non-partisan freethinker to the core, he was *thorough*; he questioned the claims of established Holocaust scholars *and* revisionists with equal diligence—and, where he saw the opportunity, with equal spleen. He was neither a denier nor an affirmer—nor was he ever more than nominally a "revisionist." He was, in the best forgotten sense of the word, a *skeptic*. He called out bullshit when he saw it, and he saw it where the best people know not to look. "The skeptic's knife cuts in all directions," said our man.

Lou lived his final years on Earth as a whiskey-drunk hermit who seemed, as my co-publisher Kevin Slaughter once put it, to have run out of fucks to give. Without an Internet connection, he was not privy to the new information—either with reference to the full-on marginalization of revisionism or to the morass of neologistic effrontery that had at the time of his death already begun to proliferate in the idiolect of web culture. Alas, his Biercian wit was never brought to bear against such new-fangled terms as "cisgender" or "critical race theory" or "woke" or "MAGA" or "minor-attracted person" or "bussy." Nor did he live to fact-check the newly benighted generation of phony fact-checkers—and wouldn't *that* have been fun? Because, to bring the irony full circle, in view of our present smug-besotten, hyper-politicized, thought-patrolled shitshow-cum-zeitgeist, L.A. Rollins was, in the sense that once mattered, a damn good fact-checker. *Sometimes, there's a man....*

ONE HONEST MAN:
L.A. ROLLINS AND REVISIONISM
Michael A. Hoffman II

For all I know, there may have been gas chambers used for the mass murder of Jews in some of the Nazi camps. But I refuse to believe in such gas chambers merely because some gang of would-be intellectual dictators tries to lay down the law.

—L.A. Rollins

IF YOU COULD HAVE KNOWN LYSANDER SPOONER, you might have a handle on L.A. "Lou" Rollins, the sometime "Holocaust" revisionist and full-time contrarian curmudgeon. I looked upon him as the ideal World War II revisionist because he didn't have a neo-Nazi bone in his body. I met him when he was on the fringe of the Southern California libertarian scene, which ran the gamut from philosopher John Hospers to science-fiction author Philip K. Dick. I stipulate "fringe" because it wasn't exactly a card-carrying movement, and who was or was not a libertarian was one of the several dozen arguments in which this loose confederation of freethinkers engaged during the late '70s and '80s.

As far as this writer can determine, Lou worked for the Institute for Historical Review (IHR) in Torrance, the Los Angeles suburb, from 1983–1986, writing essays and scathing book reviews for the Institute's *Journal* at a time when this writer was serving as assistant director. We might say of him what contemporaries observed of the reviews of Edgar Allan Poe: "He mistook his inkwell for a bottle of prussic acid."[1] Rollins and fellow libertarian-revisionist Bradley Smith reported to this writer at the IHR, and it was my job to edit their assignments and see that they met our publishing deadlines. If that datum renders yours truly a corporate literary cop, perish the thought. There was no riding herd on Rollins or Smith, who were comrades in obstreperous individualism.

I recall one occasion when they were approximately an hour late to the office and I queried Bradley, who did the driving, concerning the delay. "Four red lights in succession", Bradley reported truthfully. Well, not quite. Lou quickly interrupted, index finger planted pedantically in mid-air: "Actually, Bradley, it was three red lights. One was a yellow light that you had time to drive through but chose otherwise." He spoke those words with the scolding didacticism of an Etonian schoolmaster.

That was Rollins: a stickler for detail and a relentless, hair-splitting precision thinker who questioned the smallest details. I was supposed to be his editor but

---

[1] At this juncture, one can hear Poe's sardonic laughter from the grave: prussic acid is otherwise known as hydrogen cyanide, patented and trademarked in the 1920s Germany under the pesticide brand name "Zyklon B," a prophylactic against the potentially fatal typhus louse which infested clothing and bedding in Europe during World War II. It is the alleged killing agent supposedly used in the "gas chambers of the Holocaust."

he taught me a thing or two, including to always modulate a generalization such as "Israelis support their right-wing government" with the qualifier "Almost all Israelis...." It's a basic instruction, but delivered emphatically by Rollins, it has stuck with me throughout my writing life.

Lou execrated the idea of "the sacred." In his review of Azriel Eisenberg's *The Lost Generation: Children in the Holocaust*, he characterized the author as a "Holocaustomaniac." He wrote (page 261),

> reading Eisenberg's "eyewitness" accounts may be a good way for devout Holocaustomaniacs to experience agony and torment. But, being the cold-hearted nitpicker that I am, I wonder if reading them is a good way to find out what really happened to Jewish children under Nazi rule.
>
> ...[the] hearsay account of gassings and cremation at Birkenau is a dilly. For one thing, he said that "Once the gassing process had been completed, the floor of the chamber opened automatically and, the corpses fell into the subterranean chamber...." But Birkenau crematoria IV and V had no subterranean chambers. Crematoria II and III each had two subterranean "chambers," one of which allegedly was a gas chamber, the other allegedly an undressing room. But these two subterranean "chambers" were on the same level, at right angles to each other. There were no subterranean chambers underneath the alleged subterranean gas chambers. So this part of [the] tale just doesn't fit the facts.

> Ambrose Bierce wittily defined "reverence" as 'The spiritual attitude of a man to a god and a dog to a man." But Eisenberg and his "eyewitnesses" are not gods, nor am I a dog, although I am a Gentile. They are merely human beings, as I am. So I see no reason to revere Eisenberg and his "eyewitnesses," no reason to put them on a pedestal, above skepticism, above criticism. As far as I am concerned, the fact that some or all of Eisenberg's witnesses suffered at the hands of the Nazis does not give them a license to lie.

Euphemisms and sugarcoating played no part in Lou's "Luciferian" libertarian lexicon.

More than ever, we value and appreciate anti-censorship libertarians in this hyper-Orwellian age in which the free-speech ethics of the sixties, sanctimoniously preached by the young to their unhip, aging parents' generation, have gone up in smoke now that the hipster Left is largely in our culture's driver's seat. So it's a comfort to know that almost every up-and-coming libertarian will defend your right (or that of your blog, website, Twitter, or Facebook account) to be seen and heard unhindered. This writer can never subscribe to libertarianism, however, since that ideology generally supports buccaneer capitalism. Values like the indigenous people of the land, and the land itself, are rated by many libertarians a distant second to "free enterprise" and that strange deity they term "The Market."

But Lou was not one of that species. Following his stint as a writer for the Institute for Historical Review, he served as manuscript editor at Loompanics Unlimited, the venerable "outlaw" bookseller and publisher based in Port Townsend, Washington. There he brought my book *They Were White and They Were Slaves*, to the attention of owner Mike Hoy, recommending it as a history volume Hoy ought to distribute. Lou pointed to my sections on onerous child labor during the Industrial Revolution and the contempt with which British capitalists looked upon the white kids who slaved from ages four, five, and six in mines and factories, dawn to dusk. Like Lou, Hoy was an independent with libertarian instincts that were unclassifiable. *They Were White and They Were Slaves* became a steady seller for the company as the duo elevated Loompanics into a national powerhouse of forbidden literature that has seldom been equaled.

When Loompanics closed, to the best of my knowledge Lou failed to find another steady, decent-paying job. Holocaust revisionism was a part-time pursuit that had paid meagre sums. Meanwhile, his stream of churlish letters to the local weekly newspaper in Port Townsend, as well as the *Seattle Times*,[2] became renowned for their learned drollery. His indefatigable stream of missives were the subject of a story in the *Port Townsend Jefferson County Leader* of June 18, 1997, titled "The Man Behind the Letters." Reading the article by staff writer Miranda Bryant, who clearly warmed to her subject, the newspaper's report comes across as fair, but Lou cautioned, "Don't believe everything you read." Nonetheless, he didn't object to our reprinting Bryant's

---

[2] www.seattletimes.com/opinion/this-tells-volumes-about-the-zoo-managements-sincerity/

piece in our *Revisionist History* newsletter.

Bryant wrote,

> The self-admitted holocaust revisionist has stirred up more than his share of controversy within the *Leader*'s widely read letters-to-the-editor section. Fearless in his constant questioning of the "truth" about the genocidal killing of Jews by Nazis, he is the nemesis of many here.... Anyone who has read his letters knows one must choose words carefully when addressing him. Like a tax evader always looking for a loophole, the wordsmith reads more meaning than most into words and their placement.
>
> ...One is compelled to ask permission before affixing the label of holocaust revisionist to him. "Yeah, that's fair enough," he answers. "There are some people who call themselves that who are much more extreme and much more dogmatic than I am," Rollins begins. "They will say things like, 'There were no gas chambers that the Nazis used to exterminate people.' I don't say that because I don't know for certain."
>
> His mission, if he has one, is not to deny the holocaust, but to set the historical record about it "straight." He is simply questioning what he refers to as "the dogma" and asking for proof of the number killed... a reasoning that wouldn't be an issue itself if it were not for the

subject's "taboo," Rollins says. Self-pride in his skeptical nature is apparent... Rollins' humor has always been part of his work. However, that humor isn't likely understood or appreciated by most....

Lou eventually vacated the reasonably tolerant enclave of Port Townsend. In middle age, he settled into penury without complaint. After Loompanics, and a stint residing in his mother's backyard shed, he moved to the Midwest, where he generated a stream of public as well as private epistolary invective and erudition, promising this writer, for example, a comeuppance in his next book, founded on his perception that my Fortean[3] theses concerning "twilight language" memes and serial occult killers were flimsy, if not outright buncombe. It seems he reasoned that if revisionists like me were giving it to Zionists and "Holocaust saints and martyrs," they ought to be able to take it too.

Lou was the Ambrose Bierce of our time and difficult to dislike. His generosity (which he would have denied) was evident in the reams of handwritten letters he mailed on a nearly weekly basis to numerous correspondents, brimming with lengthy quotes from recondite material that was often of value to my research.

Toward the end of his life, he spent more time criticizing revisionists than the alleged homicidal gas chambers of Auschwitz, not because he had recanted his initial doubts but rather due to the fact that he believed

---

3   "Fortean," i.e. inspired by the writings of Charles Hoy Fort (1874–1932).

he had glimpsed a new idol being made of revisionism itself, and in him, the iconoclastic instinct was supreme.

Those who had the privilege of knowing him experienced a relationship with a fellow for whom the Greek Cynic Diogenes spent his life searching. Broke, with few close friends, yet intractably rude and obstinate to the end, L.A. Rollins was a gifted, quintessentially American thinker, and one honest man.

> Michael A. Hoffman II is a writer and the founding director of Independent History and Research.

L.A. Rollins and Michael A. Hoffman II
Port Townsend, circa 1997

Essays

There's been a lot of ... people walkin' around my ranch lately, talkin' about some hollow-cast. What's a hollow-cast? Is it like a spin-cast or a dry-cast? They don't look like fishin' types, and there ain't no water here anyhow.

—Letter to *National Lampoon*

Men become civilized, not in proportion to their willingness to believe, but in proportion to their readiness to doubt.

—H.L. Mencken

That one man or ten thousand or ten million men find a dogma acceptable does not argue for its soundness.

—David Starr Jordan

Dogma demands authority, rather than intelligent thought, as the source of opinion; it requires persecution of heretics and hostility to unbelievers; it asks of its disciples that they should inhibit natural kindness in favor of systematic hatred.

—Bertrand Russell

THE HOLOCAUST AS SACRED COW

EVERYBODY KNOWS ABOUT THE HOLOCAUST. In barest essentials, the Nazi State, on Adolf Hitler's orders, planned and attempted to kill all European Jews, and succeeded in killing six million of them, mainly in gas chambers in such death camps as Auschwitz and Treblinka. Everybody knows this.

A few years ago, I got into a discussion with the brother of a friend of mine. He had recently returned from Israel, where he had been living for a few years. (He is not Jewish but had gone to Israel with his Israeli Jewish wife.) Eventually, we ended up debating the merits of the Arab-Israeli conflict, and, in the course of that debate, he brought up the six million Jews who, so the familiar story goes, were killed by the Nazis. Since a few years before this I had become a skeptic regarding the Holocaust in general and the six million Jewish victims in particular, I asked him if he was sure that the Nazis had killed six million Jews. He then told me of a visit he had made to Yad Vashem, Israel's official memorial to the "martyrs and heroes" of the Holocaust. He told me that he had seen the names of the victims of the Nazis. I asked if he had counted the names. Of course, he had not, but he informed me that he didn't need to count the names to know that there were six million of them.

This fellow's remarkable ability to determine the number of names at Yad Vashem without counting becomes even more remarkable if one knows that, in fact, Yad Vashem has thus far managed to collect only about three million names of supposed Jewish victims of the Nazis. According to *Los Angeles Times* staff writer Dial Torgerson, in a 25 October 1980 story from Jerusalem, "In the somber Hall of Names at Yad Vashem, Israel's memorial to the victims of the Holocaust, are the names of nearly 3 million Jews who died in the Nazi death camps of the 1930s and '40s." Yet, despite this, my friend's brother somehow "knew" that he had seen six million names of Jewish victims at Yad Vashem! This fellow's will to believe in the Six Million murdered Jews was so strong that he imagined a non-fact (the six million names at Yad Vashem) to give support to his belief. Such are the absurdities of which a true believer is capable.

But this is by no means a unique case of dogmatism. For many people, the six million figure is not a fact, although they call it that; rather. it is an article of faith, believed in not because of compelling evidence in its support but because of compelling psychological reasons. For such people, the six million figure is a Sacred

Truth not to be doubted and, if necessary, to be defended with dogmatism, mysticism, illogic, fantasy, or even downright lies. (Such pious frauds, or holy lies, have a venerable pedigree, going back to the early Christians who attributed their writings to other persons better known and more revered than themselves, to the pre-Christian Jewish writers who forged pro-Jewish versions of the *Sybilline Oracles*, and to even earlier true believers.)

In April of 1982, controversy swirled about a Los Angeles teacher, George Ashley, who had reportedly told a class of students that the number of Jewish deaths in the Holocaust had been greatly exaggerated, that, perhaps, one million had died, rather than the familiar six million. Among the responses to the news reports of Ashley's heresy was a letter published in the *Los Angeles Times* signed by one Joseph Rosenfeld, which proclaimed: "All reputable scholars have accepted the 6 million figure—a figure reached painfully and painstakingly by poring over countless lists of concentration camp victims, family histories, body counts, and every conceivable heartbreaking method available to social scientists and historians."

But Rosenfeld's story of how the six million figure was arrived at is pure fantasy. In fact, as early as 1943, two years before the end of the Holocaust, the narrator of Ben Hecht's propaganda play *We Will Never Die* was already claiming that two million Jews had been killed and that four million more would die by the end of the war. Thus, the six million figure was never more than a very rough estimate of Jewish deaths. How could it have been anything more, given that, as Roger Manvell and Heinrich Fraenkel wrote in their 1967 book, *The Incomparable Crime*, "No figures have been published giving the numbers of Jews left alive in the Soviet Union; the estimates differ widely, and lie between 1.6 and 2.6 million." Of course, the number of Jews killed in the Soviet Union is a correlative of the number of Jews left alive. The more Jews that were killed, the fewer that would have been left alive. The fewer that were killed, the more that would have been left alive. If the estimates of the numbers of Jews left alive in the Soviet Union differ by as much as one million, then, by implication, the estimates of the numbers of Jews killed in the Soviet Union must also differ by as much as one million. And so I repeat: Rosenfeld's story of how the six million figure was "painfully and painstakingly" arrived at is pure fantasy. It is akin to, though not nearly as entertaining as, *Alice's Adventures in Wonderland*.

Rosenfeld's assertion that all reputable historians have accepted the six million figure smacks of a tautology. If he defines "reputable historians" to mean "historians who have accepted the six million figure," then what he says is, by definition, true, but also trivial because there is no reason why anyone else should accept such an obviously loaded definition. On the other hand, if he does not define his terms in a loaded manner, then he has the problem of explaining how French-Jewish historian Pierre Vidal-Naquet, in an essay devoted primarily to criticizing revisionism regarding the Holocaust, could say that "nothing must be considered sacred. The figure of the six million Jews exterminated, which originated at Nuremberg [not true, as I've already pointed out], has nothing sacred or definitive about it, and many historians arrived at a somewhat lower figure."

Among the historians who have arrived at lower figures are two prominent Holocaust historians (hereinafter "Holocaustorians"), Raul Hilberg and Gerald Reitlinger, both firm believers in Nazi genocide and the gas chambers. Hilberg estimated that about 5.1 million European Jews died during World War II, while Reitlinger estimated between 4.2 and 4.6 million dead. An appendix to Nora Levin's *The Holocaust* (pages 715–718) gives the estimates of Hilberg and Reitlinger as well as the more conventional estimates of the Anglo-American Committee of Inquiry Regarding the Problems of European Jewry and Palestine (5,721,500) and of Jacob Lestchinsky (5,957,000). As Levin explains,

> Reitlinger's considerably lower estimates are traceable largely to what he calls "highly conjectural estimates" of losses in territory presently controlled by the Soviet Union and losses in Romania. He has also pointed to the "widely differing estimates of the Jewish populations of Russia, Poland, Hungary, Romania and the Balkans" before the war.

One wonders if Rosenfeld would dismiss Hilberg and Reitlinger as disreputable. If so, then it would only be fair to dismiss Rosenfeld as an incorrigible dogmatist.

In any case, Nazi-hunter Simon Wiesenthal, "the avenging angel of the Holocaust," has his own fantasy about the six million figure. In the wake of a brief but favorable commentary by British author Colin Wilson on a booklet titled *Did Six Million Really Die?*, Wiesenthal wrote a letter, published in the April 1975 issue of *Books and Bookmen*. According to Wiesenthal, "Scientific researchers and historians in various countries reached the conclusion, based on German documents, that the figure of exterminated Jews was between five million eight hundred thousand and six million two hundred thousand. They agreed to a round figure of six million."

I think I've already given enough information about the widely divergent estimates of Jewish deaths to show that this is just another fairy story. The only question is: Does Wiesenthal himself actually believe it?

Another letter published in the *Los Angeles Times* concerning the aforementioned Ashley affair was signed by one Robert Glasser, self-identified as "the Anti-Defamation League's staff person handling the case of George Ashley." Glasser insisted that "the question regarding this instructor is not ... one of academic freedom. It is simply a fact that 6 million Jews were killed in the Holocaust, and any attempt to teach otherwise is akin to teaching that 1 plus 1 equals 3." But, as I've already demonstrated, the six million figure is not a fact; it is, at best, an estimate, an estimate disputed even by some prominent Holocaustorians. If Glasser is not simply a tale-spinner, his assertion can best be explained as a result of ignorance and dogmatism, which so frequently go hand-in-hand. As Montaigne said, "Nothing is so firmly believed as that which we least know."

In any case, Robert Glasser is not the only ADLer in L.A. given to making dogmatic assertions about the six million figure. *The Los Angeles Times* of 3 May 1981 quoted ADL attorney David Lehrer's comment on the claim that the Holocaust is a myth: "It's a historical fact and we're not going to debate it. Are there any reputable historians who deny that 6 million Jews were killed in the Holocaust?"

Yes, Mr. Lehrer, there are "reputable" historians, i.e., Holocaustorians, who deny that six million Jews were killed in the Holocaust. But, in any case, if the Holocaust is a historical fact, rather than an article of faith, why is Lehrer unwilling to debate it? Is it not because, as Learned Hand said, "All discussion, all debate, all dissidence tends to question, and in consequence to upset existing convictions"?

Apparently, Lehrer cannot tolerate the thought that existing convictions about the Holocaust might be upset by open discussion and debate, and so he simply refuses to debate.

My point that the six million figure is sacred to many people is explicitly confirmed by the oath sworn by attendees of the World Gathering of Holocaust Survivors in June of 1981: "We vow we shall never let the sacred memory of our perished 6 million be scorned or erased." But the belief in the six million figure is only one of the tenets comprising what might be called the Holocaust Creed. And, though some may not regard the six million figure as sacred, they may nevertheless consider other tenets of the Holocaust Creed to be sacred and unquestionable.

For example, Eugene Wetzler, a Jewish Marxist, has written an essay largely devoted to attacking Noam

Chomsky, the libertarian socialist and MIT linguist, because of his defense of the civil liberties of French Holocaust revisionist Robert Faurisson. Wetzler writes,

> The often quoted figure of 6,000,000 may be an underestimate. It was the figure given by the Allied Tribunal at Nuremberg. Studies of objective facts that tend to lower or raise the figure are acceptable ... None of this brings into question the fact that genocide was indeed committed.

For Wetzler, to raise or lower the six million figure is acceptable, but to bring into question "the fact" of genocide is not. Thus, for Wetzler, "the fact" of genocide is a Sacred Truth, not to be doubted or questioned.

But I propose to question this Sacred Truth of genocide. Did the Nazi State attempt to kill all European Jews? Consider this passage from Goebbels' diary of 27 March 1942, which is sometimes cited as evidence of Goebbels' supposed knowledge of a program to exterminate all Jews:

> Beginning with Lublin, the Jews in the General Government [German-occupied central Poland] are now being evacuated eastward. The procedure is a pretty barbaric one and not to be described here more definitely. Not much will remain of the Jews. On the whole it can be said that about 60 per cent of them will have to be liquidated whereas only about 40 per cent can be used for forced labor.

Assuming the authenticity of the passage, and assuming that "liquidated" meant "killed," then Goebbels was projecting the killing of about 60 percent of the Jews, with the others to be used for forced labor. While such an interpretation does give support to a charge of mass murder committed by certain Nazis, it does not support a charge of genocide, of total extermination.

Now consider the postwar confessions of Rudolph Höss, commandant of Auschwitz. Höss repeatedly said that in June of 1941, he received from Himmler an order for the total extermination of European Jewry. There are, however, a number of oddities in Höss' confessions, including his reference to an "extermination camp" named "Wolzek," which nobody else on Planet Earth ever heard of. Also, the confessions Höss made as a prisoner of the British and at Nuremberg differ in some respects from the confessions he later made as a prisoner of the Polish Communists. For example, in his later confessions, he reduced his estimate of the number of Jews killed at Auschwitz from about 2.5 million to about 1.25 million. And he modified his story about the extermination order he said he received from Himmler. While he still claimed to have received such an order, he also claimed that Himmler had soon modified the order to exempt from extermination Jews capable of war work. As Höss put it,

> Originally all the Jews transported to Auschwitz on the authority of Eichmann's office were, in accordance with orders of the Reichsführer SS, to be destroyed without exception. This also applied to the Jews from

Upper Silesia, but on the arrival of the first transports of German Jews, the order was given that all those who were able-bodied, whether men or women, were to be segregated and employed in war work. This happened before the construction of the women's camp, since the need for a women's camp in Auschwitz only arose as a result of this order.[1]

Putting it more succinctly, Höss wrote that

When the Reichsführer SS modified his original Extermination Order of 1941, by which all Jews without exception were to be destroyed, and ordered instead that those capable of work were to be separated from the rest and employed in the armaments industry, Auschwitz became a Jewish camp.

Whatever one may think of Höss' confessions, it is a fact, acknowledged by nearly all Holocaustorians, that many Jews were used by the Nazis for forced labor. So if there was an extermination program, it is hard to see how it could have been a program for total extermination, for genocide. Thus, Eugene Wetzler's unquestionable "fact" of genocide is questionable indeed.

Of course, dogmatism comes as easily to a Marxist intellectual like Wetzler as swimming does to a fish. But consider the way in which 34 French historians responded to the heresies of Holocaust revisionist Robert Faurisson.

---

1 *Commandant of Auschwitz*, Popular Library, 1961, pp. 178–179.

These historians signed a declaration, published in *Le Monde* on 21 February 1979, which concluded thusly:

> Every one is free to interpret a phenomenon like the Hitlerite genocide according to his own philosophy. Everyone is free to compare it with other enterprises of murder committed earlier, at the same time, later. Everyone is free to offer such or such kind of explanation; everyone is free, to the limit, to imagine or to dream that these monstrous deeds did not take place. Unfortunately they did take place and no one can deny their existence without committing an outrage on the truth. It is not necessary to ask how technically such mass murder was possible. It was technically possible, seeing that it took place. That is the required point of departure of every historical inquiry on this subject. This truth it behooves us to remember in simple terms: there is not and there cannot be a debate about the existence of the gas chambers.

But who, other than two-legged sheep, would take seriously such a dogmatic declaration? For all I know, there may have been gas chambers used for the mass murder of Jews in some of the Nazi camps. But I refuse to believe in such gas chambers merely because some gang of would-be intellectual dictators tries to lay down the law. As the late novelist-philosopher Ayn Rand once said, speaking through John Galt, the hero of her novel *Atlas Shrugged*,

> Independence is the recognition of the fact that yours is the responsibility of judgment and nothing can help you escape it—that no substitute can do your thinking, as no pinchhitter can live your life—that the vilest form of self-abasement and self-destruction is the subordination of your mind to the mind of another, the acceptance of an authority over your brain, the acceptance of his assertions as facts, his say-so as truth, his edicts as middle-man between your consciousness and your existence.

The insistence of 34 French historians that the mass murder of Jews in gas chambers was technically possible because "it took place" is reminiscent of the argument of Joseph Glanvill in *Saducismus Triumphatus* (1681): "Matters of fact well proved ought not to be denied, because we cannot conceive how they can be performed. Nor is it a reasonable method of inference, first to presume the thing impossible, and thence to conclude that the fact cannot be proved." What were the "matters of fact well proved" that Glanvill thought should not be denied? They were the well proved "facts" of the existence of witches and witchcraft.

It should be pointed out, however, that unlike those who denied the existence of witches and witchcraft because, as Glanvill said, they "presumed" it to be impossible, Robert Faurisson does not simply presume the Nazi gas chambers to have been impossible. Rather, he presents arguments based on allegedly factual information about the properties of Zyklon B, the gas allegedly used for mass murder at Auschwitz. For example, in "The Gas Chambers of Auschwitz Appear to be Physically Inconceivable,"[2] Faurisson writes that "This gas is inflammable and explosive; there must not be any naked flame in the vicinity and, most definitely, it is necessary not to smoke." He then cites the testimony of Auschwitz commandant Rudolf Höss that immediately after opening the door of a gas chamber, following the gassing, prisoners would begin to remove the corpses, smoking and eating as they worked. Faurisson asks,

> How could they smoke in a place with vapors from an inflammable and explosive gas? How could all of that be done near the doors of the crematory ovens in which they were burning thousands of bodies? [The gas chambers were allegedly housed in the same buildings as the crematory ovens.] Who are these beings endowed with supernatural powers? From what world do these tremendous creatures come? Do they belong to our world which is ruled by inflexible, known laws of the physicist, the doctor, the chemist, the toxicologist? Or do they indeed belong to the world of the imagination where all those laws, even the law of gravity, are overcome by magic or disappear by enchantment?

Assuming that Faurisson is right about the inflammability and explosiveness of Zyklon B, he has raised some pertinent (and impertinent) questions about the

---

[2] *The Journal of Historical Review*, Vol. 2 No. 4 Winter 1981, p. 321.

physical possibility of the notorious Nazi gas chambers, questions which deserve to be answered by those who maintain that those gas chambers really existed. But rather than answer Faurisson's questions, 34 French historians dogmatically insist that the alleged mass murder with Zyklon B was possible because "it took place." Such dogmatism regarding the gas chambers is the intellectual equivalent of the dogmatism of Catholic historians who insist that it was possible for the sun to plunge toward the Earth above Fatima because "it took place," as attested by thousands of eyewitnesses. As some people believe in the Holy Ghost, others believe in the Holocaust.

However, Lucy Dawidowicz, one of the leading Jewish Holocaustorians, actually approves of the French historians' dogmatic declaration, which, she says, "could well serve as a guide to American historians." Dawidowicz would undoubtedly be pleased, therefore, to know that some American academics have reacted to Holocaust revisionism with the same degree of open-mindedness as was displayed by the astronomers who refused to look through Galileo's telescope but nevertheless "knew" that he could not possibly have discovered any new heavenly bodies with it.

One of the reactions to newspaper reports about Holocaust revisionist Arthur Butz and his book, *The Hoax of the Twentieth Century*, was a letter to the *New York Times* by one Professor Gerard R. Wolfe of New York University. Wolfe said that Northwestern University, where Butz teaches electrical engineering and computer sciences, should bring him up on charges of "academic incompetence" and "moral turpitude" for having written a book whose title he gave as *Fabrication of a Hoax*. Wolfe had seen the *New York Times* story which reported this incorrect title, but he had not seen the book itself. Noam Chomsky has written that "No rational person will condemn a book, however outlandish its conclusions may seem, without at least reading it carefully ... checking the documentation offered, and so on." But Professor Wolfe is not a rational person, at least not in relation to Holocaust revisionism.

Another true believer who was moved to comment on "the Faurisson affair" was a Michael Blankfort of Los Angeles, perhaps the same Michael Blankfort who was a playwright, novelist, and screenwriter, who, in an interview given shortly before his death in July 1982, spoke of a visit he made to Israel in 1948 which resulted in "the onset of a devotion to Israel that is without parallel in my life." In a letter published in *The Nation*, Blankfort wrote, "Anyone who claims the Holocaust never happened is insane. Why shouldn't a university fire a crazy teacher who might harm his students with his criminal delusions?" Coincidentally, iconoclastic psychiatrist Thomas Szasz, in *The Manufacture of Madness*, mentioned a doctor of the Sorbonne who wrote in 1609 that the Witches' Sabbat was an objective fact, disbelieved only by those of unsound mind. The parallel is obvious—and ominous.

Blankfort's dogmatic assertion that anyone who says the Holocaust never happened is insane is an example of one of the most common ploys of Holocaust dogmatists, a fallacy Ayn Rand identified as "the Argument from Intimidation," which, as she explained, is not an argument, but a means of forestalling debate and extorting an opponent's agreement with one's un-discussed notions. It is a method of by-passing logic by means of psychological pressure.

...the psychological pressure method consists of threatening to impeach an opponent's character by means of his argument, thus impeaching the argument without debate.

The essential characteristic of the Argument from Intimidation is its appeal to moral self-doubt and its reliance on the fear, guilt or ignorance of the victim. It is used in the form of an ultimatum demanding that the victim renounce a given idea without discussion, under threat of being considered morally unworthy. The pattern is always: Only those who are evil (dishonest, heartless, insensitive, ignorant, etc.) can hold such an idea.

In Blankfort's case, "the Argument from Intimidation" took the following form: Only those who are insane can hold such an idea, i.e., the idea that the Holocaust never happened. But as Rand said, "The Argument from Intimidation is a confession of intellectual impotence."

Another true believer is my very own congressman, Representative Henry A. Waxman. In a column published in *The B'nai B'rith Messenger* of Los Angeles, Waxman waxed abusive:

To be realistic, we must note that the recognition of the horrors of the Holocaust in civilized circles has been sharply answered by an incredible repudiation of the Holocaust by those who would destroy us. How perverse, how deranged and utterly sick are the people behind the "debunking of the Holocaust?"

Who are these people who offer prizes to anyone who can prove a single Jew died in the concentration camps?

It appears that Waxman does not even know what he's talking about. The Institute for Historical Review has offered a reward of $50,000 to the first person to prove to its satisfaction, in accord with American legal standards, that Jews were *gassed* to death at Auschwitz, but no one has offered prizes "to anyone who can prove that a single Jew died in the concentration camps." In any case, Waxman's response to Holocaust revisionism is simply a variation of "the Argument from Intimidation": Only the perverse, the deranged, or the utterly sick can engage in debunking the Holocaust. Another confession of intellectual impotence.

One more variation of "the Argument from Intimidation" was employed by British writer Alan "The Loneliness of the Long Distance Runner" Sillitoe in a letter published in *Books and Bookmen*, April 1975. Responding to Colin Wilson's aforementioned favorable comments on *Did Six Million Really Die?*, Sillitoe declared, "To disbelieve that an act of colossal and monstrous injustice has been committed is an act of injustice in itself." In other words: Only the unjust can disbelieve the Holocaust. Yet another confession of intellectual impotence. Some true believers, however, are not content merely to censure Holocaust heretics; they want to censor them as well. For example, Professor Franklin H. Littell of the religious studies department at Temple University, who is a member of the US Council on the Holocaust, warned participants in a Jerusalem symposium on anti-Semitism that the damage being done by revisionists [*what* damage?] should be taken seriously. According to *The Jerusalem Post International Edition*, 19–25 October 1980, Littell announced, "You can't 'discuss' the truth of the Holocaust. That's a distortion of free speech" and was applauded when he declared, "The US should emulate West Germany, which outlaws such public exercises. We now have to deal with a minimum of violence; later, we'll have to fight them in the streets." Thus, in true Orwellian fashion, Littell declares, *Censorship is free speech*. But as Ayn Rand wrote in her book *For the New Intellectual*,

> Let no man posture as an advocate of freedom if he claims the right to establish his version of a good society where individual dissenters are to be suppressed by means of physical force. Let no man posture as an intellectual if he proposes to elevate a thug into the position of final authority over the intellect.
>
> No advocate of reason can claim the right to force his ideas on others. No advocate of the free mind can claim the right to force the minds of others. No rational society, no cooperation, no agreement, no understanding, no discussion

> are possible among men who propose to substitute guns for rational persuasion.

Since Littell proposes precisely to substitute guns for rational persuasion, no discussion of the truth of the Holocaust is possible *with him*. So I have only one thing to say to Littell: Just try and stop me from discussing the truth of the Holocaust! Wendell Phillips once said. "If there is anything in the universe that can't stand discussion, let it crack." And I say. If the Sacred Truth of the Holocaust can't stand discussion, let it crack.

Another confirmation of my point about the sacredness of the Holocaust for true believers can be found in what I call the canonization of the survivors. With rare exceptions, such as Roman Polanski, Holocaust survivors are seen as Semitic saints. Instead of halos over their heads, though, concentration camp numbers tattooed on their arms serve as the insignia of their sainthood. This canonization of survivors is reflected in their immunity from criticism, or even skepticism, by the minions of the mass media of communications. How often have you seen or read any mass-medium journalist doubting or disputing the word of a Holocaust survivor? Rarely, if ever, I'll wager.

Yet another manifestation of the sacredness of the Holocaust is revealed in the headline of a *Los Angeles Times* story about the increasing numbers of people visiting the site of the Dachau concentration camp. The headline: "Record Number Visit Shrine to Nazi Victims." Thus, Dachau is a *shrine*, one of many, to which the pious make pilgrimages. But, if for so many people, the

Holocaust is a sacred cow, a matter of blind faith, the question is: Why? I think that Jewish psychohistorian Howard F. Stein has given at least part of the answer in "The Holocaust and the Myth of the Past as History"[3]

> why, for Jews, the Holocaust? What, in sanctifying the Holocaust, do Jews not want to know about that grim era? Whatever be the "facts" of the Holocaust, it is experienced as a necessity, as part of a recurrent historic pattern. Reality must be made to conform to fantasy. Whatever did happen in the Holocaust must be made to conform to the group-fantasy of what ought to have happened. For the Jews, the term "Holocaust" does not simply denote a single catastrophic era in history, but is a grim metaphor for the meaning of Jewish history.
>
> ...the "reality" of the Holocaust is inextricably part of the myth in which it is woven—and for which myth it serves as further confirmatory evidence—for the timeless Jewish theme that the world is in conspiracy to annihilate them, one way or another, at least eventually.

Jean-Louis Tristani, one of the contributors to the book *Intolerable Intolerance*, gives an analysis which I think complements that of Howard Stein:

> The Holocaust, which represents one of the most popular themes of contemporary Judaism,

---

[3] *The Journal of Historical Review*, Vol. 1 No. 4, Winter 1980, pp 309–322.

thus falls into a long tradition. It is bound up with what it would be necessary to call the "invention of Israel," of the Israel of today. The Hitlerian genocide perpetrated in the gas chambers, the Exodus and the creation of the Israeli state, do they not attain in effect the lofty meaning which the servitude in Egypt, the Exodus, and the installation in the Promised Land once had?

Judaic scholar Jacob Neusner, in his book *Stranger at Home*, treats the Holocaust as part of a myth of "Holocaust and redemption":

> The myth is that "the Holocaust" is a unique event, which, despite its "uniqueness," teaches compelling lessons about why Jews must be Jewish, and, in consequence of that fact, do certain things known in advance (which have nothing to do with the extermination of European Jewry). The redemptive part of the myth maintains that the State of Israel is the "guarantee" that "the Holocaust" will not happen again, that it is that State and its achievements which give meaning and significance, even fulfillment, to "the Holocaust."
>
> ...so if you want to know why be Jewish, you have to remember that (1) the gentiles wiped out the Jews of Europe, so are not to be trusted, let alone joined; (2) if there had been "Israel," meaning the State of Israel, there would have been no "Holocaust"; and so (3) for the sake

of your personal safety, you have to "support Israel."

If we synthesize these three analyses, we get the following conclusions: (1) the Holocaust is a metaphor for the meaning of Jewish history, that is, that the world is in conspiracy to annihilate the Jews; (2) the Holocaust is part of a myth, comparable to earlier Jewish myths, encompassing the Holocaust, the Exodus, and the rebirth of the State of Israel; and (3) this myth explains to Jews why they must support the State of Israel.

Thus, it is not surprising to find Alfred Lilienthal reporting, in *The Zionist Connection*,

> To ingrain the State of Israel more deeply into the Jewish consciousness, the International Association of Conservative Rabbis incorporated the events of the last 2,000 years in prayer. The death of the six million as well as the establishment of Israel, the June war, and the reunification of Jerusalem was all woven into the revised liturgy.

One Holocaust prayer can be found in Bernard Martin's *Prayer in Judaism*. It is "An Elegy for the Six Million" by David Polish. (Polish, incidentally, makes use of numerous variations on the mythic theme that the fat of murdered Jews was used by the Nazis to make soap.)

As Howard Stein says, the Holocaust—the alleged Nazi extermination of European Jewry—is a metaphor for the meaning of Jewish history. The question is: is it anything more than a metaphor? In his book *Heresies*, Thomas Szasz says, "Most of the heresies in the book ... pertain to matters where language is used in two ways, literally and metaphorically: where the true believer speaks metaphorically but claims that he asserts literal truths; and where heresy may consist in no more than insisting that a metaphorical truth may be a literal falsehood."

Szasz, however, believes that the metaphor of the Holocaust expresses a literal truth, so let me be the one to commit the heresy of insisting that the metaphorical truth of the Holocaust may be a literal falsehood.

A slightly different version of this essay originally appeared in *The Journal of Historical Review*, Volume 4, Issue 1 (1983).

REVISING HOLOCAUST REVISIONISM

Author's Note (2008)

In 1974, about five years before I got interested in Holocaust revisionism, I discovered historical revisionism, particularly those strains regarding World War II and other wars. My interest grew out of my broader involvement in the early libertarian movement (which should be distinguished from the Randian or "Objectivist" movement). Libertarians such as Murray Rothbard, along with his friends, associates, and disciples, were promoting revisionism regarding various American wars in an effort to debunk, or at least defang, the propaganda and mythology that had been used to justify military intervention as a means of legitimizing State power. (Incidentally, one of these libertarian revisionists was Roy Childs, who was the "libertarian friend" to whom I refer in the opening of "Revising Holocaust Revisionism." Since Roy is dead, it occurs to me that it might not matter that I should mention that now.)

Anyway, before I waded into the swamp that has come to be known as "Holocaust revisionism"—or "denialism," as the kids say these days—I was already interested in and sympathetic to other aspects of World War II revisionist scholarship and other brands of revisionist history. I cut my chops on William Henry Chamberlin's *America's Second Crusade*, which I reviewed for Academic Associates' *Book News* when George H. Smith was the editor. I read *Containment and Revolution*, an anthology of Cold War revisionist essays edited by the pre-apostate David Horowitz, which I reviewed in the pages of *Books for Libertarians*. I read *Harry Elmer Barnes: Learned Crusader*, which discussed Barnes' seminal contribution to twentieth-century war revisionism. I read James J. Martin's *American Liberalism and World Politics, 1931–1941* and his essay collection *Revisionist Viewpoints*. Other books informing my early study of broadly "revisionist" history include *Containment and Change* by Carl Oglesby, *Free World Colossus*, also by David Horowitz, *The Lusitania*, by Colin Simpson, *The Destruction of Dresden*, by David Irving, and *American Power and the New Mandarins*, by Noam Chomsky. The point being, I was already something of a revisionist before my first brush with "Holocaust revisionism."

It may be worth noting that the term "Holocaust revisionism," as used in this essay, is actually an anachronism when used in regard to the early and middle 1970s. "The Holocaust" did not become a household word until the late '70s, when the television miniseries *Holocaust* was broadcast. Only after that event did the term "Holocaust revisionism" begin to gain currency in some circles. Thus, circa 1974, when I first encountered "Holocaust revisionism," it was actually referred to in such terms as "revisionism regarding the Nazi concentration camps and the alleged extermination of Jews by gassing." Whatever else may be said about the later term, it is certainly shorter.

I wrote "Revising Holocaust Revisionism" in 1983 for Sam Konkin's *New Libertarian* magazine. However, Konkin, after asking that I expand the piece, which I did, then held it for a year or two and ended up shelving it indefinitely. Seeing as Mr. Konkin has since gone on to feed the worms, this is its first publication.[1]

REVISING HOLOCAUST REVISIONISM (1983)

IN THE EARLY 1970S, I WATCHED the TV movie *QB VII* with a libertarian friend. The movie was based on the novel of the same name by Leon Uris, which, in turn, was based on an actual court case in England, in which Uris and his publisher were sued for libel over some statements made in Uris' earlier novel *Exodus* about a Polish-born doctor who had worked as such while imprisoned at Auschwitz.

Watching this Holocaust-related teledrama inspired my friend to tell me that James J. Martin, the revisionist historian, did not believe the widely accepted claim that the Nazis killed six million Jews. I have no vivid recollection of how I reacted to this intellectual

---

[1] Editor's Note: Rollins is here referring to the publication of "Revising Holocaust Revisionism" in *The Myth of Natural Rights and Other Essays*, Nine-Banded Books, 2008.

bombshell, but I assume that surprise and puzzlement were dominant elements.

In any case, my first substantial encounter with Holocaust revisionism came during the Labor Day weekend of 1974, when I attended one day of a two-day seminar on World War II revisionism given by none other than James J. Martin. It so happened that Dr. Martin devoted a good deal of time to presenting (quite uncritically, I realize in retrospect) some of the writings of former Buchenwald inmate and pioneer Holocaust revisionist Paul Rassinier. (It was the first time I had ever heard of Rassinier and in my notes, I misspelled his name "Recinier.") Thus, I became acquainted with some of the reasons for doubt about the Holocaust. I was by no means immediately converted into an outright denier, but my curiosity and skepticism were aroused.

A few months after attending Dr. Martin's seminar, I spotted a classified ad in *Reason* magazine for a publication called *Did Six Million Really Die?* I recognized the address as that of an English libertarian with whom I had previously corresponded. I sent off a dollar and subsequently received a booklet with the above-mentioned title, as well as a photocopy of a review of the booklet by David Ramsay Steele, apparently another English libertarian. After reading and re-reading this material, I became sufficiently intrigued by the possibility that the Holocaust might be a propaganda fabrication that I began to acquire and study the standard historical literature on the Holocaust, which I had never before bothered to read, as well as the burgeoning literature of Holocaust revisionism. I decided, with perhaps unrealistic ambitiousness, to determine for myself "the truth" about the Holocaust. Almost a decade later, my study of the controversy continues, and I have yet to determine to my own satisfaction exactly what "the truth" about the Holocaust is. As of now, I am a skeptic regarding both the Holocaust *and* Holocaust revisionism.

For reasons which can be gleaned from the above introductory remarks, it was with much interest that I read James J. Martin's essay "On the Latest Crisis Provoked by Revisionism,"[2] which was in effect a defense of the Institute for Historical Review's promotion of Holocaust revisionism. In his characteristically biting style, Dr. Martin made several points with which I could not take exception. Still, there were a number of things that bothered me. I propose to discuss some of the points in his essay—points which are, in my view, open to criticism. "Revisionism" is sometimes defined in terms of setting the record straight. Thus, I see no reason why the writings of avowed revisionists should be exempt from revisionism.

Dr. Martin is on solid ground in pointing out the "Stalinist and post-Stalinist vested interests in the Holocaust saga." Zionists are by no means alone in exploiting the Holocaust for political purposes. In fact, I would point out that the political establishments of various Western democracies also find in the Holocaust a useful ruse in justifying their legitimacy to citizens. But there are a number of problems with Dr. Martin's discussion of the Communists and the Holocaust.

---

2   *New Libertarian*, Vol. 4, No. 10, October 1981, pp. 12–15.

According to Dr. Martin,

> there are well-developed Communist legends of six million murdered in 'gas chambers' by the Germans and their allies, 1941–1944, though these largely ignore that any Jews were involved. The Polish Communist tales downplay if not exclude Jews among the deceased, and insist the dead were all Polish gentiles. The Soviet six-million story alleges they were all Soviet citizens of some ethnic composition or other and as time goes by virtually omits Jews from the totals of the dead.

But I have yet to encounter any such Soviet six-million story as alleged by Dr. Martin. Apparently, there *is* a Soviet *seven*-million story. In *The Holocaust and the Historians*, Lucy Dawidowicz writes, "According to the *Great Soviet Encyclopedia*, Soviet military and civilian losses amounted to some 20 million. Other sources estimate Soviet losses at about 11 million combatants and 7 million civilians." But this Soviet seven-million story does not allege that all the victims were killed in gas chambers, nor does it allege that all the dead were Slavs. Dawidowicz quotes a 23 June 1976 *Pravda* story about the unveiling of a monument at Babi Yar:

> A terrible tragedy broke out at Babi Yar at the end of September 1941. Tens of thousands of totally blameless, peaceful residents of Kiev, including many children, women and old people, were shot to death there within a period

of a few days. The invaders murdered Russians, Ukrainians, Jews, Byelorussians, Poles.

It is true, as Dr. Martin asserts and as Lucy Dawidowicz complains, that the Soviets commonly fail to specify Jews as among the Soviet victims of the Nazis, but it is not true, as Dr. Martin alleges, that the Soviets go so far as to claim that all the victims were Slavs.

There *is*, as Dr. Martin says, a Polish-Communist six million story, but contrary to what Dr. Martin says, it is *not* a story of six million Poles killed by the Nazis in gas chambers, nor is it a story of six million Polish gentiles killed by the Nazis. The alleged six million Polish dead are officially divided into four categories, the second half of which includes "victims of death camps, raids, executions, annihilation of ghettos, etc." The official total for this category is 3,577,000 deaths. Thus, the Polish Communists claim a maximum of 3.5 million Poles killed in gas chambers. Furthermore, while the Polish Communists, like their Soviet counterparts, commonly fail to specify Jews as being among the victims, the Polish-Communist six-million story does not explicitly exclude Polish Jews from among the dead, nor does it insist the dead were all Polish gentiles. In his essay, Dr. Martin did not bother to cite any sources that might substantiate his claims about the Polish-Communist six-million story, but in a letter of 30 July 1976, he wrote,

> A booklet I have in hand issued in English from Warsaw titled *Transfer of the German Population from Poland*, asserts on p. 1 of the introduction that "Six million Polish citizens were murdered,"

> and doesn't in the slightest mention Jews. Later on it alleges that many Jews were "exterminated," too, so their story must be a 12 million and not a six million legend.

To be clear, even if the booklet "doesn't in the slightest mention Jews" in claiming six million dead, that is still not the same thing as explicitly excluding Jews from among the dead or insisting that all the dead were Polish gentiles. But according to Dr. Martin himself, the booklet *does* mention Jews. He says it "alleges that many Jews were 'exterminated,' too." Note that the word "too" is apparently Dr. Martin's own and not the booklet's (he doesn't put it in quotation marks.) Thus, Dr. Martin really has no basis for concluding that the Polish Communists must have a 12 million story (six million Poles plus six million Jews). In fact, the Polish-Communist and Jewish six-million stories overlap. Each of them includes the three million Polish Jews who were allegedly killed by the Nazis.

According to Dr. Martin, "It was the Red Army which captured the German concentration camps in the East, and made the first astronomic claims of people done to death, not the publicity departments of the Zionist organizations." But, to my knowledge, the first astronomic claims of people done to death that originated with the Red Army were made in late July and early August of 1944, shortly after the capture of the Maidanek concentration camp near Lublin, Poland. (It was claimed that about 1.5 million people were killed at Maidanek.) And the Zionist publicity departments were making astronomic claims of people done to death as early as a year before the Red Army captured Maidanek. For example, on 26 August 1943, the Institute of Jewish Affairs of the American Jewish Congress made public their publication *Hitler's Ten Year-War on the Jews*, in which it was claimed that 1,702,500 European Jews had fallen victim to "organized murder" and that over three million had died from all causes. Dr. Martin presumably knows this. Why? Because in the article "Raphael Lemkin and the Invention of 'Genocide',"[3] he discusses this book along with another IJA publication, *Starvation Over Europe: Made in Germany*. As Dr. Martin explains,

> It is significant that these two books were published under the aegis of one Zorach Warhaftig, [a] Jewish lawyer from Warsaw, but also a fierce Zionist, who disappeared from Poland in 1939, surfacing in New York in 1943 as deputy director of this Institute for Jewish Affairs, a post he held until 1947. Feverishly active in the post-May 1945 effort to get as many as possible of Europe's displaced-person Jews to Palestine, Warhaftig subsequently followed them there. Becoming a signer of the Declaration of Independence of the State of Israel in 1948, as well as a member of the Executive Council of the World Jewish Congress, Warhaftig from 1951–1965 was Deputy Minister of Religion in various Israeli governments.

---

3   *The Journal of Historical Review*, Vol. 2 No. 1, Spring 1981, pp. 19–34.

Given Dr. Martin's familiarity with *Hitler's Ten-Year War on the Jews* and its Zionist sponsorship, one wonders why, in his *New Libertarian* essay, he nevertheless gives the Red Army "credit" for making the first astronomic claims of people done to death.

Whatever the reason, Dr. Martin's tendency to magnify the role of the Communists in the creation of the Holocaust story is evident in the following passage:

> It has been remarked that a school of historiography is indeed a peculiar one when it is based almost entirely on *confessions*. This is the case of the "Holocaust" saga in Poland, resting mainly on statements extracted from the captured German commandants of the Auschwitz and Treblinka concentration camps by their Stalinist captors.

Dr. Martin is here referring to the confessions of Rudolf Höss, commandant of Auschwitz, and Franz Stangl, commandant of Treblinka. But Rudolf Höss was captured by and made his first confessions to members of the British Field Security Police in occupied Germany. He later repeated those confessions at Nuremberg, where he was held in American custody. Only after his appearance at Nuremberg was Höss handed over to the Stalinists, i.e., the Polish-Communists, to whom he then made some more (and, in some respects, different) confessions before they honored him with a necktie party.

I recently pointed all this out to Dr. Martin in correspondence and asked him if Höss' British and/or American captors were Stalinists. I found his reply, in a letter of 12 July 1983, less than satisfactory, though entertaining. Regarding Höss, Dr. Martin writes,

> It is unimportant to me whether Höss was intercepted in the outer orbit of the planet of Neptune and interrogated by the police of Andorra and the Andaman Islands. He was hung by a piece of Communist rope in Poland and the manuscript of his 'book' was prepared in Communist Poland with the Polish KGB presumably still holding the original, which I can't remember anyone outside Communist circles ever examining or comparing with what circulates about the world in various kinds of translations. What he said to the British is immaterial; Hoggan points out that even that super Holocaustrian [sic] Reitlinger rejected that.

Thus, Dr. Martin acknowledges that Höss made his first confessions to British interrogators, but he insists that what Höss said to the British is "immaterial" because David Hoggan, author of *The Myth of the Six Million*, "points out" that even Gerald Reitlinger, author of *The Final Solution*, "rejected that." To be exact, Hoggan "points out" that "Even Gerald Reitlinger, who grasps at every straw to document the extermination program, rejects the Nuremberg trial testimony of Höss as hopelessly untrustworthy."

In his letter of 12 July 1983, Dr. Martin further says,

> I do not claim to be anything other than an interested and sometimes enthusiastic amateur

on anything related to the "Holocaust," since I cannot read Russian, Polish or Yiddish expressed in Hebrew characters. So my views are "received" insofar as they emerge from people who know the basic literature.

People like David Hoggan? Well, David Hoggan may be familiar with the basic literature on the Holocaust, but anyone who takes David Hoggan's word for anything is just plain begging to be duped. To borrow a line from boxer Randall "Tex" Cobb, Hoggan is so full of shit his eyes are brown. Even the marginally esteemed Holocaust revisionist Arthur Butz, in *The Hoax of the Twentieth Century*, called *The Myth of the Six Million* "terrible and a clear retrogression in relation to the prior work of Rassinier." And here, for good measure, is what Butz has to say about the work of Rassinier:

> it is necessary to check up on Rassinier in his interpretation of sources; some do not check out and, in addition, he employs some clearly unreliable sources at a few points. There are also some glaring but relatively irrelevant errors of fact.

If Hoggan's book is worse than the work of Rassinier, it must be terrible indeed. And indeed it is. Contrary to what Hoggan claims, Reitlinger does not reject Höss' Nuremberg testimony (for practical purposes identical to his confessions to the British) as "hopelessly untrustworthy." On pages 104–105 of the Perpetua edition of *The Final Solution*, Reitlinger rejects three specific points: First, Höss' "admission" to having murdered 2.5 million people. He also rejects the official Soviet estimate of four million killed at Auschwitz as "ridiculous" and says that "little less than a million human beings perished in Auschwitz...." Second, he rejects Höss' claim to have received orders from Himmler *in June 1941* directing the extermination of Jews at Auschwitz. (He says that "it was in the summer of 1942 that Himmler decided on Auschwitz as the extermination centre for the Jews of Western Europe.") And, third, he rejects Höss' claim that Himmler selected Auschwitz as an extermination center because of its "easy access by rail." (He says that, "In reality Himmler preferred Auschwitz to the other Polish death camps, not because of its railway junction, which was nothing exceptional, but because of the camouflage status it had acquired through the plans to make it the center of a huge synthetic oil and rubber industry.")

Reitlinger's rejection of these three claims by no means constitutes a complete rejection of Höss' Nuremberg testimony, as claimed by Hoggan. Furthermore, one of the claims rejected by Reitlinger, the claim that Höss received extermination orders from Himmler in the summer of 1941, was common to *all* of Höss' confessions, including those he made under Stalinist auspices. Thus, Reitlinger did not reject the confessions Höss gave to the British (and repeated at Nuremberg) in favor of those he later gave the Polish Communists. Like his fellow exponents of the Holocaust saga, Reitlinger basically accepts all of Höss' confessions, picking and choosing statements from among them as he finds convenient. Thus, Dr. Martin cannot legitimately dismiss Höss' confessions to the British as "immaterial" on the grounds that Reitlinger rejects those confessions. Reitlinger doesn't reject them. Furthermore, one could ask Dr. Martin, If what Höss said to the British (and then repeated at Nuremberg) is "immaterial," then why does Arthur Butz devote a sizable portion of *The Hoax of the Twentieth Century* to a dissection of the 5 April 1946 affidavit Höss signed at Nuremberg?

In any case, Dr. Martin also refers to the statements "extracted" from Treblinka commandant Franz Stangl by his "Stalinist captors." But Stangl was arrested in 1967 by Brazilian police, then extradited to West Germany, where he was imprisoned up to the time of his death while awaiting word of his appeal of the sentence he had received at his trial. If any of Stangl's captors were Stalinists, this is not self-evident. In my correspondence with Dr. Martin, I asked him if Stangl's Brazilian and/or West German captors were Stalinists. Apparently, he was unable to answer this question affirmatively, for he gave no direct reply to it.

Dr. Martin's attempt to pin the confessions of Höss and Stangl exclusively on the Stalinists is a failure. Moreover, in asserting that the Holocaust saga in Poland rests mainly on the confessions of Höss and Stangl, Dr. Martin has slighted a number of other confessions, including those of Joseph Kramer, Pery Broad and Hans Kremer, concerning Auschwitz. And he has most especially slighted the famous statements of Kurt Gerstein concerning Belzec, which are almost equal in prominence to the Höss confessions. Of course, ignoring the Joseph Kramer and Pery Broad confessions (given to the British) and the Gerstein statements (given to the Americans and the French) does serve Dr. Martin's purpose in magnifying the role of the Stalinists in all of this. But it doesn't serve historical accuracy.

According to Dr. Martin,

> Between 1945 and 1960, hundreds of persons perjured themselves (perhaps M. Rassinier was excessively charitable in describing them as "vulgar false witnesses") in German and other courts testifying to seeing "gas chambers" in various concentration camps in Germany. In 1962, their own sponsors betrayed them by admitting officially that there were not and had never been any such installations anywhere on the territory of Germany as constituted territorially in 1937.

Presumably, Dr. Martin is referring to the letter, by Dr. Martin Broszat of Munich's Institute for Contemporary History, which appeared in *Die Zeit* on 19 August 1960 (not 1962). Holocaust revisionists are fond of citing Dr. Broszat's supposed admission that there were no gas chambers located within Germany's prewar borders. But that is not precisely what Dr. Broszat "admitted." Here are the first two sentences of the Broszat letter: "Neither in Dachau, nor in Bergen-Belsen, nor in Buchenwald have Jews or other prisoners been gassed. The gas chamber in Dachau was never quite finished or put into operation." Thus, Dr. Broszat "admitted" that no prisoners were gassed in various German concentration camps, but he also referred quite explicitly to "the gas chamber in Dachau," which he said was "never quite finished or put into operation." So, in fact, Dr. Broszat affirmed the existence of at least one (unfinished and unused) gas chamber within a German concentration camp. Dr. Broszat has more recently been quoted by journalist Gitta Sereny on the subject of gas chambers, to wit "Mauthausen, Natzweiler had one. Sachsenhausen, too, I think. They used them toward the end to replace the shootings and injections of small groups of prisoners, which had become so demoralizing to the staff."[4] Neither Mauthausen nor Natzweiler was located within Germany's 1937 borders, but Sachsenhausen was. So Dr. Broszat has affirmed the existence of gas chambers at two concentration camps (Dachau and Sachsenhausen) located within those 1937 German borders. And, therefore, Dr. Martin cannot legitimately use Dr. Broszat as his authority in denouncing as perjurers *all* who ever testified to seeing gas chambers in concentration camps within Germany.

And even if Dr. Broszat actually had "admitted" that there were no gas chambers in any concentration camp within Germany, I would ask, "So what?" Dr. Broszat's *Die Zeit* letter consists only of assertions. It contains no explanation whatever of *how* he reached the conclusions asserted. Why do a few assertions of a State-supported West German historian, assertions made without any supporting argument or discussion of evidence, carry such weight as to conclusively prove that any and all testimony to the contrary by witnesses was perjured?

---

4   See "The Men Who Whitewash Hitler," *The New Statesman*, Nov. 2, 1979.

Methinks I smell an "argument from authority" here. Is it possible that Dr. Martin treats these unsupported assertions by Dr. Broszat as definitive simply because they tend to confirm what Dr. Martin wants to believe, i.e., that there were no gas chambers in the Nazi concentration camps? After all, Dr. Martin does *not* regard Dr. Broszat's assertions as definitive when Dr. Broszat asserts that the Jews were mass-exterminated in gas chambers in camps in Poland, which Dr. Broszat does assert in the very same letter—the letter in which he "admitted" there were no gassings in the camps in Germany. You can't have it both ways. Either all of Dr. Broszat's unsupported assertions are authoritative or none of them are. Take your choice.

In the following passage, Dr. Martin discusses the nature of history as an intellectual discipline:

> Students of my time who got their early training in history from tough old manuals such as the *Introduction to the Study of History* by Langlois and Seignobos were taught that history is a science of reasoning based on documents, and the degree to which an account of the past is not based on documents is the degree to which such an account cannot properly be called history.

Dr. Martin relies on this notion of what history is when he writes:

> If the Institute for Historical Review and its *Journal* are in existence to spread falsehood, it is up to its critics to prove that. And it has to be

> done with documentary evidence, not incensed testimony, hysterical opinion, and self-serving unsupported emotional allegations and affidavits.

Note the false dichotomy: EITHER documentary evidence OR *incensed* testimony, *hysterical* opinion, and *self-serving, unsupported emotional* allegations and affidavits. Apparently, in Dr. Martin's mental world, there are no such things as *non*-incensed testimony, *un*hysterical opinion, or *non*-self-serving, *non*-emotional allegations and affidavits.

Years ago, in the pages of *The Nation*, Ernest Zaugg wrote that Paul Rassinier suffered from "documentitis." Rassinier seemed to think that nothing could be proven except by means of official documents. But Dr. Martin also suffers from "documentitis." For him, documents are the only acceptable form of historical evidence. To which I say, "Bunk!" Documents, of course, are important, but they are not the *alpha* and *omega* of history. History is the attempt to know and to recount (some of) what has happened in the past. To that end, historians may legitimately use *any* relevant and credible evidence, whether documentary or not.

For example, one category of evidence which Dr. Martin implicitly rejects is what might be called "archeological" evidence. I am referring to any sort of discernible traces of human activity that are left in the wake of such activity, including tangible artifacts. Consider the question of whether or not people were gassed to death at the Maidanek concentration camp. So far as I know, there are no official German documents referring to such gassings. On the other hand, there has been a good deal of postwar testimony to the effect that people were gassed there. But perhaps most importantly, the alleged gas chambers of Maidanek are still standing and intact (unlike the alleged gas chambers of Auschwitz, Treblinka, Belzec, and Sobibor). Surely these structures, alleged to be gas chambers, constitute evidence of some sort in regard to the question of whether people were gassed at Maidanek. The *quality* of this evidence may be questioned, but evidence it is. I, for one, have long wondered why the exponents of the conventional wisdom about the Holocaust have made such little use of the evidence provided by the alleged gas chambers at Maidanek. Perhaps, for some reason, the alleged gas chambers of Maidanek do not provide convincing evidence of gassing.[5] In any case, Dr. Martin's insistence on documentary evidence to the exclusion of all other kinds of evidence is as absurd as the claim that a man cannot prove he was born unless he has a birth certificate.

There is another point to be made about documentary evidence, to wit, that it is not above criticism. The fact that something is asserted in an official document by no means guarantees that the assertion is true. By the same token, the fact that an action or event is not mentioned in any official document does not necessarily mean that no such action or event took place.

---

5 For a relatively recent revisionist study of Maidanek, see "The Gas Chambers of Majdanek," by Carlo Mattogno, in *Dissecting the Holocaust*, edited by Ernst Gauss, aka Germar Rudolf, Theses and Dissertations Press (2000).—L.A.R., 2008.

Documents are made by human beings, and human beings are fallible, capable of error. Furthermore, human beings sometimes think it in their interest to lie. From 1980 to 1981, I worked for an electronic security company, monitoring the security systems of my employer's clients. One of the duties of the job was the keeping of a log of all significant events during one's shift. I know that in many cases, the contents of that log did not accurately reflect what actually transpired. There were, for example, times when there were so many significant events happening that by the time I got around to logging them, I was no longer able to recall precisely what had happened. And there were times when I or one of my fellow monitors decided to cover up some error or failure to follow prescribed company procedure by means of intentional falsification of the log. Are those who create government documents beyond any such human shortcomings? I see no reason to think so. So just as the value of witness testimony may be vitiated by the fallibility or the dishonesty of the witness, likewise the value of documentary evidence has to be scrutinized and judged for credibility like any other form of human testimony.

Now what about Dr. Martin's challenge to critics of the Institute for Historical Review to prove that it and its *Journal* "are in existence to spread falsehood"? Well, it so happens that, overall, I support the IHR's publication and dissemination of revisionist writings. In fact, I have myself been published in the IHR's *Journal of Historical Review*. So I have no intention of trying to prove that the IHR and its *Journal* exist for the specific purpose of spreading falsehood. Nevertheless, I can prove that the IHR and its *Journal* have, in fact, spread falsehood. Or, to be more specific, I can prove that they have spread *some* falsehood along with the truth they have spread.

Consider the IHR's Winter 1982/83 booklist. Among the publications you will find offered for sale are *The Methods of Re-education*, a booklet by Udo Walendy; *The Six Million Swindle*, a booklet by Austin J. App; *Debunking the Genocide Myth*, a collection of writings by the aforementioned Paul Rassinier; and *Six Million Lost and Found*, by "Richard Harwood," i.e., Richard Verrall, which was originally titled *Did Six Million Really Die?* Demonstrable falsehoods can be found in each of these publications.

Udo Walendy's booklet contains a choice falsehood on page 7, where Walendy misquotes Sefton Delmer's autobiography, *Black Boomerang*, wherein Delmer described his wartime activities supervising Britain's "black" radio propaganda campaigns against Germany. According to Walendy, Delmer wrote that

> as we put out news bulletin after news bulletin and service programme after service programme an entire system of atrocity campaigns developed.

But Delmer *actually* wrote,

> as we put out news bulletin after news bulletin and service programme after service programme an entire system of *subversive* campaigns developed [emphasis added].

By substituting the word "atrocity" for the word "subversive," Walendy fabricated a confession by Delmer of the British use of atrocity propaganda during World War II. Ironically, in another booklet, concerning allegedly forged atrocity photos, Walendy writes that "someone who knowingly uses retouched, clipped, transposed, drawn or otherwise altered photos and alleges that they are 'authentic photographs' *is guilty of fraud or forgery*." But, of course, the same is true of someone who knowingly uses altered quotations and alleges that they are "authentic quotations." Walendy also asserts that "Scientists and official institutions who allege that falsified pictures are authentic evidence, not only make themselves suspect with regard to these pictures but with regard to all their statements." By presenting an altered Sefton Delmer quotation as authentic evidence, Udo Walendy makes *himself* suspect with regard to all his statements, including his unsupported allegation about Sefton Delmer appearing at the end of page 8 of *The Methods of Re-education*.

On the first page of *The Six Million Swindle*, Austin App declares that "a search for the truth is mandatory." But his booklet nevertheless contains at least two falsehoods. On page 28, App writes,

> On February 22, 1948, probably unconscious of the implications, and therefor [sic] objective, Hanson Baldwin and the *New York Times*, after a world-wide census, reported that "there were between 18,000,000 and 19,000,000 Jews in the world.

But, in fact, the *Times* military affairs editor Hanson Baldwin, in an article on the Middle East situation, referred to "the 15 to 18 million Jews of the world." Furthermore, the figures *actually* given by Baldwin were supposedly based on a world-wide census only according to the testimony of one Benjamin H. Freedman. But Freedman was apparently App's source for the above-quoted falsified version of Baldwin's figures. (App refers to a statement by Freedman dated October 1966.) So Freedman's claim that he visited Baldwin in 1948 and was shown the results of such a world-wide census is clearly open to doubt.

On pages 28 and 29, App refers to Ben Hecht, who, according to App, "complained that his ancestors had not hacked Jesus up and fed him to the lions, so that the symbol of the cross would not have been revered." But the statement to which App refers was made by a fictional character in *A Jew In Love*, a novel by Hecht. According to Morris Kominsky, this character "is a very offensive, reactionary, anti-Communist degenerate by the name of Boshere." During a conversation, Boshere (the fictional character) says,

> One of the finest things ever done by the mob was the crucifixion of Christ. Intellectually it was a splendid gesture. But trust the mob to bungle. If I'd have been there, if I'd had charge of executing Christ, I'd have handled it differently. You see, what I would have done was had him shipped to Rome and fed to the lions. They could never have made a savior out of mince

meat. I would do the same thing to the radicals today.

As Morris Kominksy remarked, "Just imagine what confusion and dishonesty there would be in attributing to Shakespeare himself all the utterances of characters in his plays."

Debunking the Genocide Myth, the collection of writings by Paul Rassinier, includes "The Drama of the European Jews," a reply to Raul Hilberg's *The Destruction of the European Jews*. This work alone contains enough falsehoods to choke a correspondent for *The National Enquirer*. For starters, there is Rassinier's falsehood that Hannah Arendt, in her reports on the Eichmann trial, wrote that "3 million Polish Jews were massacred during the first day of the war." What Arendt actually wrote was that "three million Polish Jews, as everyone knew, had been massacred since the first days of the war." A slight difference in meaning.

Then there is Rassinier's falsehood that "Mr. Shalom Baron ... claimed on April 4, 1961, before the Jerusalem Tribunal, that 700,000 of them [Polish Jews] were still living in 1945 when the country was liberated by Russian troops." But what Salo (not Shalom) Baron actually claimed, on April 24 (not April 4), was that "according to the census carried out by the Central Jewish Committee in Poland, in August 1945, 73,955 Jews were left."

Thus, Rassinier exaggerated the number of Polish Jewish survivors claimed by Baron by 626,045.

Then there is Rassinier's falsehood that Raul Hilberg

> wants to prove that 1.4 million Jews were exterminated by the *Einsatzgruppen*, but after having used all means to prove it (reports of unit leaders, testimonies of witnesses who survived, etc.) he is still lacking 500,000 bodies, to come to his total, so, coolly, he adds, on his own authority, 250,000 for "omissions" and 250,000 for "gaps in our sources."

Hilberg actually reached the figure of 900,000 Jews exterminated by the *Einsatzgruppen* relying only on *Einsatzgruppen* reports and not, as Rassinier claims, by also using "testimonies of witnesses who survived, etc." And, while it is true that Hilberg adds 250,000 for "gaps in our sources," it is *not* true that he adds 250,000 for "omissions." Rather, he adds 250,000 based on "other fragmentary reports, most of which we have cited in this chapter."

These are but three specific—and serious—falsehoods in *The Drama of the European Jews*. There are plenty more where they came from. Just follow the sources and see for yourself.

In the introduction to *Six Million Lost and Found*, aka *Did Six Million Really Die?*, author Richard Verrall piously declares, "The aim on the following pages is quite simply to tell the Truth." But his booklet may be the most falsehood-laden specimen of Holocaust revisionism on the IHR's booklist. It contains enough falsehoods to make any writer of Hollywood docudramas green with envy. For example, there is Verrall's falsehood that "after the war, the *New York Times*, February 22, 1948, placed the number of Jews in the world at a minimum of 15,600,000 and a maximum of 18,700,000." As I've already pointed out, Hanson Baldwin actually referred to "the 15 to 18 million Jews of the world." Verrall makes Baldwin's figures more precise and larger than they actually were.

Then there is Verrall's attempt to discredit the Kurt Gerstein statements by claiming that "Gerstein's sister was congenitally insane and died by euthanasia, which may well suggest a streak of instability in Gerstein himself." But it was Gerstein's *sister-in-law*, Berta Ebeling, who allegedly was "congenitally insane," which suggests absolutely nothing about Gerstein himself.

Moving on, there is Verrall's falsehood that "The Russians refused to allow anyone to see Auschwitz until about ten years after the war, by which time they were able to alter its appearance and give some plausibility to the claim that millions of people were murdered there." But on pages 123–128 of *Ashes and Fire* (copyright 1947), Jacob Pat describes a tour of Auschwitz that he and some friends made. He recounts that Polish troops allowed him and his friends entrance to the camp after showing a "special military pass." Walter Lippmann, according to biographer Ronald Steel, visited Auschwitz in 1947. And in his 1948 book, *I Saw Poland Betrayed*, Arthur Bliss Lane, US Ambassador to Poland from 1944 to 1947, briefly describes the visit he made to Auschwitz during October of 1945 (if I have understood Lane's chronology accurately). Contrary to Verrall, *some* people *were* allowed to visit Auschwitz fairly soon after the war.

Verrall discusses the book *Under Two Dictators* by

Margarete Buber, a German-Jewish woman who had been imprisoned in a Russian labor camp before being deported to Germany in 1940. Verrall's discussion contains the falsehood that "[Buber] noted that she was the only Jewish person in her contingent of deportees from Russia who was not straight away released by the Gestapo." But this is a distortion of what Buber actually wrote. According to Buber,

> At the end of the second week in Lublin, all our women were taken one by one to the Gestapo—except me. They each returned with a form on which it said that they were to return at once to their home town, wherever it was, and report there to the Gestapo within three days of their arrival ... And then they went off, leaving me alone in the cells feeling terribly downhearted and abandoned.

Buber goes on to say that "Out of the 150 who had been handed over by the Russians, the Gestapo had retained forty men and myself. We were to go to the Police Presidium in Berlin under Gestapo escort." Buber does not say how many of those forty men were Jewish, but at least one of them was, as indicated by her reference to one of them as "the Jew from Hungary."

Then there is Verrall's falsehood that "Rassinier mentions [Eugen] Kogon's claim that a deceased former inmate, Janda Weiss, had said to Kogon alone that she had witnessed gas chambers at Auschwitz, but of course, since this person was apparently dead, Rassinier was unable to investigate the claim." But here is what

Rassinier actually says about the matter:

> To my knowledge this Janda Weiss was the only person in the whole of the concentration camp literature who was said to have been present at such exterminations [by gas] and whose exact address [Brno, Czechoslovakia] was given. Unfortunately, by unhappy chance, he was in the Russian zone and only Eugen Kogon has profited by his statements.

Clearly, Rassinier did not say that Janda Weiss was either dead or apparently dead but that he (not "she") was in the Russian zone.

By selling these publications by Walendy, App, Rassinier, and Verrall, the Institute for Historical Review is in fact spreading falsehood. And it should be added that the Institute's *Journal of Historical Review* and other IHR publications have also spread falsehood. One need only to turn to Volume 2, Number 3 of the flagship *Journal*, wherein were published several letters written by former IHR Director "Lewis Brandon," i.e., David McCalden. There one can find McCalden's falsehood contending that "Since 1960, all exterminationists have agreed that there were no gassings in the German camps; just in the Polish camps." Not true. There are yet "exterminationists" who do not regard Dr. Broszat's previously discussed and oft-misconstrued "admission" to be correct. See, for example, Germaine Tillion's book *Ravensbrück*, especially appendices 1–3.

Then there is McCalden's falsehood that Gitta Sereny "wrote in the *New Statesman* of 2 November 1979

88 | Outlaw History

… that many Holocaust 'memoirs' are faked." Consult the source, and you will discover that Sereny actually wrote that "some" (not "many") Holocaust memoirs have been faked, and she specifies only two such faked memoirs.

It might be noted that McCalden is no longer affiliated with the IHR. Nevertheless, McCalden's separation from the IHR did not precipitate an end to the publication of falsehoods by the IHR.[6] Consider just a few falsehoods to be found in post-McCalden IHR publications.

First, see page 4 of the IHR's October/November 1981 *Revisionist Newsletter*. There one will find an item concerning a column by Rabbi Yaacov Spivak in the August 21, 1981, *Jewish Press*. Spivak had discussed the taping of an episode of the *Phil Donahue Show*, the guests of which included several Holocaust survivors. According to the IHR's newsletter,

> Spivak reports what happened that day during the taping: "In the middle of the show, one of the producers—obviously quite shaken—walks on camera with the startling information that 7 out of 8 callers phoning the Chicago-based program said they were sick of hearing about the Holocaust, claimed it never happened, and made many blatantly anti-Semitic statements!" Were the millions of folks who watch the Donahue show made aware of this surprising response? Of course not, which is one good reason such shows are always taped.

---

6 Nor did it result in an end to the publication of falsehoods by David McCalden, but that's another story.

There are at least two falsehoods in this. The first may be found in Rabbi Spivak's distorted account, quoted accurately by the IHR, of what the *Donahue* show producer stated concerning what seven out of eight callers had said about the Holocaust survivors. Although the producer, Sherry Singer, did say that some of the callers said, "Let's not hear about it anymore," she did *not* say that any of the callers had claimed the Holocaust never happened. But there is another falsehood in the IHR's item, to wit, the claim that millions of folks who watch the *Donahue* show were not made aware of the "surprising response" of the callers. In fact, Sherry Singer's report that seven out of eight callers were "totally unsupportive" of the Holocaust survivors was *not* edited out of the show, as implied by the IHR. I myself saw and heard Ms. Singer making those statements when the program was broadcast in Los Angeles on August 11, 1981. Since Rabbi Spivak said nothing about Singer's comments being kept hidden from Donahue's viewers, this falsehood is the IHR's baby.

Now see page 308 of Volume 2, Number 4 of *The Journal of Historical Review*. There one can find, in a previously unpublished letter to *The Nation*, Paul Rassinier's falsehood that "the only document which speaks of gas chambers in these camps [Chelmno, Sobibor, Treblinka] is the Gerstein document." But if Gerstein's statements count as a document, then the various Rudolf Höss confessions must count as well. And at least one of the Höss confessions speaks of gas chambers at Chelmno, Treblinka, Sobibor, Belzec, and Maidanek. Furthermore, the depositions of Wilhelm Pfannenstiel speak of gas chambers at Belzec. According to both the Gerstein statements and the Pfannenstiel depositions, Pfannenstiel accompanied Gerstein to Belzec, where, despite their differing accounts, they both claimed to have witnessed the gassing of Jews.

Want more? On pages 280–281 of Vol. 3, No. 3 of *The Journal of Historical Review*, Issa Nakhleh, representative of the Arab Higher Committee and Permanent Representative of the Palestine-Arab delegation in New York, tells the following tale:

> The proof that Egypt was not prepared or preparing for war [in 1967] is the fact that, in the evening of June 4, 1967, a party was held for the airforce graduates in Anshas (former Farouk palace and gardens), where practically every important officer in the Egyptian airforce and all its commanders were present in that party until the early hours of the morning of June 5, when the Israelis attacked at 4 a.m. According to unimpeachable evidence in our possession, Egyptian agents of the Israeli intelligence were able to put LSD in the drinks and coffee served to most important officers and top command of the Egyptian airforce. When Israeli airplanes struck at 4 a.m. on the morning of June 5, most of the Egyptian airforce officers were asleep and incapacitated by LSD. We have also unimpeachable evidence that the Israeli airplanes dropped LSD-25, a nerve gas, on Egyptian forces in Sinai and on Egyptian military airports, and were

> able to incapacitate the Egyptian armed forces. These facts prove that the Israeli armed forces won the 1967 war by deception, conspiracy, and using LSD-25 nerve gas.

Well, the Israeli forces may have used deception and conspiracy to win the 1967 war, but Nakhleh's unsubstantiated allegations, supposedly based on unspecified "unimpeachable evidence"—he calls these allegations "facts"—prove absolutely nothing. And Nakhleh's allegations cannot be true as stated, since they depend upon the falsehood that LSD and LSD-25 are two different things. According to Nakhleh, LSD is the infamous drug, while LSD-25 is a nerve gas. But LSD-25 is not a nerve gas. LSD-25 is simply LSD. That is, LSD-25 is simply a more specific designation for the drug more commonly known as LSD. There are other reasons for skepticism about Nakhleh's tale of Israeli intrigue and chemical warfare,[7] but his falsehood that LSD-25 is a nerve gas, rather than the well-known psychoactive drug, is sufficient reason to impeach his "unimpeachable evidence."

If Issa Nakhleh actually has unimpeachable evidence to back up his accusations, I'll hump a camel.

As I write this, it is August of 1983, and the IHR has recently published a leaflet entitled "66 Questions and Answers on the Holocaust." The first question the leaflet asks is, "What proof exists that the Nazis practiced genocide or deliberately killed six million Jews?" The leaflet answers, "None." This is elaborated with two

---

7   Editor's Note: See Rollins' definition of "Irrefutable Evidence" in *Lucifer's Lexicon: Expanded and Revised Edition* (Underworld Amusements & Nine-Banded Books, 2018).

falsehoods, the first of which states, "The only evidence is the testimony of individual 'survivors.' This testimony is contradictory and no 'survivor' claims to have actually witnessed any gassing." Contrary to the IHR's leaflet, however, the testimony of survivors is not the only evidence. The testimony of Rudolf Höss, Franz Stangl, Joseph Kramer, Pery Broad, Johann Paul Kremer, and Kurt Gerstein has already been mentioned. In addition, incriminatory testimony was also given by Wilhelm Hoettl, Dieter Wisliceny, Otto Ohlendorf, and other former minions of the Third Reich. And, again contrary to the IHR's leaflet, some survivors *do* claim to have witnessed gassings. For example, in *One Year in Treblinka*, originally published in May of 1944, Jankiel Wiernik claims to have witnessed gassings at Treblinka. Sophia Litwinska also claims to have witnessed a gassing at Auschwitz. In fact, she claims to have been pulled out of a gas chamber while a gassing was in progress! And in his book, *Eyewitness Auschwitz*, Filip Müller claims to have witnessed gassings at Auschwitz I and Birkenau while he was a member of the *Sonderkommando*.

The falsehoods I have pointed out suggest the possibility that some revisionists aim not to set the record straight but to bring the record into alignment with their own preconceptions. If "revisionism" means bringing history into accord with facts, as Harry Elmer Barnes put it, then some of what passes for revisionism is not revisionism at all.

It is unfortunately true that the *Journal of Historical Review* and other IHR publications, ostensibly intended for "lovers of historical truth," have indeed spread falsehood. But, in fairness, the *Journal* has sometimes also provided a forum for exposing the falsehoods of revisionists. For example, I was able to expose Paul Rassinier's falsehood concerning Salo Baron in the *Journal*'s pages.[8]

Nevertheless, the IHR has spread falsehood via some of the publications it sells as well as its own publications. This speaks to the validity of a point made by Steven Springer in his introduction to *Reason* magazine's special revisionism issue in February 1976. After making the case for revisionism, Springer provides a caveat: "This is not to say, however, that the works of anyone calling himself a revisionist should be accepted without question. People can get carried away by their theories ... and invent or distort facts accordingly." Q.E.D.

However—and I want to emphasize this—I am prepared to demonstrate that exponents of the standard Holocaust narrative have themselves spread many, many falsehoods. Neither side in the Holocaust controversy claims a monopoly on falsehood. That is why I generally believe nothing I read on this subject unless and until I can verify it to my own satisfaction. This is one reason why, after almost a decade of following the controversy, I remain skeptical of both sides.

I say: Down with Holocaust dogmatism, regardless of the source.

I say: Up with Holocaust *skepticism*.

---

[8] Review of Azriel Eisenberg's Witness to the Holocaust, *Journal of Historical Review*, Vol. 4, No. 1, Spring 1983.

SOURCES

App, Austin J., *The Six Million Swindle: Blackmailing the German People for Hard Marks with Fabricated Corpses*. Boniface Press, 1976.

Arendt, Hannah, *Eichmann in Jerusalem*. Viking Compass, 1965.

Baldwin, Hanson, "Armies for Palestine: Need for International Force of 70,000 Believed Indicated as U. N. Faces Decision," *New York Times*, 22 February 1948, p. 4.

Brandon, Lewis, et al., "Unanswered Correspondence," *Journal of Historical Review*, Vol. 2, No. 3, Fall 1981.

Brecher, Edward M., *Licit and Illicit Drugs*. Little Brown & Co., 1972.

Broszat, Martin, Dr., Letter in *Die Zeit*, 19 August 1960, p. 16.

Buber, Margarete, *Under Two Dictators*. Dodd and Mead, 1949.

Butz, Arthur R., *The Hoax of the Twentieth Century: The Case Against the Presumed Extermination of European Jewry*. Institute for Historical Review, 1980.

Dawidowicz, Lucy S., *The Holocaust and the Historians*. Harvard University Press, 1981.

Delmer, D. Sefton, *Black Boomerang*. Viking Press, 1962.

Donat, Alexander, ed., *The Death Camp Treblinka*. Holocaust Library, 1979.

Friedländer, Saul, *Kurt Gerstein: The Ambiguity of Good*. Alfred A. Knopf, 1969.

Harwood, Richard, *Six Million Lost and Found*. Institute for Historical Review, 1979.

Hecht, Ben, *A Jew In Love*. Covici-Friede, 1931.

Hilberg, Raul, *The Destruction of the European Jews*. Quadrangle Books, 1967.

Höss, Rudolf, *Commandant at Auschwitz*. Popular Library, 1959.

Hoggan, David L., *The Myth of the Six Million*. The Noontide Press, 1969.

Institute for Historical Review, "66 Questions and Answers on the Holocaust" (Leaflet published by The Institute for Historical Review), 1983.

Institute for Historical Review, "Other Revisionist News," *Revisionist Newsletter*, 1981, p. 4.

Joffroy, Pierre, *A Spy for God: The Ordeal of Kurt Gerstein*. Harcourt Brace Jovanovich, 1971.

Kominsky, Morris, *The Hoaxers: Plain Liars, Fancy Liars and Damned Liars*. Branden Press, 1970.

Lane, Walter Bliss, *I Saw Poland Betrayed*. Western Islands, 1965.

Martin, James J., "On the Latest Crisis Provoked by Revisionism," *New Libertarian*, Vol. 4, No. 10, October 1981, pp. 12–15.

Martin, James J., Personal correspondence with the author, 12 July 1983.

Martin, James J., "Raphael Lemkin and the Invention of Genocide," *The Journal of Historical Review*, Vol. 2, No. 1, Spring 1981, pp. 19–34.

Müller, Filip, *Eyewitness Auschwitz: Three Years in the Gas Chambers*. Stein & Day, 1979.

Nakhleh, Issa, "Memorandum to the President," *The Journal of Historical Review*, Vol. 3, No. 3, Fall 1982, pp. 280–281.

Naumann, Bernd, *Auschwitz*. Frederick A. Praeger, 1966.

North, Gary, "World War II Revisionism and Vietnam," *Reason*, February 1976, pp. 34–39.

Pat, Jacob, *Ashes and Fire*. International Universities Press, 1948.

Rassinier, Paul, *Debunking the Genocide Myth: A Study of the Nazi Concentration Camps and the Alleged Extermination of European Jewry*. The Noontide Press, 1978.

Rassinier, Paul, "Letter to *The Nation*," *Journal of Historical Review*, Vol. 2, No. 4, Winter 1981, p. 305.

Reitlinger, Gerald R., *The Final Solution*. Perpetua / A.S. Barnes & Company, 1961.

Rollins, L.A., "The Holocaust as Sacred Cow," *Journal of Historical Review*, Vol. 4, No. 1, Spring 1983.

Rollins, L.A., Review of Lawrence Dennis' and Maximilian St. George's *A Trial on Trial*, *Journal of Historical Review*, Vol. 6, No. 1, Spring 1985, p. 123.

Rollins, L.A., Review of Azriel Eisenberg's *Witness to the Holocaust*, *Journal of Historical Review*, Vol. 4, No. 1, Spring 1983.

Sereny, Gitta, "The Men Who Whitewash Hitler," *New Statesman*, 2 November 1979.

Shub, Boris, ed., *Hitler's Ten-Year War on the Jews*. Institute of Jewish Affairs of the American Jewish Congress, World Jewish Congress, 1943.

Shub, Boris, ed., *Starvation Over Europe: Made in Germany*. Institute of Jewish Affairs of the American Jewish Congress, World Jewish Congress, 1943.

Springer, Steven, Editorial Introduction, *Reason*, February 1976, p. 4.

Steele, Ronald, *Walter Lippmann and the American Century*. Little Brown & Co., 1980.

Tillion, Germaine, *Ravensbrück*. Anchor Press, 1975.

Walendy, Udo, *Forged War Crimes Malign the German Nation*. Kolle-Druck, 1979.

Walendy, Udo, *The Methods of Re-education*. Verlag fur Volkstum und Zeitgeschichtforschung, 1979.

Wiernik, Jankiel, *A Year in Treblinka*. American Representation of the General Jewish Workers' Union of Poland, 1944.

Zaugg, Ernest, "The Nazi Whitewash," *The Nation*, No. 195, 14 July 1962.

Zeiger, Henry, A., *The Case Against Adolf Eichmann*. Signet Books, 1960.

Book Reviews

DEIFYING DOGMA
Denying History
Michael Shermer and Alex Grobman
University of California Press, 2000

Author's Note (2008)

When I wrote "The Holocaust as Sacred Cow" and "Revising Holocaust Revisionism" in the early 1980s, there was, as yet, no debate between revisionists and orthodox Holocaustorians. The Holocausters, for years, were content to call the revisionists names, denounce the imputed motives of the revisionists, lie about what the revisionists were claiming, and to make dogmatic pronouncements about the overwhelming and indisputable Truth of Holocaust orthodoxy.

However, beginning sometime in the late 1980s, a kind of debate began to emerge, as a few orthodox Holocaust scholars provided serious critical appraisals of revisionist—or "negationist"—arguments. Some anti-revisionist texts which, despite their shortcomings, might ultimately prove to be of significant value include Pierre Vidal-Naquet's *Assassins of*

Memory, Jean-Claude Pressac's *Auschwitz: Technique and Operation of the Gas Chambers*, and *The Case for Auschwitz* by Robert Jan van Pelt.

Denying History by Michael Shermer of the Skeptics Society and Alex Grobman of the Simon Wiesenthal Center is an altogether different kettle of gefilte fish. Simply stated, it is one of the worst would-be refutations of Holocaust revisionism that I have yet encountered (though some of the others are pretty bad). As a general rule, shitty books are best ignored and forgotten. However, since Grobman and Shermer made the mistake of smearing me—*moi!*—in the pages of their meretricious, pseudo-skeptical screed, I was willing, even eager, to review it and to point out some of the many instances where they go wrong.

In "Revising Holocaust Revisionism," I concluded my critical assessment of certain revisionist claims by stating that I *could* just as easily point out falsehoods in the writings of orthodox Holocaust historians. With "Deifying Dogma," I believe I have made good on this. Both revisionists and anti-revisionists have peddled falsehoods; it just so happens that Grobman and Shermer are swimming in them.

If Shermer and/or Grobman ever responded to my review, they didn't bother to notify me, so, as far as I know, my critique of this dynamic duo of Holocaust orthodoxy remains unanswered.

DEIFYING DOGMA (2000)

MICHAEL SHERMER IS THE FOUNDER and editor of *Skeptic* magazine, director of the Skeptics Society, and adjunct professor of the History of Science at Occidental College in Los Angeles, as well as the author of *Why People Believe Weird Things* (1997) and *How We Believe: The Search for God in the Age of Science* (1999).

Alex Grobman is the author and editor of a number of books on the Holocaust, including *Rekindling the Flame: American Jewish Chaplains and the Survivors of European Jewry*. He is also the founding editor of the *Simon Wiesenthal Annual*.

In *Denying History*, Shermer, a self-described "professional skeptic," and Grobman, a professional Jew, have teamed up to tell the hoi polloi what they're supposed to think about various unorthodox historical claims, primarily the claims of Holocaust revisionism, or "Holocaust denial," as they prefer to label it.

In his foreword to Grobman and Shermer's egregious opus, prominent scholar-activist Arthur Hertzberg effuses, "They take up the contentions of the Holocaust deniers, point by point, and refute them down to the smallest detail." Shermer and Grobman likewise promise a thorough refutation of the revisionists, er, I mean, "deniers."

So how does this dynamic duo accomplish such an amazing feat of intellectual heroism? First and foremost, they have "thoroughly refuted" the revisionists by *ignoring most of what revisionists have written*. Thus, a number of significant revisionist studies are neither cited in the authors' bibliography nor mentioned in their text. There is no reference, for example, to *The Auschwitz Myth* by William Stäglich, nor to Carlo Mattogno's *Auschwitz: The End of a Legend*, nor to Walter Sanning's *The Dissolution of European Jewry*, nor to Samuel Crowell's *The Gas*

Chamber of Sherlock Holmes, nor to Michael A. Hoffman II's *The Great Holocaust Trial.* These are substantial omissions which seriously undermine Grobman and Shermer's claim to having put forth anything approaching a "thorough" refutation of revisionist arguments.

Revisionist books that are mentioned get short shrift. A prime example is *The Hoax of the Twentieth Century* by Arthur Butz. *Hoax* gets mentioned only four times, and in three of these instances, Shermer and Grobman falsely cite arguments that Butz does not make. As for their one reasonably accurate reference concerning Butz's interpretation of the Wannsee Protocol, they don't bother to discuss what he actually wrote. Nor do they bother to mention the German government documents that Butz cites in support of his interpretation. The vast bulk of *The Hoax of the Twentieth Century*, like the vast bulk of revisionist scholarship, is given the silent treatment. But again, in Grobman and Shermer's world, this is how you "thoroughly refute" an argument—by pretending it isn't there.

Another example of Grobman and Shermer's "thorough refutation" can be seen in their treatment of Fred Leuchter's conclusions regarding the infinitesimal or non-existent traces of hydrogen cyanide compounds in the alleged homicidal gas chambers of Auschwitz and Birkenau. On pages 129–130 and 132, Shermer and Grobman make the false assertion that all of those alleged gas chambers are nothing but rubble and have been completely exposed to the elements since 1945.

In fact, this is not true of the alleged gas chamber of the crematorium of Auschwitz, nor is it true of the alleged gas chamber of Crematorium II of Birkenau.

Further, the authors assume that exposure to the elements would reduce the amount of any residue of hydrogen cyanide compounds, including ferric ferrocyanide. Jewish revisionist David Cole challenged this unproven assumption in his manuscript *46 Important Unanswered Questions Regarding the Nazi Gas Chambers*. Cole asked why Zyklon B blue staining, indicative of the presence of hydrogen cyanide, is still present on the *outside* of a brick delousing building at Majdanek, against which clothing and blankets were beaten to remove gas residue after delousing (a standard prophylactic against the typhus louse, which plagued parts of Europe during WWII). Why weren't *these* blue stains washed away by the weather?

On page 132, Shermer and Grobman do offer a reply to Cole on this point:

> His question sounds reasonable, but when we visited Majdanek we could see that the blue staining on the outside bricks is minimal. Moreover, a roof overhang has protected the bricks from rain and snow, so that the bricks at Majdanek are nowhere near as weathered as the open rubble [of the alleged homicidal gas chambers] at Auschwitz. In addition, Cole gives no citations for some of his claims.

But Shermer and Grobman give no citation for some of *their* claims, such as their assertion that exposure to the elements will reduce or remove residue of hydrogen cyanide compounds, including ferric ferrocyanide. While giving the impression of having answered

Cole's question about Majdanek, they have not answered a similar question regarding the dark-blue staining still present on an outside wall of a delousing building at Birkenau.[1]

The delousing building at Birkenau has a roof overhang of, at most, only several inches. The darkly stained outside wall of the delousing building at Birkenau has not been protected from rain, snow, or other weather by the roof overhang. Why then are those dark blue stains still present after all these years? You won't find any answer to that question in *Denying History*.

The authors have "thoroughly refuted" Leuchter, Cole, et al. by pretending to reasonably answer one question while refusing to respond to a similar and more difficult question.

Another of their glaring omissions relates to Paul Grubach's article "The Leuchter Report Vindicated,"[2] in which Grubach rebuts criticism of Leuchter made by Jean-Claude Pressac. Although Shermer and Grobman parrot many of Pressac's arguments against Leuchter, they omit any mention of Grubach's counter-arguments. Grubach's article is listed in their bibliography, however, indicating that their evasion is conscious and deliberate.

Giving the silent treatment to so much of the revisionist literature is far from the only act of intellectual dishonesty in *Denying History*. Another method favored by Shermer and Grobman is to make false claims about the content of revisionist studies.

---

[1] *Cf.* Jean-Claude Pressac, *Auschwitz: Technique and Operation of the Gas Chambers*, The Beate Klarsfeld Foundation, 1989, p. 59.

[2] "The Leuchter Report Vindicated," *The Journal of Historical Review*, Vol. 12, No. 4, Winter 1992, p. 445.

In three of the four instances in which they condescend to refer to the contents of Arthur Butz's *The Hoax of the Twentieth Century*, Shermer and Grobman falsely attribute to Butz arguments that he does not make. For example, on page 178, they write, "Deniers claim that no extermination camp victim has given eyewitness testimony of gassings. If so many millions of Jews were exterminated surely someone could tell us what happened, Butz insists." In their footnote for this assertion (p. 278), they cite *The Hoax of the Twentieth Century*, pages 10–12. But there is nothing even vaguely resembling the argument they have attributed to Butz on these pages (or, for that matter, anywhere in his book that I recall).

On page 61 of *Denying History*, the authors falsely attribute to Butz the apparently contradictory statement "that Raul Hilberg's 1961 classic work, *The Destruction of the European Jews*, was fraudulent in its reliance on eyewitness accounts of gassings at Auschwitz." Actually, this "claim" appears to be a grossly distorted version of what Bradley Smith wrote in his memoir, *Confessions of a Holocaust Revisionist*.[3]

In addition to Butz, victims of Shermer and Grobman's misrepresentation include Paul Rassinier, Robert Faurisson, Mark Weber, and yours truly. Shermer and Grobman libel me on pages 84–85 of their tome. Quoting two definitions from my satirical dictionary, *Lucifer's Lexicon*, they declare that I have advanced "a

---

3   Smith was attempting to discern the meaning of a reference Butz had made, in the foreword to *The Hoax of the Twentieth Century*, to pp. 567–571 of Hilberg's *The Destruction of the European Jews*.

peculiar and paradoxical denial of mass extermination along with a hint that Hitler should have finished the job."

Now, I can understand that some very obtuse persons lacking an appreciation of satire might conceivably misconstrue my humorous definition of "The Holocaust" as being a denial of "mass extermination," even though, in reality, I don't deny "mass extermination" at all.[4] What I find hard to fathom, however, is how these two cheese puffs have managed to detect any "hint" in *Lucifer's Lexicon* "that Hitler should have finished the job." There is no such suggestion or implication in my book. Shermer and Grobman simply fabricate the accusation in order to defame me. To facilitate their smear, they quote me selectively. They publish my definition of "Zionist Propaganda" ("Hebrew National baloney") but overlook my definition of "Nazi Propaganda" ("Goebelled information. Lies that limp as they goosestep").

The deceit continues on pages 137–139 where the duo discuss the postwar "confessions" of SS *Unterscharführer* (Sergeant) Pery Broad, who had been stationed at Auschwitz. After his arrest by the British on May 6, 1945, and while working for them as an interpreter, Broad allegedly wrote a "memoir" which was "passed on" to British intelligence in July 1945. The "Broad Report" contains an account of Auschwitz as an "extermination camp," in which some two or three million Jews were murdered.[5]

---

4   Mass extermination is not necessarily equivalent to "The Holocaust," which, according to Shermer and Grobman, signifies the destruction of at least five million Jews by means of gas chambers and other weapons as part of an intentional plan.

5   Shermer and Grobman, who claim that about one million

In order to convince readers of the authenticity of the "Broad Report," Shermer and Grobman assert, "In April of 1959 Broad was called to testify at a trial of captured Auschwitz SS members and acknowledged authorship of the memoir, confirmed its authenticity and retracted nothing."

Actually, Broad was *arrested* in April 1959 and was subsequently one of the defendants in the "Auschwitz trial," which convened in Frankfurt in January 1964. As for what Broad actually said about the "Broad Report" of 1945 when questioned in 1964, here is what can be found on page 162 of *Auschwitz*, Bernd Naumann's account of the trial:

> After some hesitation Broad admits that he is the sole author of this report, but he says that he cannot stand behind everything in it because some of the things he wrote were based on hearsay.[6]

Since Naumann's book is listed in Shermer and Grobman's bibliography, the authors presumably know that their description of Broad's trial testimony is largely false. Yet the authors seem determined to compound their fraudulent misrepresentation, as they go on (p. 138) to quote statements from the 1945 "Broad Report" while pretending they are quoting from Broad's 1964 trial testimony!

Jews died at Auschwitz, do not mention this discrepancy.

6   *Auschwitz: A Report on the Proceedings Against Robert Karl Ludwig Mulka and Others Before the Court at Frankfurt*, Praeger, 1966.

108 | Outlaw History

Next, the authors assume the mantle of word sleuths. On pages 205–206, they write of

> Another piece of evidence in our pantheon, [Pantheon? Do they really liken each piece of evidence for the Holocaust to a god?] is a word that appears in numerous Nazi documents referring to Jews, *ausrotten*, which means "to extirpate or exterminate." In *Hitler's War*, David Irving claims that *ausrotten* really means "stamping out" or "rooting out." For instance, he translates a conversation between Hitler and Alfred Rosenberg, the Nazi Reich Minister for the eastern occupied territories. In Rosenberg's discussion of handling the Jews, Irving takes *ausrotten* to mean "stamping out" and then concludes that Rosenberg meant transporting Jews out of the Reich. But modern dictionaries say *ausrotten* means "to exterminate, extirpate, or destroy." Irving's response to this is, "The word *ausrotten* means one thing now in 1994, but it meant something very different in the time that Adolf Hitler uses it." Yet a check of historical dictionaries shows that *ausrotten* has always meant "exterminate."

In the footnote to the final sentence just quoted, the authors write, "See for example *Langenscheidt's German–English, English–German Dictionary* (Berlin: Langenscheidt, 1942.) Under *ausrotten*, the dictionary gives 'root out; extirpate; exterminate.'"

On the one hand, this 1942 dictionary definition

tends to substantiate Shermer and Grobman's claim that *ausrotten* has always meant "exterminate." So if Irving actually said that *ausrotten* never denoted "exterminate" during the Nazi era, then he was wrong on that point. On the other hand, this 1942 definition upholds Irving's assertion that *ausrotten* means "rooting out" (at least in some cases).

Yet *Denying History* denies, by clear implication, that *ausrotten* ever meant "root out" or anything other than "exterminate," "extirpate," or "destroy." But the 1942 dictionary definition buried in a footnote in the back of their book shows that they are wrong on this point and that *they know they are wrong*. Thus, Shermer and Grobman are lying to their readers when, in various places in their text, they insinuate or insist that *ausrotten* means only "exterminate, extirpate, destroy," or even "murder" (p. 191) and has never had any other meaning.[7,8]

Furthermore, although *ausrotten* does not necessarily mean "exterminate," the word "exterminate" can have more than one meaning and does not automatically signify genocide. When British Colonel Spottiswood

---

7   For more on this subject, see L.J. Rather, *Reading Wagner: A Study in the History of Ideas*, Louisiana State University Press, 1990, pp. 212–213.

8   Incidentally, Shermer and Grobman's page 191 claim that "*Ausrotten* meant murder" follows a supposed quotation from a lecture by SS chief Heinrich Himmler to his *Gruppen-führers* (lieutenant-generals) in January 1937, in which he implied, according to their translation, that the Nazi State was murdering [*ausrotteten*] the Communists. Unfortunately for Shermer and Grobman, in January 1937 there definitely was not any Nazi State policy of murdering the Communists. The policy was to imprison them in concentration camps, which, as least at that early date, were in no sense "death camps."

110 | Outlaw History

addressed a group of German civilians ordered to visit the Bergen-Belsen concentration camp on April 24, 1945, he stated, "What you will see here is the final and utter condemnation of the Nazi Party. It justifies every measure which the United Nations will take to exterminate that Party."[9] Was Spottiswood saying that the United Nations intended to kill all members of the Nazi Party?

Winston Churchill, in a memorandum written on July 8, 1940, said that he could see only one way to defeat Germany and therefore proposed "an absolutely devastating, exterminating attack by very heavy bombers from this country upon the Nazi homeland."[10] Was Churchill proposing to *kill all Germans* by his use of this phrase?

Many of the familiar arguments which Shermer and Grobman use in attempting to make their case against Holocaust skepticism will bore seasoned revisionists. But in one instance, they claim to have discovered new evidence to vindicate gas-chamber orthodoxy. This involves two aerial photos of Birkenau taken on May 31, 1944, which appear as figure 21 on page 149 of *Denying History*. In their caption for these photographs, Shermer and Grobman write,

> image enhancement enables us to decipher a group of people seemingly being marched into Crematorium V. [It's actually Crematorium IV.] The front of the long line is turning into the Crematorium grounds through an opening in

---

9 *Cf.* Jon Bridgman, *The End of the Holocaust: The Liberation of the Camps*, Areopagitica Press, 1990, p. 54.

10 Quoted in Max Hastings, *Bomber Command*, Dial Press/J. Wade, 1979, p. 116.

the fence; comparison of these two shots reveals some movement in the line into the crematorium grounds.

In order to interpret these photos as evidence of mass extermination by gassing, the authors make the unproven assumption that the only likely reason for a line of people to have been moving into the yard of the crematorium was to go into the crematorium to be "gassed." But even if one were to accept this unproven assumption, there would still be problems with the authors' thesis.

Examining these photos with the naked eye, I see no evidence of movement whatsoever. The dark blotches that Shermer and Grobman interpret as a queue of people in movement appear to be in the same place in both photos. In contrast, people in movement *are* evident to the naked eye in two sets of aerial photographs of Auschwitz taken on August 25, 1944, which Shermer and Grobman reproduce on pages 147–148 as figures 19 and 20 (the lines of people in those photos are not alleged to be headed toward any homicidal gas chamber).

It does not seem to have occurred to the authors, who like to pose as scientific historians, to compare the two Birkenau photos of May 31, 1944, with similar Birkenau photos taken on other dates to see if any dark blotches are visible in the same places as in the May 31 photos. If the dark blotches do appear in the same places in photos of Birkenau taken on other dates, then that would indicate a very high probability that the dark blotches in question are not people but some sort of stationary objects, such as trees or shrubs (there were trees in the vicinity of the facilities in 1944).

So I did what Shermer and Grobman apparently did not bother to do. I consulted revisionist researcher John Ball's book, *Air Photo Evidence*.[11] On page 70, I found a photo of Birkenau taken on June 26, 1944, which shows most, though not all, of the area visible in the May 31 photos. Lo and behold! This photo does show dark blotches in roughly the same places as in the May 31 photos.[12]

Do Shermer and Grobman wish to disregard the statistical probabilities and absurdly claim that the May 31 aerial photos and the June 26 photo show two different groups of people, each headed toward "Crematorium V" [sic], who just happen to be in at least approximately the same place? If not, then they can kiss this supposed new evidence of gassings goodbye.[13]

It should be conceded that *Denying History* does contain a few legitimate criticisms of revisionist claims and arguments. But considering the great number of revisionist claims and arguments that Shermer and Grobman refuse to confront, their criticisms of revisionism, legitimate or otherwise, amount to mere hypocritical sniping.

This is hypocrisy on their part because almost all of the fallacies they rightly or wrongly attribute to

---

11 Ball Resource Services, 1992.
12 I say "roughly" because this photo is of poorer quality than the May 31 photos; hence, the correspondence is not exact.
13 It should be noted in this regard that Shermer and Grobman argue that mass gassings did not occur as often as many people assume. This is their way of explaining why none of the aerial photos of Auschwitz, taken on several different days during 1944, show any smoke or flame emanating from the crematoria "chimneys."

revisionists—quoting out of context, selective quotation, selective use of evidence, the "snapshot fallacy," making unsupported assertions, engaging in speculation—are committed by Shermer and Grobman themselves in *Denying History*.

There is also an aspect of hypocrisy in this book that pertains solely to Shermer, who claims to be a "skeptic." While Shermer is extremely skeptical toward the unorthodox doubts which Holocaust revisionists harbor toward the homicidal-gas-chamber stories, he exhibits no similar skepticism toward the claims of his fellow true believers in Holocaust orthodoxy. Indeed, he reveals himself to be a dogmatic and deceitful defender of this orthodoxy.

Shermer is skeptical concerning the Doubting Thomases of his time but clings to faith in the deified dogma put forth by the consensus of his time. Shermer's self-promoted status as a "professional skeptic" is a fraud.

I do not claim to have "thoroughly refuted" the contents of *Denying History*. Nor do I claim to have proven anything whatsoever about what occurred in Europe during the Second World War. Unlike Shermer and Grobman, I am not trying to defend any dogma at all. All I have attempted to do is to show that *Denying History* fails miserably to live up to the hyperbolic claims that the authors and their credulous supporters have advanced in promoting it. The skeptic's knife cuts in every direction.

A slightly different version of this essay originally appeared in *Revisionist History*, Number 16, October–November (2000).

WITNESS TO THE HOLOCAUST
Witness to the Holocaust
Azriel Eisenberg
The Pilgrim Press, 1981

WITNESS TO THE HOLOCAUST is a collection of "eyewitness accounts of a brutal period in history" compiled and edited by Dr. Azriel Eisenberg, "a leading Jewish scholar," who has provided introductions to each of the 27 chapters and to many of the selections contained therein. As psychohistorian Howard Stein has written, "Between 1933 and 1945 some awesomely terrible things took place in Europe—*to everyone*. It is, however, another matter to view the entire sordid era through the eyes of a single group—the Jews—and to accept this interpretation as the only valid one." But that is pretty much what *Witness to the Holocaust* does; it views the entire Nazi era almost exclusively through the eyes of a single group—the Jews—and accepts this Judeocentric interpretation as the only valid one.

Eisenberg's Judeocentrism comes out, for example,

in his dogmatic proclamation (p. 5) that "The Holocaust was unique." Of course, in a trivial sense, the Holocaust was unique, for, as Harry Elmer Barnes once wrote, "Every historical situation is essentially unique, never again to be repeated in its entirety." But Eisenberg's proclamation is supposed to be a *significant* truth. So in what significant sense was the Holocaust unique? According to Eisenberg (p. 2), "it was the Jews that were singled out for *total* destruction." But as readers of this journal know, this assertion is, at best, debateable. And Eisenberg makes no attempt whatever to prove this, at best, debateable assertion. But even if the Jews were slated for total destruction by the Third Reich, that doesn't necessarily make the Holocaust unique. According to the Old Testament, the Hittites, the Amorites, the Canaanites, the Perizzites, the Hivites and the Jebusites were all marked out for total destruction by the Lord God of Israel:

> "And so Joshua defeated the whole land, the hill country and the Negeb, and the lowland and the slopes, and their kings. He left none remaining, but utterly destroyed all that breathed, as the Lord God of Israel commanded." (Joshua 10:40).

Furthermore, Eisenberg himself contradicts his claim that the Jews were singled out for total destruction. In the very next paragraph after the one in which he makes that claim, he turns around and says,

> One people that shared the fate of the Jews were the Gypsies. They, too, had been persecuted

> through the ages, and like the Jews, the Gypsies were isolated and liquidated, country by country.... When the bloodbath was over, only pitiful remnants were left alive.... Except for the few survivors, a whole people, unique in its lifestyle, language, culture, and art, was wiped off the face of the earth. There are no memorials to their dead or commemorations of their tragedy. The death of the Gypsy nation was more than physical; it was total oblivion. (p. 2)

Thus, Eisenberg contradicts Eisenberg. The implication, of course, is that the Holocaust, the alleged extermination of the Jews, was not unique. Nevertheless, three pages later, Eisenberg is insisting, "The Holocaust was unique."

Why the doublethink? Why this insistence on the uniqueness of the Holocaust? Well, as Eric Hoffer observed in *The Passionate State of Mind*,

> Monotheism—the adherence to a one and only God, truth, cause, leader, nation and so on—is usually the end result of a search for pride. It was the craving to be a one and only people which impelled the ancient Hebrews to invent a one and only God whose one and only people they were to be.
>
> Whenever we proclaim the uniqueness of a religion, a truth, a leader, a nation, a race, a party or a holy cause [or a holocaust], we are also proclaiming our own uniqueness.

Azriel Eisenberg and all the other Jews who proclaim the uniqueness of the Holocaust are also proclaiming their own uniqueness. What is the nature of this uniqueness? As Howard Stein puts it, "To Jews, the Holocaust ... interweaves two elements of the doctrine of Chosenness: (a) election as moral superiority, and (b) election to suffer." In fact, we find both of these elements of the doctrine of Chosenness explicitly affirmed in one of Eisenberg's selections. In "The Time Was Midnight," Zionist rabbi Joachim Prinz reminisces about his life in Nazi Germany during the 1930s:

> I told them from the pulpit, in every sermon, that to be a Jew is to be beautiful, great, noble, and that we had every right to feel superior.... There are times when people who have been degraded and humiliated have to say that in reality they are "beautiful." Sometimes I exaggerated. But it was planned exaggeration. I spoke about the Jewish face, the beauty of the Jew as a human being; I spoke about the Jewish contribution to civilization and that the world could not really exist without us, and that Christianity and Islam were indebted to us. All of this was designed not merely to reject the Nazi propaganda, but to replace it with a sense of superiority—moral, cultural, religious and human.
>
> ...I spoke about hammer and anvil, and the hammer had to be rejected and detested. It hurt to be the anvil, but it was morally superior. I often preached about "pity the prosecutor," and

how superior are the people who are subjected to persecution, how much pride there is in suffering because we believe that in the end hammers and persecutors will be discarded while we shall continue to live. (pp. 92–93)

As Holocaustomania goes, Eisenberg's case is extreme. We are told that he "has devoted much of his life to a study of the Holocaust." And, apparently, he wants every other Jew to do likewise. He says, "we must study the Holocaust; the deaths of six million Jews have charged us to live, to learn, to remember, and to tell the world." And, he says, "We should be furious with our peers who are apathetic and to whom this catastrophe is irrelevant to their daily lives." In other words, to be a good Jew, and to avoid Eisenberg's fury, one must be as obsessed with the Holocaust as he is. Now that's Holocaustomania!

Although Eisenberg wants Jews to study the Holocaust, he wants them to study it in approximately the manner in which Catholics study the catechism. He actually has the nerve to tell his readers, "This is not just another book on a heartrending chapter of modern history; it is a scroll of agony and heroism. As such, it must be studied with awe and reverence." And, he declares, "The *Shoah* [a Hebrew term which is used interchangeably with "Holocaust"] cannot be intellectualized." In other words, Eisenberg is telling his readers, Don't think; don't question; don't criticize. Just *feel* and *believe*.

I wonder if Eisenberg has ever read Ayn Rand's

novel *The Fountainhead*. Here is Ellsworth Toohey, the villain of the novel, explaining his methods of achieving power over others:

> If you get caught at some point and somebody tells you that your doctrine doesn't make sense—you're ready for him. You tell him that there's something above sense. That here he must not try to think, he must feel. He must believe. Suspend reason and you play it deuces wild. Anything goes in any manner you wish whenever you need it. You've got him. Can you rule a thinking man? We don't want any thinking men.[1]

When Eisenberg tells his readers the Holocaust cannot be intellectualized (viewed intellectually), that is his way to suspend reason and play it deuces wild. And play it deuces wild he does. I've already shown how he asserts the uniqueness of the Holocaust while making other claims contradicting this assertion. But when it comes to the fate of German Jews under Nazism, Eisenberg goes hog wild playing it deuces wild. According to Eisenberg, "Between 1933 and 1938, 300,000 Jews emigrated [from Germany], 40,000 died, and 160,000 were murdered." This is ridiculous inasmuch as there were about 500,000 German Jews in 1933, so Eisenberg's statistics imply the gross falsehood that there were no Jews left in Germany as of 1939. In fact, Eisenberg's ridiculous statistics are contradicted by those that were published

---

1   25th Anniversary Edition, Signet Books, 1968, p. 638.

in 1943 by the Institute of Jewish Affairs of the World Jewish Congress and which are reprinted by Eisenberg on page 115. The IJA cited a June 1933 census (not including the Saar) showing 499,682 German Jews and a May 1939 unpublished census showing 235,000 Jews remaining in Germany. These figures indicate a decline in the German Jewish population of almost 300,000, Eisenberg's figure for the number who had emigrated from Germany during roughly the same period. But while the IJA said 235,000 Jews remained in Germany in May 1939, Eisenberg says 200,000 had died or been murdered between 1933 and 1938. This is confusing enough, but Eisenberg achieves total confusion when, on page 605, he informs us that in the early 1950s, the Bonn government agreed that "Germany must pay a billion dollars to cover the expenses of integrating the surviving half-million German Jews into Israeli society...." Come again? The surviving half-million German Jews? In other words, *all* the Jews of Germany survived both the Third Reich and the Second World War! Presumably, the 200,000 who died or were murdered between 1933 and 1938 had all been resurrected in time to collect reparations from the West German government, beginning in the '50s. Quite a miracle! But, of course, in the magical, mystical kingdom of the Holocaust, "anything goes in any manner you wish when ever you need it."

One of the reasons Eisenberg advances for studying the Holocaust is that "We must be prepared to challenge the prevarications and downright falsifications expressed in books, movies, and plays by dodgers of guilt." But what about the prevarications and downright falsifications expressed by *mongers* of guilt—for example, Eisenberg? On the page preceding his claptrap about challenging prevarications and falsifications, he himself expresses the following flaming falsehoods: "As the Nazi armies overran Europe, Jews were immediately hunted down, transported, and liquidated. The whole Nazi war machine, even when overtaxed and facing certain defeat, was bent on destroying them." But the "Nazi" armies invaded western Poland in 1939 and Norway, northern France, and the Low Countries in 1940. Since the alleged extermination of Jews did not begin until mid-1941 (Eisenberg, for reasons known only to Eisenberg, says on page 134 that "the mass deportations to the death factories began ... at the end of 1942"), the Jews of western Poland, Norway, northern France, and the Low Countries were not "immediately hunted down, transported, and liquidated." And, if "the whole Nazi war machine ... was bent on destroying" the Jews, then who the hell was fighting against the Allied war machines? This is a "leading Jewish scholar"? This is a *misleading* Jewish scholar.

On page 40, in an excerpt from Friedrich Percyval Reck-Malleczewen's *Diary of a Man in Despair*, there is this bit of gossip about Hitler from 1936: "[Hitler] has taken to spending his nights in his private projection room, where his poor projectionists have to show sex films for him, night after night." Aha! Hitler the voyeur! But if one consults the Collier Books edition of Reck-Malleczewen's *Diary*, one finds this on page 26: "he has taken to spending his nights in his private projection room, where his poor projectionists have to show six films for him, night after night." So the actual gossip, itself almost certainly exaggerated, was that Hitler watched *six* films, not sex films, every night. Admittedly, this particular falsification might have occurred accidentally. Nevertheless, there it is, waiting to mislead any devout Holocaustomaniac reading Eisenberg's book with the necessary "awe and reverence."

Another falsification concerning Hitler can be found on page 33, where Eisenberg asserts, "Hitler glorified the 'big lie.' In his book, *Mein Kampf*, he wrote, 'The [people] more readily fall victims to the big lie than the small lie.'" [Bracketed insertion by Eisenberg.] That Hitler did not glorify the "big lie" can be seen quite clearly if one reads his remarks on the subject in their full context:

> It required the whole bottomless falsehood of the Jews and their Marxist fighting organization to lay the blame for the collapse on that very man who alone, with superhuman energy and will power, tried to prevent the catastrophe he foresaw and save the nation from its time of deepest humiliation and disgrace. By branding Ludendorff as guilty for the loss of the World War, they took the weapon of moral right from the one dangerous accuser who could have risen against the traitors to the fatherland. In this they proceeded on the sound principle that the magnitude of a lie always contains a certain factor of credibility, since the great masses of the people in the very bottom of their hearts

tend to be corrupted rather than consciously and purposely evil, and that, therefore, in view of the primitive simplicity of their minds, they more easily fall victim to a big lie than to a little one, since they themselves lie in little things, but would be ashamed of lies that were too big. Such a falsehood will never enter their heads, and they will not be able to believe in the possibility of such monstrous effrontery and infamous misrepresentation in others; yes, even when enlightened on the subject, they will long doubt and waver, and continue to accept at least one of these causes as true. Therefore, something of even the most insolent lie will always remain and stick—a fact which all the great lie-virtuosi and lying—clubs in this world know only too well and also make the most treacherous use of.

The foremost connoisseurs of this truth regarding the possibilities in the use of falsehood and slander have always been the Jews; for after all, their whole existence is based on one single great lie, to wit, that they are a religious community while actually they are a race-and what a race! One of the greatest minds of humanity [Schopenhauer] has nailed them forever as such in an eternally correct phrase of fundamental truth: he called them "the great masters of the lie." And anyone who does not recognize this or does not want to believe it will never in this world be able to help the truth to victory.[2]

"Monstrous effrontery?" "Infamous misrepresentation?" Not exactly *glorification* of the "big lie." The irony is positively exquisite. Hitler accused "the Jews" of being the foremost practitioners of the "big lie." So how does Azriel Eisenberg respond? *With a big lie*, to wit, that Hitler "*glorified*" the "big lie." How's that for *chutzpah*?[3]

On page 133, Eisenberg informs us,

> The SS used the famine [in Warsaw] as a fiendish trap to ensnare more Jews for extermination. Thus in Warsaw, in July 1942, they posted a notice that those "who will present themselves for selection for resettlement will receive three kilograms of bread and one kilogram of marmalade." Hungry and desperate Jews flocked to the railroad station, where they were packed into deportation trains without food. Why feed people who were soon to die?

Ah, the "fiendish deviousness" of the Nazis! But wait. Here is how Warsaw ghetto survivor Vladka Meed describes the Nazis' "diabolic tactics" in *On Both Sides of the Wall* (p. 44): "Hunger drove famished Jews to the bread line, where each received his three kilograms of bread—before being pushed into the waiting railroad

---

[2] *Mein Kampf*, Sentry edition, Houghton Mifflin Company, 1943, pp. 231–232.

[3] For the record, I want to point out that Hitler did not pretend to be a paragon of veracity; he did defend deception in political propaganda. See, for example, *Mein Kampf*, Sentry edition, p. 182.

cars." And here is what Alexander Donat says in *The Death Camp Treblinka* (p. 13): "Despite some initial apprehensions, most of the Jews of Warsaw really believed that this was no more than a bona fide resettlement. This belief was enhanced by the fact that at one point every Jew who volunteered for 'resettlement' received three kilograms of bread and one kilogram of marmalade." Eisenberg asks, "Why feed people who were soon to die?" But since the Nazis *did* feed the volunteers for resettlement (according to Meed, Donat, and others), Eisenberg's question actually suggests the possibility that those people were *not* soon to die. What do you have to say about *that*, Dr. Eisenberg?

In any case, Eisenberg's distorted account of Auschwitz includes the following (p. 216): "It is estimated that the ovens 'processed' as many as seven million people." Oh, really? Seven million? But, pray tell, Dr. Eisenberg, estimated by whom? Even the official Soviet estimate, the largest that I recall seeing previously, was "only" four million. I suspect that what Eisenberg has done is to calculate 10,000 killed and cremated daily for almost two years, from early 1943 to late 1944, the period during which the four large crematoria of Birkenau were in use. The figure of 10,000 killed and cremated daily is commonly given as the peak figure for Auschwitz, supposedly reached during the period of the Hungarian deportations in the spring and summer of 1944. But apparently Eisenberg has taken this peak figure and turned it into the norm for the entire period during which the crematoria were operating. Thereby he exaggerates the already exaggerated death toll for

Auschwitz. Good work, Dr. Eisenberg. But why settle for seven million victims at Auschwitz? Why not estimate eight million, nine million, ten million, or even 100 million? After all, those who read your book with the appropriate awe and reverence will surely swallow everything you serve up.[4]

But perhaps Eisenberg does think there are limits to what his readers will swallow. Perhaps that is why his edited version of the Gerstein statement omits Gerstein's claim that 25 million people were killed by gassing. (While Eisenberg normally indicates his editorial omissions with the customary ellipses, he does not indicate this particular omission from the Gerstein statement with an ellipsis.)

In any case, it is interesting to note that Gerstein's purported eyewitness account of the gassing of Jews at Belzec is the only such eyewitness account of the gassing of Jews to be found in Eisenberg's 649-page tome. So how reliable is this account? Paul Rassinier wrote, "If it is not true that the gas chambers at Belzec, Treblinka, and Sobibor could asphyxiate between 15,000 and 25,000 persons a day; if it is not true that a gas chamber 25 meters square could hold 700 to 800 persons; if it is not true that a train with 45 cars could transport 6,700 persons; and if it is not true that Hitler was at Belzec on 15 August 1942, I ask what does it contain that is true since it contains nothing else?"[5] Before concluding that it contains nothing that is true, revisionists should

---

[4] See Saul Friedlander, *Kurt Gerstein: The Ambiguity of Good*, Alfred A. Knopf, Inc., 1969, pp. 117–118.

[5] *Debunking the Genocide Myth*, Noontide Press, 1978, pp. 269–270.

consider the deposition of Dr. Wilhelm Pfannenstiel, who, according to both the Gerstein statement and his own deposition, accompanied Gerstein on his fateful visit to Belzec. In his deposition of 6 June 1950, Pfannenstiel claims to have witnessed a gassing of Jews at Belzec. Here is his description of it:

> a shipment of Jews—men, women, and some children—arrived.... They were ordered to strip completely and to hand over their possessions. They were informed that they were to be incorporated into a working process and must be deloused to prevent epidemics. They would also have to inhale something.
>
> After the women's hair had been cut off, the whole shipment of people was taken to a building containing six rooms. On that occasion, to my knowledge, only four were used. After these people had been shut up in the rooms, the exhaust gas from the engine was piped in. Gerstein stated that it took about eighteen minutes before quiet was restored inside. While the Jews were being taken in, the rooms were lit up with electric light and everything passed off peacefully. But when the lights were turned off, loud cries burst out inside, which then gradually died away. As soon as everything was quiet again, the doors in the outside wells were opened, the corpses were brought out, and, after being searched for gold teeth, they were stacked in a trench. Here, too, the work was

done by Jews. No doctor was present. I noticed nothing special about the corpses, except that some of them showed a bluish puffiness about the face. But this is not surprising since they had died of asphyxiation.[6]

Interestingly enough, Pfannenstiel went on to comment on the Gerstein statement: "I know that Dr. Gerstein gives an entirely different description of this gassing scene. That version is false. It is full of exaggerations."[7]

Thus, Pfannenstiel pretty much agreed with the revisionists about the Gerstein statement but, nevertheless, claimed to have witnessed a gassing of Jews at Belzec. Thus far, revisionists have been content to attack the extremely dubious Gerstein statement and have not seen fit to even mention the Pfannenstiel deposition, which appears to be somewhat more credible.[8]

For his own rather different reasons, Eisenberg includes a lengthy excerpt from the Gerstein statement in his book but not a single syllable from the Pfannenstiel deposition. This despite his pious asseveration that he has "endeavored to include the latest significant data which appeared before this book went to press."

The Pfannenstiel deposition was made over 30 years

---

6   See Saul Friedlander, *Kurt Gerstein: The Ambiguity of Good*, Alfred A. Knopf, Inc., 1969, pp. 117–118.

7   The reader is referred to Friedlander's book, pp 119–120, for Pfannenstiel's entire criticism of the Gerstein statement.

8   I presume that Arthur Butz, for example, knows about the Pfannenstiel deposition, since his bibliography in *The Hoax of the Twentieth Century* includes Friedlander's book on Gerstein.

ago, and the well-known Friedlander book which quotes it was published in 1969, but, apparently Eisenberg still doesn't know about it. That's what I call keeping up with the latest developments![9]

In a chapter entitled "Grim End and Judgment Day," Eisenberg tries to paint a pretty picture of various "war crimes" trials. Regarding the Eichmann trial, he tells us,

> Argentina complained that Israel had violated its sovereignty by abducting Eichmann from Buenos Aries. Others challenged Israel's right to try Eichmann. The trial, however, was meticulously fair. Eichmann was represented by the defense counsel of his choice, all the normal judicial procedures were maintained, and the world press was constantly in attendance.

---

9 The question of the reality of gassing at Belzec is complicated by the testimony of another self-proclaimed eyewitness, Jan Karski, a wartime member of the Polish resistance who claimed to have infiltrated Belzec, disguised as a camp guard, in early October of 1942, not quite two months after the supposed visit by Gerstein and Pfannenstiel. Although Karski's supposed infiltration of Belzec was supposedly organized by leaders of Jewish resistance groups precisely in order for Karski to observe and then bear witness to the supposed extermination of the Jews, Karski did not report seeing any gas chambers or gassings of Jews. Karski said he saw Jews being herded into railroad cars which then left Belzec. Karski claimed that the Jews were killed by leaving them in the railroad cars until they died of suffocation, starvation, or whatever, but he did not claim to have seen this. And what he did claim to have seen is consistent with the revisionist claim that Belzec was a transit camp for Jews being sent "to the East," not an extermination camp. Eisenberg includes an excerpt from Karski's 1944 book, *The Story of a Secret State*, but it is Karski's description of the Warsaw ghetto, not his account of Belzec.

So the Eichmann trial "was meticulously fair." But here's a second opinion on the Eichmann trial, from Lenny Bruce:

> Eichmann really figured, you know, "The Jews—most liberal people in the world—they'll give me a fair shake." Fair? Certainly. "Rabbi" means lawyer. He'll get the best trial in the world, Eichmann. Ha! they were shaving his legs while he was giving his appeal! That's the last bit of insanity, man.[10]

In a more serious vein, consider some of Hannah Arendt's revelations in *Eichmann in Jerusalem*. She says "it is among the minor mysteries of the new State of Israel that, with its high percentage of German-born people, it was unable to find an adequate translator into the only language the accused and his counsel could understand."[11] Arendt also reports that in Israel "rabbinical law rules the personal status of Jewish citizens, with the result that no Jew can marry a non-Jew...."[12] Then she goes on to comment,

> Whatever the reason, there was something breathtaking in the naïvete with which the prosecution denounced the infamous Nuremberg Laws of 1935, which had prohibited intermarriage and sexual intercourse between the Jews and Germans. The better informed among the

---

10 *The Essential Lenny Bruce*, Ballantine Books, 1967, p. 35.
11 *Eichmann in Jerusalem*, Viking Press, 1964, p. 3.
12 *Op. cit.*, p. 7.

correspondents were well aware of the irony, but they did not mention it in their reports. This, they figured, was not the time to tell the Jews what was wrong with the laws and institutions of their own country.[13]

So, even if, as Eisenberg says, "the world press was constantly in attendance" at the trial, it may have done nothing to guarantee fairness for Eichmann. In any case, according to Arendt, "The journalists remained faithful for not much more than two weeks, after which the audience changed drastically."[14] Arendt reports,

> The story [of the Final Solution] was confirmed by sworn and unsworn statements usually given by witnesses and defendants in previous trials and frequently by persons who were no longer alive. (All this, as well as a certain amount of hearsay testimony, was admitted as evidence....)[15]

So much for Eisenberg's claim that "all the normal judicial procedures were maintained." Arendt continues,

> It quickly turned out that Israel was the only country in the world where defense witnesses could not be heard [since they were threatened with prosecution under the Nazis and Nazi Collaborators Law], and where certain

---

13 *Op. cit.*, 7–8.
14 *Op. cit.*, p. 8.
15 *Op. cit.*, p. 220.

witnesses for the prosecution, those who had given affidavits in previous trials, could not be cross-examined by the defense. And this was all the more serious as the accused and his lawyer were indeed not "in a position to obtain their own defense documents."[16]

Despite all this, Eisenberg has the gall to assert that the Eichmann trial "was meticulously fair." As Lenny Bruce said, "Ha!"

Eisenberg's tedious tome does contain a few tidbits of interesting information. For example, there is an account of a Purim celebration in a displaced-persons camp in 1946 (pp. 551–553). This account mentions a poster which announced, "At 6:30 p.m. a public burning of *Mein Kampf* will take place in the Square." Eisenberg does not denounce this book-burning as "a medieval spectacle," his characterization of the Nazis' public burning of books written by "Jews, Christian liberals, and humanitarians" on 10 May 1933. As he says on page 628, "We must guard the freedom of the press and must protect the basic rights of all; at the same time, we must make sure that freedom is not turned to license and used against us."

Another interesting tidbit, necessitating a revision of revisionism, is an excerpt from Salo W. Baron's 1961 book, *A Historian's Notebook: European Jewry Before and After Hitler* (pp. 498–500). What is of interest is Baron's statement (p. 498) that "According to the survey prepared by the Central Jewish Committee in Poland on

---

16   *Op. cit.*, p. 221.

August 15, 1945, there were altogether 73,955 Jews left in that country including some 13,000 serving in the Polish army and 5,446 recorded in 10 camps in Germany and Austria." This is of interest because it tends to confirm something I was told by a correspondent some years back, to wit, that Paul Rassinier was wrong in asserting that "Mr. Shalom [sic] Baron, brandishing his title of Professor of Jewish History at Columbia University, claimed on April 4, 1961, before the Jerusalem Tribunal, that 700,000 of them [Polish Jews] were still living in 1945 when the country was liberated by Russian troops...."[17] Since Rassinier, on the supposed authority of Baron, employs this figure of 700,000 Jews in postwar Poland in his demographic study in *The Drama of the European Jews*, that demographic study must be revised. If this 700,000 figure is discarded as spurious, then the highest Jewish estimate, mentioned by Rassinier, of Jews surviving in Poland is the estimate of 500,000 which Rassinier attributed to the World Center of Contemporary Jewish Documentation.[18] Therefore, Rassinier's calculations of the total number of Jewish survivors must be revised downward by 200,000. And his calculations of the total number of Jewish deaths must be revised upward by the same amount.

Because of space limitations, there are a number of aspects of *Witness to the Holocaust*, such as its strong pro-Zionist bias and its anti-assimilationist conclusion, which I shall not discuss.

---

17 *Debunking the Genocide Myth*, Noontide Press, 1978, p. 219.
18 In his demographic study, Rassinier restricted himself to using statistics from Jewish sources.

Over 2,000 years ago, Cicero insisted that "The first law is that the historian shall never dare to set down what is false; the second, that he shall never dare to conceal the truth; the third that there shall be no suspicion in his work of either favoritism or prejudice." If Cicero's "laws" for the writing of history were enforced by my enemy, the State, then Azriel Eisenberg, misleading Jewish educator, would be in jeopardy of the maximum penalty. *Witness to the Holocaust* is, in several senses, including the literal one, a heavy book. As a work of history, however, it makes a good doorstop.

A slightly different version of this essay was originally published in The Journal of Historical Review, Vol. 4, No. 1, pp. 108–118 (1983).

A LEGACY OF HATE
A Legacy of Hate: Anti-Semitism in America
Ernest Volkman
Franklin Watts, 1982

"SOME PEOPLE GO AROUND smelling after anti-Semitism all the time," wrote George Orwell in a letter to a friend. Orwell then opined that "More rubbish is written about this subject than any other I can think of." Ernest Volkman is a "prize-winning journalist" who has dedicated himself to proving the aptness of Orwell's remarks. For some time, he has gone around smelling after anti-Semitism, and he has written a load of rubbish about it.

This load of rubbish, titled *A Legacy of Hate: Anti-Semitism in America*, purports to be "a study of the more modern forms of anti-Semitism in this country, the one place in the world where this ancient disease should not have happened, and where it should not be happening." But what it is, primarily, is an exercise in fear-mongering, an attempt to conjure up the specter of calamity for American Jews as a possible consequence of a supposed new outbreak of anti-Semitism. And, secondarily, the book is an exercise in smear-mongering, in which numerous individuals, groups, movements, and institutions are tarred with Volkman's mile-wide brush of anti-Semitism.

Volkman's main theme, not exactly an original one, is that "there is a new anti-Semitism afoot." But this "new anti-Semitism" is a strange beast. As Volkman puts it, "There are expressions of anti-Semitism, but paradoxically, they are not expressed out of hatred, but because of something even more hateful: simple ignorance." But, as Volkman *also* says,

> Anti-Semitism, then, is hatred of the Jews as a people. It should be distinguished from anti-Jewish feelings. People who do not like Jews for one reason or another are not necessarily anti-Semites; there is no compelling reason for Jews to be universally liked, any more than Americans, Chinese, Catholics or Buddhists are to be universally liked. Voltaire, that great humanist, plainly did not like Jews (he regarded them as odd and superstitious), but took pains to note that he thought burning Jews at the stake was uncalled for. Anti-Semites, however, progress over that critical step beyond dislike to pathology, hating Jews for being Jews.

If anti-Semitism is "hatred of the Jews as a people," then there can be no "expressions of anti-Semitism" that "are not expressed out of hatred." Thus, Volkman's "new anti-Semitism" is not anti-Semitism at all. Volkman attempts to pass his self-contradiction off as a "paradox." Rather, it is an example of his inability, or unwillingness, to think straight. (He has a similar problem with getting his facts straight, but more on that anon.)

As I've said, Volkman's main theme is the rise of a "new anti-Semitism." There are two varieties of this "new anti-Semitism": "indifferent anti-Semitism" and "casual anti-Semitism." The first of these is the subject of a chapter titled "A Callous Indifference." Volkman probably took this title from a phrase used in a 1974 book titled, coincidentally, *The New Anti-Semitism*, an opus perpetrated by Arnold Forster and Benjamin Epstein, who Alfred Lilienthal has aptly dubbed the high priests of the "Anti-Defamation" League's cult of *anti*-anti-Semitism. Here is the context in which Forster and Epstein used the phrase:

> This book represents an attempt to survey the American domestic and world scenes and properly identify the current sources, modes and extent of anti-Jewish behavior. The task will involve, necessarily, some re-defining of traditional notions of anti-Semitism and serious reorientation of long-held convictions about the nature of its sources. But more important, we propose to examine as well behavior that can only be properly defined as an insensitivity to these problems rather than anti-Semitic either by the definitions that have existed or by new and more inclusive descriptions. It includes,

often, a callous indifference to Jewish concerns expressed by respectable institutions and persons here and abroad—people who would be shocked to think themselves, or have others think them, anti-Semites.[1]

Forster and Epstein did not go so far as to include "a callous indifference to Jewish concerns" within their new (and improved?) definition of "anti-Semitism." But, in a case of the student surpassing the teacher, Volkman has done just that. With Volkman, "a callous indifference to Jewish concerns" becomes one of the two varieties of "the new anti-Semitism." This is progress indeed. I can hardly wait for the day to arrive when this ever-expanding concept of "anti-Semitism" will have come to encompass everything under the sun.

In the meantime, Volkman has sniffed out numerous instances of "a callous indifference." The Reagan administration, it seems, was guilty of "a callous indifference" in nominating Warren Richardson to the post of assistant secretary for legislation of the Department of Health and Human Services, because Richardson, from 1969 to 1973, had been general counsel and chief lobbyist for Liberty Lobby, "one of the more notorious anti-Semitic organizations in the country." Volkman rhetorically asks, "[H]ow was it possible for an administration to nominate for a high-ranking domestic policy post, a man who at the very least had served an avowedly anti-Semitic organization?" But, elsewhere in the book, he mentions Liberty Lobby's "recent assertion

---

1   *The New Anti-Semitism*, McGraw-Hill, 1984, p.5.

that it is 'not anti-Semitic, only anti-Zionist.'" Thus, Liberty Lobby is not an *avowedly* anti-Semitic organization, and Volkman knows it.

In any case, it was Richardson who was nominated, not the Liberty Lobby. And even assuming the Liberty Lobby is anti-Semitic, that does not necessarily mean that Richardson is anti-Semitic (unless, of course, one believes in guilt by association), and Volkman's evidence of Richardson's alleged anti-Semitism is tenuous at best. It consists of two items: (1) an article by Richardson critical of American Middle East policy which concluded, "Liberty Lobby will not tag along with the cowards who would rather countenance another national disaster than brave the screams of the pro-Zionist 'free press' in America," and (2) a joint interview Richardson gave with Curtis Dall, then head of the Liberty Lobby, in 1970, during which Richardson referred to "the international money order." But if this is enough to convict a man of anti-Semitism, then my name is Isadore Lipschitz. The article on Middle East policy, even assuming Richardson wrote the above-quoted conclusion, which he denies, is evidence only of anti-Zionism, not anti-Semitism. Volkman treats anti-Zionism as a manifestation of "the new anti-Semitism," but, as I've already pointed out, "the new anti-Semitism" is not anti-Semitism. As for Richardson's reference to "the international money order," taken out of context it is not proof of much of anything (what did Richardson say about "the international money order?"), let alone proof of anti-Semitism. Volkman claims that the phrase is "an old right-wing code word for Jews, by which is meant 'international

Jewish money.'" Of course, one can convict a person of anything by putting the necessary incriminating words in their mouth. But Robert Anton Wilson, in an interview given to *Conspiracy Digest* and reprinted in his book *The Illuminati Papers*, makes some relevant comments about a similar matter:

> it has been impossible to talk about bankers' conspiracies since the 1930s without most of your audience thinking you are a Nazi or, at least, an anti-Semite. This is what is called a conditioned association, or uncritical inference, and, however illogical it is, it is very widespread. I've been attacking the bankers since about 1962, and I never stop getting mail from two groups of idiots: Jewish idiots who think I'm secretly an anti-Semite, and are angry at me for it; and anti-Semitic idiots who also think I'm a secret anti-Semite, and are glad to welcome me to their loathsome club.[2]

I don't know if Volkman is a Jewish idiot, but he is, in any case, an anti-anti-Semitic idiot.

Most of Volkman's examples of "callous indifference" are episodes in which the US government has failed to act as a running dog lackey of the Zionist State of Israel. He is willing to go to ridiculous lengths to condemn the Carter administration for insufficient zeal in defending Israel. During the Carter administration, says Volkman, "the Americans sat on their hands while a

---

2   *The Illuminati Papers*, And/Or Press, 1980.

series of events took place that should have aroused the strongest US protest." Such as? One such "incident took place at the June 1980 meeting of the Organization of African Unity, when Israel was referred to in the group's official documents merely as 'the Zionist entity.'" Oh, dear! How horrendous! But, pray tell, why should the US government jump up and down, pull out its hair and scream "No! No! No!" because some other governments refer to Israel as "the Zionist entity?"

According to Volkman, the second variety of "the new anti-Semitism" is what he calls "casual anti-Semitism." Let's see how he derives this pseudo-concept. He begins by noting that the results of recent public opinion surveys suggest that anti-Semitism is declining. But, he asks,

> if anti-Semitism is supposedly disappearing, why are there so many instances of open expression of anti-Semitism? Because it is what we might call casual anti-Semitism, a new form that is most often expressed by people who claim no animosity toward Jews. For the most part they're telling the truth; whether they are making such statements in the name of "truth" or "objectivity" or "realism" or "historical fact," they very seldom have malicious intent (pp 82–83).

Thus spake Volkman. But, irony of ironies, Volkman's own words can be quoted to question the meaningfulness of this pseudo-concept of "casual anti-Semitism." In a chapter on the history of anti-Semitism in America,

Volkman reports that historian Oscar Handlin "went so far as to claim that anti-Semitism in this country did not really begin until the early part of this century and that any anti-Semitic incidents before then were 'without malicious intent' (whatever that means)." But if, as Volkman is snidely suggesting, it is meaningless for Handlin to write about anti-Semitic incidents "without malicious intent," then it is likewise meaningless for Volkman to write about expressions of anti-Semitism by people who "very seldom have malicious intent." Nevertheless, Volkman devotes an entire chapter of this book to doing just that.

Volkman says that "casual anti-Semitism is expressed out of ignorance or because there is simply no awareness that such a statement might be considered in the least anti-Semitic." So "casual anti-Semitism" is, in some cases, expressed out of ignorance. But Volkman's prime example of "casual anti-Semitism" is revisionism regarding "the Holocaust," a subject about which his own ignorance is such that he is obviously incompetent to judge anyone else's knowledgeability about the subject. As for Volkman's statement that "casual anti-Semitism" is sometimes expressed "because there is simply no awareness that such a statement might be considered in the least anti-Semitic," this seems to imply that it is "casual anti-Semitism" to make any statement that "might be considered" anti-Semitic. But with anti-anti-Semitic bloodhounds like Volkman on the prowl, any statement that is in the least critical of Israel, Zionism, organized Jewry, the American Jewish lobby, "Holocaust" historiography, individual Jews, etc.

might be considered anti-Semitic, whether or not it really is. In effect, Volkman is saying, *Keep your mouth shut*. Don't you dare criticize Israel, Zionism, organized Jewry, the American Jewish lobby, "Holocaust" historiography, individuals Jews, etc., or he'll accuse you of "casual anti-Semitism." What Volkman is trying to pull is a variation of what the late novelist-philosopher Ayn Rand called the "Argument from Intimidation," which, as she explained,

> is not an argument, but a means of forestalling debate and extorting an opponent's agreement with one's undiscussed notions. It is a method of by-passing logic by means of psychological pressure.
>
> ...the psychological pressure method consists of threatening to impeach an opponent's character by means of his argument, thus impeaching the argument without debate.
>
> The essential characteristic of the Argument from Intimidation is its appeal to moral self-doubt and its reliance on the fear, guilt or ignorance of the victim. It is used in the form of an ultimatum demanding that the victim renounce a given idea without discussion, under threat of being considered morally unworthy. The pattern is always: "Only those who are evil (dishonest, heartless, insensitive, ignorant, etc.) can hold such an idea."

In Volkman's case, the "Argument from Intimidation" takes this form: Only those who are anti-Semitic—at least, "casually" so—can hold such an idea. Rand observed that "The Argument from Intimidation is a confession of intellectual impotence." Volkman's performance confirms that.

As I've said, Volkman's primary example of "casual anti-Semitism" is "Holocaust revisionism," or, as he puts it, "the disturbing attempt to disprove one of the touchstones of modern Jewry, the Holocaust." True to the method of "the Argument from Intimidation," Volkman makes no attempt to come to grips with and rebut the arguments of the "Holocaust revisionists." Instead, he labels (libels?) "Holocaust revisionism" as "casual anti-Semitism" and then presents an incredibly distorted, error-ridden version of the history of "Holocaust revisionism," throwing in some choice invective along the way ("insanity," "hopelessly muddleheaded," "this poison ... evil works," etc.).

According to Volkman, Paul Rassinier "had been imprisoned at Buchenwald, an experience which somehow led him to conclude that no atrocities went on in Nazi concentration camps, and if any Jews were killed, they were murdered by Jewish Kapos (camp trustees)." But, in fact, Rassinier, who was imprisoned at Buchenwald, never asserted that no atrocities went on in the Nazi concentration camps. And if one consults Lucy Dawidowicz's "Lies About the Holocaust,"[3] which is Volkman's source of information about Rassinier, one finds a rather different, and more accurate, characterization of what Rassinier concluded. As Dawidowicz puts it, Rassinier concluded that "the atrocities committed

---

3   *Commentary;* Vol. 70, No. 6, Dec 1, 1980, p, 31.

in the Nazi camps had been greatly exaggerated by the survivors." Volkman has somehow managed to get the facts wrong even though his source got them right. This is a prize-winning journalist? In any case, Volkman is also wrong in claiming Rassinier concluded that "if any Jews were killed, they were murdered by Jewish *Kapos* (camp trustees)." This is, in fact, a distortion of something Rassinier wrote about Buchenwald:

> The S.S. no longer had any need to hit men, since those to whom they delegated their power did the hitting better; nor to steal, since their minions stole better and the benefits were the same; nor to kill slowly to make order respected, because others did that for them, and order in the camp was all the more perfect for it.[4]

As you can see, Rassinier did not specify Jewish prisoners or Jewish Kapos. Volkman has once again managed to get the facts wrong. But this time he did so by accurately repeating an inaccurate statement by Lucy Dawidowicz.

According to Volkman, Arthur Butz, in *The Hoax of the Twentieth Century*, "included what he considered to be incontrovertible evidence that all the Jews who were supposed to have died [during "the Holocaust"] were in fact still alive, carefully hidden from view." That Butz did not assert this can be verified by consulting page 239 of his book, where he states that "The Jews of Europe suffered during the war by being deported to the East,

---

4 *Debunking the Genocide Myth*, Noontide Press, 1978, p. 127.

by having had much of their property confiscated and, more importantly, by suffering cruelly in the circumstances surrounding Germany's defeat. They may even have lost a million dead." This is another instance in which Volkman got his facts wrong by parroting Lucy Dawidowicz. Of course, he might have avoided this error if he had taken the trouble to read the Butz book rather than relying on a second-hand description from a biased, hostile source. But But *nooooooo!* Not *this* prize-winning journalist! Not *this* self-righteous hypocrite, who even has the *chutzpah* to condemn Northwestern University for defending Butz's academic freedom, because—now get this—"it did not seem to occur to Northwestern that equally cherished standards of academia were being trampled in the process, including truth, research and facts." "Truth, research and facts"? Let's examine some further evidences of Volkman's concern for "truth, research and facts."

According to Volkman, "Anne Frank died in the Nazi gas chambers for the crime of being Jewish...." But Ernst Schnabel, who researched the fate of Anne Frank for his book *Anne Frank: A Portrait in Courage*, found that she and her family were deported to Auschwitz, from which she and her sister were transferred to Belsen, where they both died of typhus. Schnabel's findings about Anne Frank's fate are summarized in the commonly available paperback editions of what purports to be her diary. Volkman says that the diary "remains one of the great documents of humanity." But has he actually read it?

Concluding a plea for more extensive treatment

of Jewish history, and especially "the Holocaust," in high-school and college textbooks, in order to eradicate the "appalling ignorance" about such matters, Volkman invokes "the memory of the famous historian Simon Dubonow [sic] who, as the Nazis took him from the Riga ghetto in 1941 to be gassed at Buchenwald, called out: 'Brothers! Write down everything you see and hear. Keep a record of it all!'"

Volkman cites *The Holocaust and the Historians* by Lucy Dawidowicz as his source of information about Dubnow. But here is Dawidowicz's version of this incident:

> In December 1941, when the German police entered the Riga Ghetto to round up the old and sick Jews, Simon Dubnow, the venerable Jewish historian, was said to have called out as he was being taken away: "Brothers, write down everything you see and hear. Keep a record of it all" (p. 125).

Notice that Volkman took the liberty of adding two exclamation points to the Dubnow quotation. Notice also that in Dawidowicz's version, Dubnow "was said to have called out," but in Volkman's version, Dubnow "called out." But, most importantly, notice that Dawidowicz said nothing about Dubnow being taken "to be gassed at Buchenwald." So why then does Volkman say Dubnow was taken "to be gassed at Buchenwald," *where there never was a gas chamber?* The explanation undoubtedly lies in Volkman's dedication to "truth, research and facts."

Volkman's dedication to "truth, research and facts" also shows up in his handling of a speech made by Charles Lindbergh on 11 September 1941, in which Lindbergh, an opponent of American intervention in the war in Europe, said, "The three most important groups who have been pressing this country toward war are the British, the Jewish, and the Roosevelt administration." Volkman responds that "many influential Jews were in fact isolationists," even though Volkman's source, *The Warhawks* by Mark Lincoln Chadwin, concedes that "many influential Jews were *interventionists*." (Italics in original.) Volkman is so concerned about "truth, research and facts" that he substitutes the word "isolationists" for "interventionists" to create a non-fact with which to rebut Lindbergh.

Volkman's concern for "truth, research and facts" is manifest throughout *A Legacy of Hate*, and there are many examples of that concern that I will not mention specifically. Suffice it to say that Volkman's dedication to "truth, research and facts" is such that one should never take his word for anything.

In his search for anti-Semitism, Volkman covers a lot of ground, and the list of those he indicts on this charge is a long one. The culprits include George Ball (an advocate of a tougher US policy with respect to Israel and a critic of the American Jewish lobby who, interestingly enough, works for the investment banking house of Lehman Brothers, Kuhn Loeb), Paul McCloskey, James Abourezk, both *Time* and *Newsweek* magazines, the Hilton hotel chain, the *60 Minutes* television program, David Irving, Truman Capote, Vanessa Redgrave,

Richard Nixon, Spiro Agnew, Jerry Falwell, the National Council of Churches, Daniel Berrigan, Mobil Oil, and—hold onto your hats—the Anne Frank Foundation!

Volkman discusses anti-Zionism in a chapter titled "Anti-Zionism: The Easy Disguise." Here he dogmatically spouts the Zionist line and makes unsubstantiated, inaccurate generalizations about anti-Zionism and anti-Zionists. According to Volkman, "a reading of the vast literature produced by anti-Zionists is persuasive that anti-Zionism is certainly motivated by anti-Semitism, and there is not much point in trying to claim (as many do) that anti-Semitism and anti-Zionism are two very different things." But if Volkman has actually read "the vast literature produced by anti-Zionists," then I'll eat my yarmulke. None of this literature, is included in Volkman's bibliography, and there is nothing in his text to indicate any familiarity with it. If Volkman had read the anti-Zionist literature, he might have known that the anti-Zionists include Alfred Lilienthal, Moshe Menuhin, Rabbi Elmer Berger, Murray Rothbard, Rabbi Moshe Schonfeld, and Uri Avneri, and he might have thought twice about equating anti-Zionism with anti-Semitism (while vehemently denouncing those who equate Zionism with racism).

At one point, Volkman writes that "it is possible to tell the history of Judaism by simply reciting one long dirge of anti-Semitism." Possible, yes. But truthful? To tell the history of Judaism as one long dirge of anti-Semitism is to practice what Salo W. Baron called the "lachrymose" presentation of Jewish history. In this version, Jewish history is a history of suffering, persecution and martyrdom at the hands of hate-ridden Gentiles. Or, in other words, the Jew is the eternal victim and, furthermore, never a victimizer. Of course, there are problems with this view. On the one hand, it has to ignore or minimize the various "Golden Ages" that Jews have enjoyed during their history, for example, their five-century-long "Golden Age" in Moslem-ruled Spain. On the other hand, it has to ignore or minimize such things as the Hebrew conquest of Canaan, the forced conversion to Judaism of the Idumeans under John Hyrcanus, Jewish persecution of the early Christians (considered blasphemers for deifying a man), the prominent role of Jews in the slave trade during the early Middle Ages, etc. In line with this one-sided, lachrymose view of Jewish history, Volkman blithely dismisses the victimization of Palestinian Arabs at the hands of Zionist/Israeli Jews. "However much anyone wants to believe that the Palestinians' plight is cause for some concern, it obviously bears no resemblance to the very real plights of the Cambodian refugees, the Vietnamese boat people, the Soviet Jews and the many victims of the torture chambers of Latin America." Thus, while the Soviet Jews' plight is a very real plight, the plight of the Palestinians is no cause for concern. How's that for bias and insensitivity?

And this is not the only manifestation of Volkman's one-sided view of Jewish Gentile relations. Another is Volkman's abrupt dismissal of the claim that "classical Jewish texts were violently anti-Christian" as a manifestation of "anti-Semitism" while he himself claims that classical Christian texts are anti-Semitic. Is Volkman's reference to "the scriptural anti-Semitism" of Gospel accounts of the trial of Jesus a manifestation of anti-Christian prejudice? If not, then why is the claim that classical Jewish texts were violently anti-Christian necessarily a manifestation of anti-Semitism? I suggest that Volkman open up Hannah Arendt's *The Origins of Totalitarianism* (which he lists in his bibliography) and read the preface to Part One, "Anti-Semitism." There he can find Arendt writing that

> it was Jewish historiography, with its strong polemical and apologetic bias, that undertook to trace the record of Jew-hatred in Christian history while it was left to the anti-Semites to trace an intellectually not too dissimilar record from ancient Jewish authorities. When this Jewish tradition of an often violent antagonism to Christians and Gentiles came to light, "the general Jewish public was not only outraged but genuinely astonished," so well had its spokesmen, succeeded in convincing themselves and everybody else of the non-fact that Jewish separateness was due exclusively to Gentile hostility and lack of enlightenment.

In short, classical Jewish texts (some of them anyway) were violently anti-Christian, just as some classical Christian texts were anti-Jewish.

Volkman seems almost oblivious to the reality that anti-Semitism is but one side of a coin, the other side of which is anti-Gentilism. But let him consider the following statement, made by a George Mysels of Hollywood in a letter printed in *The Los Angeles Herald Examiner* of 4

January 1982: "I am not lighting a candle for the Polish people because nobody ever lit candles for the millions of Jews who have been murdered by the Poles since Polish history began." Millions of Jews murdered by the Poles? How's that for a "blood libel"? That Mr. Mysels is not simply anti-Polish but anti-Gentile, is confirmed by a letter printed in the same newspaper the very next day in which he wrote that "The only friends of Jews are other Jews and a number of apparent Gentiles who are aware of the existence of a least one Jew in their lineage." And let Volkman consider this item from The *Los Angeles Times* of Monday, 11 October 1982:

> TEL AVIV (AP)—Police investigating the fire that destroyed Jerusalem's Baptist church have detained two suspects, Israel radio said Sunday.
>
> The radio said the suspects are Jews, one of them a foreigner. There was no immediate police comment on the radio report.

One can't help but wonder if this church-burning was the work of Rabbi Meir Kahane's Kach ("Thus") movement. It was a member of Kahane's movement who was recently convicted of plotting to blow up the Dome of the Rock shrine, the mosque at Islam's third holiest site. And it was the Kach movement which, according to *The Los Angeles Times* of 25 October 1982, printed a poster "describing the massacre of Palestinians in Beirut as divine retribution for the past murders of Jews" and saying, "'What we ourselves should have done was done by others.'" Contrary to the image Volkman seeks to create, hatred in Gentile–Jewish relations is not a one-way street; it travels in both directions.

A Legacy of Hate is an awesomely bad book. Amusingly enough, one of Volkman's mentors, Lucy Dawidowicz, in the October 1982 *Commentary*, calls it "a shoddy book" which "tries to exploit the ripple of anti-Semitic incidents by sounding a general alarm in a chapter called, of all things, 'Kristallnacht.'" And, says Dawidowicz, "Stretching evidence is only one of this book's flaws." True. It has lots of other flaws, including factual inaccuracies, unsupported assertions, incoherent arguments, specious reasoning, and internal contradictions. Shoddy indeed. But then, what do you expect from a prize-winning journalist?

A slightly different version of this essay was originally published in The Journal of Historical Review, Vol. 3, No. 4, pp. 469–478 (1983).

WHY THE GOYIM?

Why the Jews? The Reason for Antisemitism
Dennis Prager and Joseph Telushkin
Simon & Schuster, 1983

> *Jews have suffered, and Christians have suffered. Mankind has suffered. There is no group with a monopoly on suffering, and no human beings which have experienced hate and hostility more than any other. I must say, however, that it is my impression that Jewish history has been taught with a whine and a whimper rather than with a straight-forward acknowledgment that man practices his inhumanity on his fellow human beings....*[1]
> —Rabbi Richard E. Singer,
> Highland Park, Illinois,
> Lakeside Congregation

IN *WHY THE JEWS?*, Dennis Prager and Joseph Telushkin perform a disingenuous duet of whining and whimpering. The basic premise of the book, which I dispute, is that (p. 17) "Hatred of the Jew has been humanity's great hatred. While hatred of other groups has always existed, no hatred has been as universal, as deep or as permanent as antisemitism."

But all of Prager and Telushkin's arguments in support of their assertion of the "uniqueness" of Jew-hatred are rendered at best inconclusive by a fundamental defect in their discussion. This defect is their failure to acknowledge the reality of another form of hatred that has been as universal, deep, and permanent as Jew-hatred. I'm talking about Goy-hatred.

---

[1] Quoted by Alfred Lilienthal, *The Zionist Connection*, Dodd, Mead, 1978, p. 401.

Space limitations preclude my documenting the phenomenon of Goy-hatred in the detail that I would like to. But right now I will quote just one piece of Jewish testimony concerning Goy-hatred. Writing under the name "Avner," a former member of LEHI, also known as the Stern Gang, a Jewish terrorist organization in Mandatory Palestine, described his joining the group:

> Tsfoni handed us each a heavy revolver and said in a harsh voice which immediately acquainted us with the spirit of the adventure we were embarking on:
> "No pity for the Goys."
> I experienced an inner surge of emotion.
> It was years since I had heard this word. It was never used in the kibboutz because there was no place for it in Marxist terminology. For the European Jew, the term is not necessarily one of abuse. It is the way in which it is said which gives it its character. For the Lehi, on the other hand, an Englishman would always be a filthy Goy, who could be killed for this reason alone, but if one in particular was necessary—the Polish pogrom and the Hitler camps. Later, I saw this biological hatred appear in the course of operations, as in the case of the eighteen-year-old Sabra who, after having fired a burst of submachinegun fire point-blank at a policeman, instead of running away, lingered a long while battering the already cooling body

with the butt of his weapon.[2]

In the course of this review, I will present some additional evidence of the existence of Goy-hatred throughout Jewish history.

Their failure to acknowledge the reality of Goy-hatred is not the only defect in Prager and Telushkin's discussion of the alleged uniqueness of Jew-hatred. Another defect is their penchant for magnifying the extent of Jew-hatred by promiscuously labeling as Jew-hatred (or "antisemitism") any opinion concerning Jews that they find troublesome and by endorsing false or exaggerated Jewish accusations against the Goyim.

As an example of their promiscuous use of the "antisemitism" label, consider this statement (p. 17), intended to illustrate the allegedly unique nature of Jew-hatred: "Jews who live in non-Jewish societies have been accused of having dual loyalties, and Jews who live in the Jewish state have been condemned as 'racists.'" But inasmuch as it is true that some Jews who live in "non-Jewish" societies *do* have dual loyalties and some Jews who live in the Jewish state *are* racists, saying so does not necessarily indicate Jew-hatred.

Prager and Telushkin's endorsement of false or exaggerated Jewish accusations against the Goyim is well illustrated by their discussion (pp. 18–19) of various alleged attempts to annihilate the Jewish people:

> The basic source of ancient Jewish history, the Bible, depicts two attempts to destroy the

---

[2] *Memoirs of an Assassin: Confessions of a Stern Gang Killer*, Thomas Yoseloff, 1959, p. 78.

Jewish people, the attempt by Pharaoh and the Egyptians (Exodus 1:15–22) and that of Haman and the Persians (Book of Esther). While it is true that the historicity of these biblical accounts has not been proven or disproven by nonbiblical sources, few would dispute the supposition that in ancient times attempts were made to destroy the Jews. Indeed the first recorded reference to Jews in non-Jewish sources, the Mernephta stele, written by an Egyptian king about 1220 B.C.E., states "Israel is no more."

Jewish writings from the earliest times until the present are replete with references to attempts by non-Jews to destroy the Jewish people. Psalms 83:5 describes the enemies of the Jews as proponents of genocide: "Come, and let us cut them off from being a nation, that the Name of Israel may no more be remembered." Just how precarious Jews have viewed their survival is reflected in a statement from the ancient and still recited Passover Haggadah: "In every generation they rise against us in order to annihilate us."

On two occasions in the last 350 years annihilation campaigns have been waged against the Jews: the Chmelnitzky massacres in Eastern Europe in 1648–49, and the Nazi destruction of Jews throughout Europe between 1939–1945.

...In both instances all Jews, including

infants, were targeted for murder; the general populaces nearly always joined in the attacks; and the torture and degradation of Jews were an integral part of the murderers' procedures.

Contrary to Prager and Telushkin, nonbiblical sources do disprove the historicity of the biblical account of Haman's alleged plot to annihilate the Jews of Persia. Theodore H. Gaster, a scholar of religions and civilizations of the Near East, has written,

> Scholars have long since pointed out that the story of Esther, as related in the Bible, is simply a piece of romantic fiction and cannot possibly represent historical fact. None of the Persian kings called Xerxes had a wife named Esther, and none had a vizier named Haman. What is more, the whole story of Ahasuerus' marrying a Jewish maiden is factually preposterous, for we happen to know from the Greek historian Herodotus and from other sources that the Persian king was permitted to marry only into one of the seven leading families of the realm, and the pedigree of the bride was therefore submitted to the most searching examination.[3]

---

3   *Festivals of the Jewish Year: A Modern Interpretation and Guide,* 2nd printing, William Morrow, 1972, pp. 215–216. Parenthetically, I will point out that if, as Prager and Telushkin claim, biblical accounts of attempts to destroy the Jewish people are evidence of the depth of Jew-hatred, then, by the same token, the biblical account (Book of Joshua) of how "the children of Israel," led by Joshua, "utterly destroyed" the inhabitants of Jericho, Ai, Makkedah, Libnah,

The Chmelnitzky massacres of the 1640s did, in fact, occur, with Poles and Germans among the victims, not only Jews. But, contrary to Prager and Telushkin's claim that "all Jews, including infants, were targeted for murder," Paul E. Grosser and Edwin G. Halperin have said,

> The roving bands of [Cossack] rebels allowed only those who converted to the Greek Orthodox faith to survive. Jews living in the Kiev area fled to the Tatar camps and surrendered.[4]

Prager and Telushkin's claim that "all Jews, including infants, were targeted for murder" during "the Nazi Holocaust" has been convincingly disputed by a number of writers. Rather than open up that particular subject in this review, I will refer readers especially to the works on this question by Arthur Butz and Robert Faurisson.[5]

Lachish, Eglon, Hebron, Debir, and Hazor must be evidence of the depth of Goy-hatred. Maybe that is why Prager and Telushkin do not mention Joshua or his perhaps mythical massacres.

4 *Anti-Semitism: The Causes and Effects of a Prejudice*, Citadel Press, 1979, p. 180.

5 Arthur R. Butz, *The Hoax of the Twentieth Century*, 5th ed. (Costa Mesa, CA: Institute for Historical Review, 1983). This is the expanded edition, which includes, as appendices, the essays "The International 'Holocaust' Controversy" and "Context and Perspective in the 'Holocaust' Controversy." Robert Faurisson, "The Mechanics of Gassing," *Journal of Historical Review* Vol. 1, No. 1 (Spring 1980), pp. 23–30; "Confessions of SS Men Who Were at Auschwitz," *JHR* Vol. 2, No. 2 (Summer 1981), pp. 103–36; "The Gas Chambers of Auschwitz Appear to be Physically Inconceivable," *JHR* Vol. 2, No. 4 (Winter 1981), pp. 311–17; "The Gas Chambers: Truth or Lie?," *JHR* Vol. 2, No. 4 (Winter 1981), pp. 319–73. The most complete exposition of Faurisson's views is, of course,

At least some of the five alleged attempts to annihilate the Jewish people specifically mentioned by Prager and Telushkin are totally or partially fictional. But even if all five were completely factual, that would not make true the Passover Haggadah's defamatory accusation against the Goyim: "In every generation they rise against us in order to annihilate us."

Why then do Prager and Telushkin cite the Passover Haggadah's defamation of the Goyim as evidence of the depth of Jew-hatred, when, if it is evidence of anything, it must be evidence of Goy-hatred? After all, they treat false and defamatory accusations against the Jews as evidence of Jew-hatred. But by the same token, false and defamatory accusations against the Goyim can with equal justification be viewed as evidence of Goy-hatred. So if Prager and Telushkin are right to interpret

---

found in his books and those of his supporters, which have been published in France and Italy: Serge Thion [With Robert Faurisson], *Vérité historique ou vérité politique? Le dossier de l'affaire Faurisson: La question des chambres à gas* (Paris: La Vieille Taupe, 1980); Faurisson, *Mémoire en défense contre ceux qui m'accusent de falsifier l'Histoire* (Paris: La Vieille Taupe, 1981); *Réponse à Pierre Vidal-Naquet*, 2nd ed. (Paris: La Vieille Taupe, 1983); Jean-Gabriel Cohn-Bendit, Eric Delcroix, Claude Karnoouh, Vincent Monteil, and Jean-Louis Tristani, *Intolérable Intolérance* (Paris: Editions de La Différence, 1981); Anon., *De L'Exploitation dans les camps a L'Exploitation des camps: Une mise au point de "La Guerre sociale,"* supplement au numero 3 (Paris: La Guerre sociale, 1981); "Le Citoyen," *L'incroyable Affaire Faurisson: Les petits supplements au Guide des droits des victimes* No. 1 (Paris: La Vieille Taupe, 1982). See also: Andrea Chersi (ed.), *Il caso Faurisson* (Castenedolo, Italy: Andrea Chersi, 1982), and Anon., *Note rassinieriane* (con appendice sulla persecuzione giudiziaria di R. Faurisson) (Rome: Estratto da L'Internazionalista, 1982).

anti-Jewish libels as evidence of Jew-hatred, then their own endorsement of various anti-Gentile libels must be evidence of their own virulent, violent Goy-hatred.

The main point of *Why the Jews?* is to present Prager and Telushkin's explanation of Jew-hatred. They reject various explanations that have been proposed, including (p. 20) "economic factors, the need for scapegoats, ethnic hatred, xenophobia, resentment of Jewish affluence and professional success, and religious bigotry." They assert that none of these things provides an ultimate or universal explanation of Jew-hatred. And they assume there must be such an ultimate, universal explanation. Why must there be? They say (p. 21), "Antisemitism has existed too long and in too many disparate cultures to ignore the problem of ultimate cause and/or to claim that new or indigenous factors are responsible every time it erupts." But to deny that there is any ultimate, universal cause of Jew-hatred is not necessarily to imply that "new and indigenous factors are responsible every time it erupts." To prove their point, Prager and Telushkin must prove that new and indigenous factors are never responsible for Jew-hatred. This they have not done.

Nevertheless, Prager and Telushkin proceed to endorse "the age-old Jewish understanding of antisemitism," which they express (ibid.) thusly: "Throughout their history Jews have regarded Jew-hatred as an inevitable consequence of their Jewishness." Or, as they also put it (p. 22), "The ultimate cause of antisemitism is that which made Jews Jewish—Judaism." But if, as they assert, Judaism is the cause of Jew-hatred, then what (or who) is the cause of Judaism?

In any case, Prager and Telushkin specify (pp. 22–23) four reasons why Judaism has caused Jew-hatred: 1) the Jews' allegiance to "God, Torah, and Israel" has been regarded by "non-Jews (often correctly) as challenging the validity of the non-Jews' god(s), law(s), and/or national allegiance"; 2) the Jewish mission "to perfect the world under the rule of God" and the Jews' consequent practice of making "moral" demands upon others "has constantly been a source of tension between Jews and non-Jews"; 3) "Judaism has also held from the earliest time that the Jews were chosen by God to achieve the mission of perfecting the world"; and 4) "As a result of the Jews' commitment to Judaism, they have led higher quality lives than their non-Jewish neighbors in almost every society in which they have lived," a fact which "has challenged non-Jews and provoked profound envy and hostility." "For these reasons," say Prager and Telushkin (p. 24), "Jews have always seen antisemitism as the somewhat inevitable and often quite rational, though of course immoral, response to Judaism."

In Chapter Two, "Antisemitism: The Hatred of Judaism and Its Challenge," Prager and Telushkin elaborate upon the first two of the four reasons why, they say, Judaism causes Jew-hatred. They state (p. 27), "Judaism consists of three components: God, Torah (laws and teachings), and Israel (Jewish nationhood). Throughout Jewish history, the Jews' affirmation of one or more of these components has challenged, often threatened, the gods, laws, and nationalism of non-Jews among whom the Jews have lived."

Jewish monotheism has challenged the validity of

worshiping any god but Yahweh. As Prager and Telushkin explain (pp. 27–28),

> In the ancient world, every nation but the Jews worshiped its own gods and acknowledged the legitimacy of others' gods. The Jews declared that the gods of the non-Jews were nonsense: "They have mouths but cannot speak, eyes but cannot see, ears but cannot hear..." (Psalms 115:5–6). There is but one God and He had revealed himself to mankind through the Jews. One need not be a theologian or historian to understand why these doctrines bred massive anti-Jewish resentment.

True enough. But Prager and Telushkin seem to overlook something. While Jewish monotheism challenges the legitimacy of any god but Yahweh, every other form of religion (and every form of irreligion) similarly challenges the legitimacy of Jewish monotheism. While Goyim have felt their religions threatened by Judaism, Jews have also felt Judaism threatened by other religions (or irreligions). Just as Goyim have hated Jews for this reason, so have Jews hated Goyim. Prager and Telushkin cite as a manifestation of Jew-hatred a ruling of the Synod of Elvira in 306 A.D. that Jews and Christians were not permitted to eat together. But in an interview in *The Jerusalem Post International Edition* (26 February–3 March 1984, p. 22), the Sephardic and Ashkenazic Chief rabbis of Israel, discussing Christian missionaries, "stressed that it was forbidden for Jews to have anything to do with such people" (p. 105). And the Chief rabbis' stated attitude is relatively moderate. According to Norman Kempster in the *Los Angeles Times* (18 March 1984, p. 1), "Amid the religious graffiti covering the walls of Mea Shearim, the home neighborhood of Israel's most militantly Orthodox Jews, someone has plastered dozens of copies of a handbill with the jarring message: 'Death to the Missionaries.'" Kempster also reports, "Within the last six months, the meeting place of a Christian congregation in Jerusalem was set on fire and Christian worshipers by the Sea of Galilee were showered with stones, including a potentially lethal seven pound chunk of concrete that injured a woman seriously enough to send her to a hospital." All of which is further evidence that Prager and Telushkin's whining and whimpering about the alleged uniqueness of Jew-hatred is simply so much kosher baloney.

According to Prager and Telushkin, the Jews, via their "ethical monotheism," have challenged the values of their neighbors. They quote (p. 28) the Reverend Edward H. Flannery: "It was Judaism that brought the concept of a God-given universal moral law into the world...." But, they say (ibid.), "The world to which the Jews have introduced God and His moral demands has always resented this challenge." And they conclude, "A basic element of anti-Semitism is, therefore, a rebellion against the thou shalts and thou shalt nots introduced by the Jews in the name of a supreme moral authority."

Though Prager and Telushkin have provided no proof of this, there may be some truth to it. Perhaps some Goyim do resent the challenge of Jewish "morality." But in any case, some Goyim do not resent it. They simply reject it as a hoax, a camouflage for the advancement of Jewish interests. And such "amoralism" need not mean hatred of Jews. It may simply mean a refusal to be manipulated by Jewish moralizers such as Prager and Telushkin.

Prager and Telushkin discuss resentment of Jewish "morality." They do not discuss resentment of Jewish "immorality." The Ten Commandments include the commandment that thou shalt not steal. But have Jews always felt bound by this commandment in their relations with Goyim? In *The Jerusalem Post International Edition* (25–31 March 1984, p. 14), Dr. Reuven Hammer, of the Jewish Theological Seminary of America, writes, "When the Romans complained to Rabban Gamaliel that Jewish law was most praiseworthy except for the fact that it permitted theft from non-Jews, he promptly made an enactment forbidding it." Thus, prior to Gamliel's amendment, the prohibition against stealing was interpreted so as to allow stealing from Goyim. It is only natural that Goyim would have resented such "immorality" towards them.

This may have been one reason why some Romans accused the Jews of hating mankind. Prager and Telushkin mention this pagan "antisemitic" allegation a number of times, but they never deign to refute it. Nor do they ever mention that Jewish law once permitted theft *from* Goyim. Why, though, did Jewish law allow this, if not due to hatred of the Goyim?

According to Prager and Telushkin, Jews constitute not only a religion but also a nation. Although attempts have been made to eliminate nationhood from Judaism, they insist (pp. 35–36) that "Judaism cannot survive without nationhood, since without this component it is by definition not Judaism but a new religion." And, for some reason, they assume that Judaism (as defined by them) must survive rather than be replaced by any such new religion.

Jewish nationhood, however, renders the patriotism of Jews outside Israel suspect in the eyes of their neighbors. But Prager and Telushkin say that such suspicions are unfounded. They deny (pp. 38–39) that Jews outside Israel have a "dual loyalty":

> "Jews who affirm the national component of Judaism, both in fact and Jewish legal obligation (*dina dimalkhuta dina*, the law of the land is the law according to the Talmud) live as every other good citizen in accordance with the constitution and laws of the country in which they reside, presuming, of course, that the government is not a dictatorship and does not pass immoral laws."

But, as a matter of "fact," this is mere assertion. Prager and Telushkin make no attempt whatever to refute any of the specific allegations about "dual loyalty" that have been made by anti-Zionists, in some cases Jewish anti-Zionists.[6]

As to the matter of "Jewish legal obligation," Prager and Telushkin's qualification creates a loophole wider

---

6   See, for example, "Dual Loyalty," Chapter Four of Alfred Lilienthal's *The Other Side of the Coin*, New York: Devin-Adair, 1965.

than the Mississippi River. Specifically what sort of laws would they consider "immoral"? Who knows? Within the pages of their book, "morality" and "immorality" are completely nebulous terms with no clear-cut meaning.

Chapter Three is devoted to "The Chosen People Idea as a Cause of Antisemitism." Prager and Telushkin assert that the Jewish belief that they are "the Chosen People" has caused anti-Jewish feelings ever since Goyim became aware of it. They say (p. 42), "Reactions to the Jewish belief in chosenness have been often so negative that some Jews have actually called for elimination of this belief from Judaism...." But they insist that "chosenness is an integral belief of Judaism" and proceed to "explain" (p. 43) the belief in order to give their readers "a proper understanding of the doctrine."

> Jewish chosenness has always meant that Jews have believed themselves chosen by God to spread ethical monotheism to the world and to live as a moral "light unto the nations" (Isaiah 49:6). All other meanings imputed to Jewish chosenness are non-Jewish.
>
> The Hebrew Bible, where the concept originates in its entirety, neither states nor implies that chosenness means Jewish superiority or privilege.

Apparently, the following passage in my King James Version of the Bible is a mistranslation:

> The LORD shall establish thee an holy people unto himself, as he hath sworn unto thee, if

> thou shalt keep the commandments of the LORD thy God, and walk in his ways.
>
> And all people of the earth shall see that thou are called by the name of the LORD; and they shall be afraid of thee.
>
> And the LORD shall make thee plenteous in goods, in the fruit of thy body, and in the fruit of thy cattle, and in the fruit of thy ground, in the land which the LORD sware unto thy fathers to give thee.
>
> The LORD shall open unto thee his good treasure, the heavens to give the rain unto thy land in his season, and to bless all the work of thy hand: and thou shalt lend unto many nations, and thou shalt not borrow.
>
> And the LORD shall make thee the head, and not the tail; and thou shalt be above only, and thou shalt not be beneath; if that thou shalt hearken unto the commandments of the LORD thy God, which I command thee this day, to observe them and to do them.... (Deuteronomy 28:9–13)

Of course, there are other passages of a similar nature in the Bible. And the Bible is not the only Jewish source in which Jewish chosenness has meant superiority or privilege. In "Meta-Myth: The Diaspora and Israel," Rabbi Jacob B. Agus has written,

> It is axiomatic in Kabbalistic writings that the higher souls of Jewish people are derived from the divine *pleroma*—the realm of

Sefirot—whereas the souls of all other nations are derived from the "shells." Rabbi Hayim Vital does not exempt converts from this rule (*Aitz Hayim* 7, 10, 7) (*Aitz Hadaat, Bemidbar*). The "Tanya" of Rav Sheneur Zalman was written for the general public. Its view of Gentile souls is in Chapter 6. The Zohar follows the same line, save that in the *Midrash Haneelam*, we note a certain effort to account for this difference. Before Adam sinned, he possessed the higher soul; after his sin, only his animal soul remained. Thereafter, the divine soul comes only to those who are preoccupied with Torah, entering the body of the Jewish male at age 13 (Zohar Hodosh, Bereshit 18b–19a, Midrash Hane'elam).[7]

So much for Prager and Telushkin's insistence (p. 203) that, historically, "The Jews saw their superiority as an existential fact, not a theological premise...." In fact, to this very day, some Jews continue to hold the views mentioned by Rabbi Agus. This *very* day, it so happens, I received the 30 March 1984 issue of the *B'nai B'rith Messenger*, in which columnist Gershon Winkler criticizes such views. Winkler's column, entitled "The Goy," begins, "I've heard this once too often: If a shopkeeper unknowingly gives you back too much change for your purchase, you must return the money to him only if he is Jewish. This, too, I've heard once too often: A

---

7   Etan Levine [ed.], *Diaspora: Exile and the Jewish Condition*, Jason Aronson, 1983, p. 139.

non-Jew has an 'animal' soul, not a 'Godly' soul like that of a Jew."

To judge from Prager and Telushkin's discussion of Jewish chosenness, the "ethical monotheism" that they espouse does not require them to tell the truth. Or perhaps "God" simply made a mistake in choosing Prager and Telushkin to be a light unto the nations?

Why the Jews? is more than an exercise in whining and whimpering; it also contains its share of bragging and boasting. Thus, Chapter Four concerns "The Higher Quality of Jewish Life as a Cause of Anti semitism." According to Prager and Telushkin (p. 46), "In nearly every society in which Jews have lived for the past two thousand years, they have been better educated, more sober, more charitable with one another, committed far fewer violent crimes, and had a considerably more stable family life than their non-Jewish neighbors."

There may be a good deal of truth in these claims, but even so, I dispute the assumption that this means that (p. 47) "Jews generally have led higher quality lives...." Prager and Telushkin go so far as to assert (p. 56) that "The higher quality of Jewish life is objectively verifiable." But, at best, they have objectively verified only that Jewish life has generally been of higher quality *in terms of a handful of specific criteria of evaluation*. And these particular criteria are not the only ones by which the quality of a life, or a peoples' collective life, may be evaluated. Jews may have generally been more sober, but have they generally had more fun? Jews may have generally committed far fewer violent crimes, but have they generally committed fewer non-violent crimes, such as fraud and embezzlement? Perhaps Jews have generally been better educated, but have they generally been more physically fit, healthier, or more athletically accomplished? If Prager and Telushkin wish to demonstrate the objectively higher quality of Jewish life, then they must demonstrate the higher quality of Jewish life in every respect.

In proclaiming the higher quality of Jewish life, Prager and Telushkin focus on certain positive aspects of Jewish life, never acknowledging that they might have any negative aspects to complicate the simple picture painted. This despite the fact that their book is largely devoted to whining and whimpering about how Judaism has caused Jews to be victims of the greatest hatred in history, almost always suffering from discrimination, persecution, violence, murder or annihilation campaigns, and so on. But if, as Prager and Telushkin assert, Jew-hatred is the inevitable consequence of Judaism, then why don't they take into account Jew-hatred and all its manifestations when calculating the overall quality of Jewish life?

Part Two of *Why the Jews?* is supposed to "document the thesis that Judaism, with its distinctiveness and moral challenge, is at the root of Jew-hatred" (p. 81). But this it does not do. It merely presents yet another one-sided account of Jewish history, bewailing hatred of the Jews and ignoring hatred of the Goyim.

For example, in Chapter Seven, "Antisemitism in the Ancient World," Prager and Telushkin tell us (p. 85),

In 167 B.C.E., the first recorded antisemitic

persecution in the postbiblical period took place. The Hellenic ruler of Syria and Palestine, Antiochus Epiphanes, incited in part by certain assimilated Jews, attempted to destroy Judaism, which he correctly perceived as the basis of the Jewish opposition to his leadership. Owing to their religious beliefs, the Jews rejected Antiochus' claim to being the "god manifest" ("Epiphanes" in Greek). Consequently, according to the biblical Apocrypha, Antiochus sent an emissary to Judea "in order to force the Jews to transgress the laws of their fathers and not to live according to God's commandments." (*Maccabees II* 6:11). He renamed the Holy Temple in Jerusalem after Zeus Olympus, prohibited the observance of the Sabbath and circumcision, and forced the Jews to participate in the festival procession in honor of Dionysus.

Such measures sparked the Maccabean revolt, which eventually led to Judean independence from Syrian rule. As George W. Robnett has commented,

What Antiochus Epiphanes did to the Jews in pressing Hellenism upon them is the kind of thing the Jews have capitalized down through the centuries as "oppression"—and since realism shows that most human problems are two-way streets, it is interesting to contrast the disposition of Antiochus with a Jewish leader just a few years afterwards. John Hyrcanus (of the Jewish Hasmonean-Maccabean line) came to power in Judea in 135 B.C. (under the new freedom won by the revolt). He conquered the small country of Edom to the south and (according to Graetz) gave the inhabitants (Idumeans) "the choice between acceptance of Judaism or exile." They accepted Judaism in order to keep their homes.[8]

Prager and Telushkin do not even mention the Maccabean revolt, let alone John Hyrcanus and his forcible conversion of the Idumeans to Judaism. But if Antiochus Epiphanes' actions show that he hated the Jews, then by the same token, John Hyrcanus' actions must show that he hated the Idumeans. In which case, Why the Idumeans?

In Chapter Nine, "Islamic Antisemitism," Prager and Telushkin quote (p. 128) French-Jewish novelist Albert Memmi's characterization of the status of Jews under Islam in the 20th century: "Roughly speaking and in the best of cases, the Jew is protected like a dog which is part of man's property, but if he raises his head or acts like a man, then he must be beaten so that he will always remember his status." But even if this characterization is accurate, there is a parallel in the attitude of Orthodox Jewish settlers toward Arabs in the West Bank. In *The Fateful Triangle*, Noam Chomsky discusses an article by Yedidia Segal in the 3 September 1982 issue of *Nekudah*, the journal of the religious West Bank

---

8   *Zionist Rape of the Holy Land*, Crown City Publishing Co., rev. ed., 1976, p. 386.

settlers. According to Chomsky,

> The scholarly author cites passages from the Talmud explaining that God is sorry that he created the Ishmaelites, and that Gentiles are "a people like a donkey." The law concerning "conquered" peoples is explicit, he argues, quoting Maimonides on how they must "serve" their Jewish conquerors and be "degraded and low" and "must not raise their heads in Israel but must be conquered beneath their hand... with complete submission."[9]

According to Prager and Telushkin (p. 128), "It is the Jews' refusal to accept this subordination [to Moslems] that is at the heart of the Arab-Muslim hatred for Israel." If so, however, then, by the same token, the Arabs' refusal to accept such subordination to Jews must be at the heart of the Jewish-Israeli hatred for Arabs.

In Chapter Fourteen, Prager and Telushkin ask the musical question, "What Is to Be Done?" Or, in other words (p. 179), "What, if anything, can Jews do to eradicate, diminish, or at the very least, individually avoid antisemitism?"

They say (p. 182) that assimilation, defined as "ceasing to be a Jew," is "a rational and viable way to escape antisemitism for individuals, not to the Jewish people as a whole. Many Jews will never assimilate, which alone invalidates assimilation as a solution to antisemitism."

Thus, Prager and Telushkin are looking for a *total*

---

9   South End Press, 1983, p. 124.

(final?) "solution to antisemitism." Furthermore (pp. 181–82), "A solution to antisemitism must by definition include the survival of Jewry, just as a solution to an illness must by definition include the survival of the patient. We seek solutions to antisemitism which enable Jews to live as Jews." But if, as they assert elsewhere in the book, Jew-hatred is an inevitable response to Judaism, then how can there be any total "solution to antisemitism" which enables Jews to live as Jews? The only possibility that comes to mind is the elimination of all "non-Jews," one way or another.

Prager and Telushkin do not, in fact, advocate such a solution. Instead, after showing that some other solutions (Zionism, seeking converts, fighting "antisemitism" a la the ADL) are not total solutions, they announce (p. 191) the following "solution to anti-semitism": "if the goal is to put an end to antisemitism, then Jews must also attempt to influence the moral values of non-Jews so that no aspect of Judaism any longer threatens the non-Jews' values." What does this mean in practical terms? Here's the closet that they come to answering this question (*ibid*.): "Jews must therefore resume their original task of spreading ethical monotheism... This means in essence that the Jews must make the world aware of two basic principles: ethics need God, and God's major demand is ethics."

But Prager and Telushkin don't tell us how they are going to get the world to accept "ethical monotheism." Furthermore, they don't clearly explain how such acceptance of "ethical monotheism" will necessarily end "antisemitism." After all, there have been many Christian and Moslem "ethical monotheists" who nevertheless, in Prager and Telushkin's opinion, have been "antisemites." I suggest the Prager and Telushkin's "solution to antisemitism" is as illusory as their "God" and his commandments.

If a "solution to antisemitism" is in fact possible, its discovery will require a more honest consideration of the problem than Prager and Telushkin have given it. This means, among other things, that the problem of Jew-hatred cannot be divorced from the problems of Goy-hatred. If there is to be a solution to the former problem, there must be a solution to the latter problem as well. So rather than devoting themselves exclusively to whining and whimpering, "Why the Jews?," I suggest that Prager and Telushkin finally begin to ask themselves, "Why the Goyim?"

A slightly different version of this essay was originally published in The Journal of Historical Review, Winter 1984 (Vol. 5, Nos. 2,3,4), pages 375–387.

ELIE WIESEL: MESSENGER TO ALL HUMANITY

Elie Wiesel: Messenger to All Humanity
Robert McAfee Brown
University of Notre Dame Press, 1983

Pushkin claims a beautiful lie is superior to a debasing truth. I don't agree: Truth alone elevates man, even when it hurts. The task of the writer is, after all, not to appease, or flatter, but to disturb, to warn, to question by questioning oneself.[1]

—Elie Wiesel

ROBERT McAFEE BROWN IS A PROFESSOR of theology and ethics at the Pacific School of Religion. In relation to "Holocaust survivor" Elie Wiesel, however, Brown regards himself as "the pupil" and refers to Wiesel as his "rebbe," or teacher (p. xii).

But although his teacher has written that the task of a writer is not to appease or flatter, Brown flatters his teacher outrageously in *Elie Wiesel: Messenger to All Humanity*, his study of Wiesel's writings. Indeed, this literary lickspittle tells his readers right away (*ibid*), "This is not a 'critical' appraisal of Wiesel, and I make no apologies for the fact...."

Rather than criticize Wiesel, Brown has devoted himself to brown-nosing his teacher. Thus, for example,

---

1   Elie Wiesel, *A Jew Today*, translated by Marion Wiesel, Vintage, 1979, p. 130.

he tells us that Wiesel "does not evade ghastly revelations of human depravity, nor will he let us do so." But this is hogwash, if only because of the fact that Wiesel routinely evades ghastly revelations of Jewish "depravity."

In an open letter entitled "To a Young Palestinian Arab," Wiesel pretends to denounce "the injustice endured by Arab refugees in 1948."[2] But, like any other Zionist propaganda hack, Wiesel puts the entire blame on *Arab* leaders, who supposedly "incited the Arab population to mass flight in order to return 'forthwith' as victors."[3] Wiesel makes not the slightest mention of the massacre of about 250 women, children, and old men in the Arab village of Deir Yassin by Irgun and Stern Gang terrorists, commanded by those incipient statesmen Menachem Begin and Yitzhak Shamir on April 9, 1948, shortly before the Israeli "declaration of independence." Anti-Zionist author Alfred Lilienthal cites various sources regarding the impact of this massacre:

> Jon Kimche, the Zionist writer, calling the incident "the darkest stain on the Jewish record throughout the fighting," stated, "The terrorist justified the massacre of Deir Yassin because it led to the panic flight of the remaining Arabs in the Jewish state area." Jewish writer Don Peretz described the result of Deir Yassin as a "mass fear psychosis which grasped the whole Arab community." Arthur Koestler wrote, this

---

2   *A Jew Today, op cit.*, p. 122.

3   *Ibid.*

"bloodbath ... was the psychologically decisive factor in the spectacular exodus of Arab refugees."[4]

According to Brown (p. 192), "Wiesel seeks to enlist us in the ongoing struggle of light against darkness, of memory against indifference." Here he parrots Wiesel's phony rationale for habitually harping on "the Holocaust"—the importance of "memory." But the Deir Yassin massacre is just one of many episodes of Jewish history which Wiesel finds eminently forgettable.

Thus, Wiesel has written, "There were never any religious persecutions instigated, organized or implemented by Jews."[5] Down the Orwellian "memory hole" goes the forcible conversion to Judaism of the Idumeans by John Hyrcanus. Also consigned to oblivion is the participation of Jews in instigating persecutions of Christians during the rule of pagan Rome. According to Bernard Lazare, the French-Jewish anarchist who later became a Zionist,

> The Church, in those evil days, could not count on its rival, the Synagogue, for assistance; in some places where the struggle between the Jews and Christians had reached an acute stage the Jews, recognized by Roman legislation and possessed of vested rights, would join the citizens of the towns in dragging the Christians before the court. In Antioch, for example, where

---

4 *The Zionist Connection*, Dodd, Mead & Co., 1978, p. 156.
5 *A Jew Today, op. cit.*, p.210.

the enmity between the two sects was most bitter, in all probability, the Jews, like the pagans, demanded the trial and execution of Polycarp. They are said to have fed with great eagerness the stake upon which the bishop was burned.[6]

Mister Memory has also forgotten the Jewish persecution of Jewish heretics. According to Lazare,

> In 1232, Rabbi Solomon of Montpellier issued an anathema against all those who would read the *Moreh Nebukhim* [*Guide of the Perplexed* by Maimonides] or would take up scientific and philosophic studies.... The fanatical rabbis appealed to the fanaticism of the Dominicans, they denounced the *Guide of the Perplexed* and had it burned by the inquisition. At the instigation of a German doctor, Asher ben Yechiel, a synod of thirty rabbis met at Barcelona, with ben Adret in the chair, and excommunicated all those who read books other than the Bible and the Talmud, when under twenty-five years.
>
> A counter-excommunication was proclaimed by Jacob Tibbon, who, at the head of the Provencal rabbis, boldly defended condemned science. All was in vain: those wretched Jews, whom everybody tormented for their faith, persecuted their coreligionists more cruelly and severely than they had ever been persecuted. Those whom they accused of indifference

---

6   *Antisemitism*, Britons, 1967, p. 37.

had to undergo the worst punishments; the blasphemers had their tongues cut; Jewish women who had any relations with Christians were condemned to disfigurement: their noses were subjected to ablation.[7, 8]

Despite these and similar facts, including some about the present-day State of Israel, Wiesel denies that Jews have ever perpetrated any religious persecutions. Indeed, he also denies that Jews have ever hated their enemies, or become executioners when they have had power and their enemies none. And he denies that any of the "notorious" killers in history were Jews.[9]

Robert McAfee Brown, wretched creature that he is, studiously ignores Wiesel's brazen whitewashing of Jews. Meanwhile, he obsequiously echoes Wiesel's accusations against Gentiles, as well as Wiesel's hypocritical denunciations of those who deny his accusations.

To deny the truth of the "Holocaust" story is an "ugly way" to avoid involvement," says Brown (p. 8). "There is no greater indignity," he tells us (p.10), "than to say to a suffering person, 'Your suffering is a fake.... You invented it to gain sympathy.... You are an impostor.'" Furthermore (p. 11), "attempts to deny a past Holocaust almost ensure that there will be a future one." Brown even approvingly quotes Wiesel's characterization of revisionist writings as (ibid) "the recent attempts to kill

---

7   *Antisemitism*, *op. cit.*, p. 64.
8   The dictionary definition of "ablation" is "the surgical removal of a growth, organ, or part of the body." Therefore, Lazare presumably meant that their noses were cut off.
9   *A Jew Today*, *op. cit.*, p. 210.

the victims again."[10]

Brown declares, "In the face of those who 'speak obscenely' by attempting to deny the story, we too must register disgust. And having done so, turn our backs on those who disgust us and listen no longer, listening instead to Elie Wiesel telling the story once more, a story that supplies its own credentials." Is this (pp. 11–12) Brown's euphemistic way of telling us that Wiesel's tall tales about "the Holocaust" are *self-evidently* true? Apparently so. Wiesel, it should be noted, does not claim to have been an eyewitness to any of the alleged mass gassings of Jews by the Nazis. Indeed, he only claims to have seen one event relevant to the allegations about mass extermination—the burning alive of a truckload of babies in a flaming pit on the night that he arrived at Birkenau. Obviously, it's a hell of a story. But is it true?

Consider what Wiesel himself has said in an anti-revisionist lecture given at Northwestern University:

> The boy that began to talk to you tonight, where is he? Did he dream or live his dreams of fear and fire? Did he really witness the agony of mankind, through the death of his community? Did he really see the triumph of brutality, did he hear or imagine the laughter of the executioner? Did he really see killers throwing children, Jewish children, into the flames alive? I rarely speak about this, but in this place we must. For

---

[10] I sometimes wonder if Wiesel isn't a resurrected victim of the homicidal "steam chambers" of Treblinka—he's so full of hot air!

> a very long while I resisted accepting this story as mine. For years and years I clung to the belief that it was all a dream, a nightmare. No, I did not see the children. I did not see the flames.
>
> It was no dream. It was real. Jewish children, living Jewish children were thrown into the flames in order to save money because the gas was costly.[11]

Wiesel does not tell us when or how or why he decided that the incident was real and not a dream. He simply expects us to accept without question his present assertions about the matter. That may be good enough for Robert McAfee Brown, who revels in groveling before the Shrine of the Sacred Weasel. But for those of us who are not oblivious to Wiesel's obvious hypocrisy and dishonesty, his unsupported assertions are not conclusive evidence of anything. And, as a matter of fact, there are some positive reasons for doubt about Wiesel's story of children being burned in pits at Birkenau, though, for the time being, I'm going to keep those reasons for doubt up my sleeve.

As for Robert McAfee Brown, like the whale that swallowed Jonah, he swallows Wiesel's "Holocaust" stories whole. From that starting point, he devotes the bulk of his book to Wieselian weaseling about the moral, religious and theological "implications" of "The Event." He faithfully follows all the twistings and turnings of Wiesel's non-Aristotelian "Auschwitz logic." Paradoxes

---

11 *Dimensions of the Holocaust*, Northwestern University, 1977, pp. 17–18.

parade past the reader. "The Event" is relentlessly made mysterious.

And yet, through the mist of mystification, some conclusions shine through quite clearly: the incomparable importance of "The Event", the necessity of giving special attention to Jews as victims of "The Event", and the guilt of Christians for complicity in "The Event." All the fundamental dogmas of Wiesel's brand of "Holocaust" fundamentalism.

Brown, a member of the US Holocaust Memorial Council, of which Wiesel is the chairman, was not content to compose this book-length hymn of praise to Elie Wiesel. He had to dedicate it to him as well. In his dedication, he tells Wiesel, "At every stage" of the writing "it seemed a tampering with things I had no right to touch." For this reason, "I tried very hard, my friend, not to write this book." He should have tried harder—much, much harder.

A slightly different version of this essay was originally published in The Journal of Historical Review, vol. 6, no. 3, pp. 373–377 (Fall 1985).

THE FATEFUL TRIANGLE
The Fateful Triangle:
The United States, Israel & The Palestinians
Noam Chomsky
South End Press, 1983

THE FATEFUL TRIANGLE IS A FACT-FILLED, insightful look at the "special relationship" between the United States and Israel. Noam Chomsky, professor of linguistics at M.I.T., examines the origins of this "special relationship," its disastrous consequences for the Palestinian (and other) Arabs, and its danger for everyone.

Concentrating mainly on Israel's 1982 invasion of Lebanon, Chomsky provides a wealth of ideas and information in conflict with the Zionist mythology which pretty much predominates in the mass media and academia. The result is a devastating debunking of one-sided Zionist propaganda.

The pro-Zionist bias of most American journalists and scholars is one particularly obvious aspect of the aforementioned "special relationship." As Chomsky puts it, "The truth of the matter is that Israel has been granted a unique immunity from criticism in mainstream journalism and scholarship, consistent with its unique role as a beneficiary of other forms of American support" (p. 31). He cites numerous examples of this immunity from criticism, including the silence and/or misrepresentation about Israel's terrorist attacks on US facilities in Egypt (the Lavon affair) and the "clearly premeditated" attack on the "unmistakably identified" USS *Liberty*, an attack which, according to Chomsky's count, left 34 American crewmen dead and another 75 wounded. Chomsky asks (p. 32), "Can one imagine that any other country could carry out terrorist bombings of US installations or attack a US ship, killing or wounding 100 men with complete impunity, without even critical comment for many years?"

Of course, as Chomsky acknowledges, Israel did come in for an unprecedented amount of criticism because of "Operation Peace for Galilee," the 1982 invasion of Lebanon. But he debunks the attempt by some die-hard Zionist apologists to blame such criticism on—get this—media bias *against* Israel! As Chomsky shows, there was (and is) no widespread anti-Israel bias in the American mass media, although there was, temporarily at least, a reduction in the usual degree of pro-Israel bias. As Chomsky writes (p. 289),

> The charge that the American media were "pro-PLO" or "anti-Israel" during the Lebanon war—or before—is easily unmasked, and is in fact absurd. It suffices to compare their coverage of the occupied territories, the war, the treatment

of prisoners, and other topics, with what we find in the Hebrew press in Israel, a comparison always avoided by those who produce these ridiculous charges. Again, the annals of Stalinism come to mind, with the outrage over Trotskyite "critical support" for the "workers' state." Any deviation from total obedience is intolerable to the totalitarian mentality, and is interpreted as reflecting a "double standard," or worse.

Among those accusing the media of anti-Israel bias was the self-styled Anti-Defamation League of B'nai B'rith, which, as Chomsky points out (p. 14), "specializes in trying to prevent critical discussion of policies of Israel by such techniques as maligning critics, including Israelis who do not pass its test of loyalty...." Chomsky has himself been a victim of defamation by the Anti-Defamation League and knows whereof he speaks.

It is somewhat unusual for an American author, especially a Jewish one, to blow the whistle on the ADL's propaganda antics. But it is even more unusual to see public criticism of bigtime "Holocaust" survivor and pseudo-saint Elie Wiesel and his Wiesel words regarding Israel's less lovely activities.

Regarding Israeli policies in the occupied territories, for example, Wiesel has said (p. 161):

> What to do and how to do it, I really don't know because I lack the elements of information and knowledge ... You must be in a position of power to possess all the information ... I don't have that information, so I don't know....

Similarly, after the Sabra and Shatila massacres, Wiesel said (p. 386), "I don't think we should even comment [on the massacre in the refugee camps] since the [Israeli judicial] investigation is still on .... We should not pass judgment until the investigation takes place."

Wiesel, of course, is well known for passing judgment on the actions of other governments, but when it comes to the State of Israel, he whistles a different tune. In fact, Wiesel has said (p. 16), "I support Israel—period. I identify with Israel—period. I never attack, I never criticize Israel when I am not in Israel."

Chomsky points up Wiesel's hypocrisy in the following passage (p. 387):

> Recall Wiesel's unwillingness to criticize Israel beyond its borders, or to comment on what happens in the occupied territories, because "You must be in a position of power to possess all the information." Generalizing the principle beyond the single state to which it applies for this saintly figure, as we should if it is valid, we reach some interesting conclusions: it follows, for example, that critics of the Holocaust while it was in progress were engaged in an illegitimate act, since not being in a position of power in Nazi Germany, they "did not possess all the information."

Of course, one of Wiesel's repeated accusations against "the world" is that it did not say (or do) enough about "the Holocaust" while it was in progress. One wonders how Wiesel will weasel out of this contradiction in his position.

In any case, as you may have noticed, Chomsky does not dispute the historical reality of "the Holocaust." But even so, I think that anyone who will publicly criticize the hypocrisy of such a sacred cow (or, should I say, sacred weasel?) as Elie Wiesel merits the attention of revisionists.

It should be noted that while Chomsky is highly critical of Israeli policies and actions, he is not fundamentally anti-Israel. He supports (p. 3) "a two-state political settlement that would include recognized borders, security guarantees, and reasonable prospects for a peaceful resolution of the conflict." From this position, he criticizes Israel's consistent "rejectionism"—the rejection of any political settlement accommodating the "national rights" of the Palestinian Arabs.

Chomsky also criticizes the American policies which make Israeli rejectionism possible. And he points out the hypocrisy involved in criticizing Israeli policies while supporting their subsidization with billions of dollars of American aid each year. As Chomsky puts it (p. 2),

> Clearly, as long as the United States provides the wherewithal, Israel will use it for its purposes. These purposes are clear enough today, and have been clear to those who chose to understand for many years: to integrate the bulk of the occupied territories within Israel in some fashion while finding a way to reduce the Arab population; to disperse the scattered refugees and crush any manifestation of Palestinian nationalism or Palestinian culture; to gain control

> over Southern Lebanon. Since these goals have long been obvious and have been shared in fundamental respects by the two major political groupings in Israel, there is little basis for condemning Israel when it exploits the position of regional power afforded it by the phenomenal quantities of US aid in exactly the ways that would be anticipated by any person whose head is not buried in the sand. Complaints and accusations are indeed hypocritical as long as material assistance is provided in an unending and ever-expanding flow, along with diplomatic and ideological support, the latter, by shaping the facts of history in a convenient form. Even if the occasional tempered criticisms from Washington or in editorial commentary are seriously intended, there is little reason for any Israeli government to pay any attention to them. The historical practice over many years has trained Israeli leaders to assume that US "opinion makers" and political elites will stand behind them whatever they do, and that even if direct reporting is accurate, as it generally is, its import will gradually be lost as the custodians of history carry out their tasks.

Chomsky's got a point here, and it's an important one. What better way would there be to moderate Israeli policies than to cut off (or at least drastically reduce) American aid to Israel? But even if so, how is such an aid cut-off (or reduction) to be accomplished? That is the question. Unfortunately, I don't know the answer. And, as far as I can see, neither does Chomsky.

Of course, there is much more to *The Fateful Triangle* than I have been able to indicate in this review. To mention just one more subject, those who are interested in some of the more extreme examples of Zionist thinking will find them here, especially in the section on "The Rise of Religious-Chauvinist Fanaticism." In this section, Chomsky quotes (p. 155) the following notable statement:

> We will certainly establish order in the Middle East and in the world. And if we do not take this responsibility upon ourselves, we are sinners, not just towards ourselves but towards the entire world. For who can establish order in the world? All of those western leaders of weak character?

No, this is not a passage from the plagiaristic *Protocols of the Elders of Zion*. The statement was made by Rabbi Elazar Valdmann of Gush Emunim in the pages of *Nekudah*, the journal of the religious-chauvinist West Bank settlers. There is a pop song on the radio these days which says, "Everybody wants to rule the world." I don't know if everybody wants to rule the world, but obviously the good rabbi wants to do so. I wish him the worst luck possible in getting what he wants.

Despite some shortcomings, *The Fateful Triangle* is one of the best exposés of Zionist mythology now available. Even those who have read Alfred Lilienthal's *The Zionist Connection* will probably find Chomsky's book an excellent supplement. It is, in any case, a worthy example of what James J. Martin has dubbed "inconvenient history."

A slightly different version of this essay was originally published in The Journal of Historical Review, vol. 6, no. 2, pp. 240–244.

A TRIAL ON TRIAL
A Trial On Trial: The Great Sedition Trial of 1944
Lawrence Dennis and Maximilian St. George
Institute for Historical Review, 1984

ABOUT 15 YEARS AGO, in the midst of the raging debate over American involvement in the Indochina War, which I had come to oppose, I wrote a heated denunciation of the Chicago Conspiracy Trial of 1969. At that time I knew nothing of the Great Sedition Trial of 1944, which was, in some ways, a strikingly similar judicial farce.

Of course, the Sedition Trial of 1944 has been consigned to the Orwellian memory hole by America's post–World-War-II political, economic, intellectual, cultural, academic and media establishments. After all, a basic and unquestioned premise of all postwar establishment, thinking has been the necessity and nobility of Franklin Roosevelt's interventionist warmongering. And the reality of the mass Sedition Trial of 1944 rather glaringly conflicts with at least one aspect of the mythological version of Roosevelt's War—the myth that the Roosevelt regime displayed an unusually tender solicitude for civil liberties during wartime. The IHR's reprinting of Dennis and St. George's classic work on the 1944 Sedition Trial is an important contribution to the task of "blasting the historical blackout" that still keeps most Americans in the dark about Roosevelt's War.

Lawrence Dennis was himself one of the 29 defendants charged with conspiring to undermine the morale of the armed forces in violation of the Smith Act of 1940. His co-author, Maximilian St. George, was a defense attorney for Joseph McWilliams, another of the defendants in the trial.

The book is not so much an account of the trial as an analysis of it. Dennis and St. George identify the people and the purposes behind the trial and how and why it came about. And they devote much of the book to a dissection of the government's case against the accused seditionists. This detailed legal discussion is, perhaps inevitably, somewhat repetitious and, therefore, somewhat tedious. But there is much here that should be of interest to civil libertarians as well as revisionists.

The prosecutor, O. John Rogge, accused the defendants of membership in a worldwide Nazi conspiracy. His case consisted largely of out-of-context quotations from the writings of the defendants. These quotations were supposed to show that the defendants agreed with Nazi criticisms of communism, democracy, Jews, and/or the warmongering Roosevelt regime. Thus, agreement with the Nazis on one or more points was made out to be the equivalent of full-fledged, conscious participation in a conspiracy to Nazify the planet. Dennis and St. George painstakingly debunk this ludicrous attempt to prove guilt-by-association. They also include a chapter calling for an end to the abuse of the charge of "conspiracy." Perhaps those revisionists with a penchant for parroting conspiracy theories based on similar guilt by association arguments will take heed of the author's views.

Dennis and St. George point out (p. 83) that

> One of the many ironies of the mass Sedition Trial was that the defendants were charged with conspiring to violate a law aimed at communists and a communist tactic, that of trying to undermine the loyalty of the armed forces. What makes this so ironical is that many of the defendants, being fanatical anti-Communists, had openly supported the enactment of this law.

How's that for being hoisted with one's own petard? As the authors go on to say, "The moral is one of the major points of this book: laws intended to get one crowd may well be used by them to get the authors and backers of the law. This is just another good argument for civil liberties and freedom of speech."

Perhaps the backers of the prosecution of Ernst Zündel in Canada for publishing "false news" about "the Holocaust" should contemplate this particular point. Imagine how many Canadian Holocausters would end up behind bars if the law against publishing "false news" about "the Holocaust" were ever used against *them*. There wouldn't be enough jails to hold 'em.

Here is another of the ironies of the Sedition Trial. As Dennis and St. George pointed out for the benefit of the "extremists of the left" who supported the trial, the same sort of guilt-by-association argument could easily be used to make a similar case against those same leftists. They write (p. 211),

> If anti-Semitism equals Nazism and Nazism equals conspiracy to cause insubordination, any brand of socialism can be made to equal Russian communism and, if popular feeling were aroused against Russia, Russian communism could equal conspiracy to commit almost any crime in the catalogue.

This is a rather prescient statement, considering it was first published in 1945. Three years later, with the Cold War in full swing, the Truman regime indicted twelve top Communist leaders (including Eugene Dennis) under the Smith Act.

In Chapter XIX, "Beating an Improper Prosecution," Dennis and St. George give their advice on how to fight a free-speech battle in American courts. Thus, at a time when the Zionist inquisitors are resorting more and more to outright governmental censorship to stamp out historiographical heresy, *A Trial on Trial* takes on increasing practical importance. I recommend it highly.

A slightly different version of this essay was originally published in The Journal of Historical Review, Spring 1985 (Vol. 6, No. 1), pages 123–124.

YEHUDA BAUER AND THE "POLEMICAL AND APOLOGETIC BIAS" OF JEWISH HISTORIOGRAPHY

A History of the Holocaust
Yehuda Bauer
Franklin Watts, 1982

HANNAH ARENDT ONCE POINTED OUT the "strong polemical and apologetic bias" of Jewish historiography. Yehuda Bauer is professor of Holocaust studies at Jerusalem's Hebrew University and, according to Dr. Franklin H. Littell, "one of the world's top authorities on the Holocaust," but *A History of the Holocaust*, Yehuda Bauer's latest contribution to Jewish historiography, is no exception to Hannah Arendt's observation.

The book begins with a fairly lengthy overview of Jewish history. (We do not even reach the beginning of the Third Reich until page 93.) Bauer's bias is already apparent by page 4, where he tells us,

> In the ancient world, as well as later, the concept of one God meant that all humans were His children—that all men are equal, a

> revolutionary idea indeed.
>
> The laws that bear the imprint of the Mosaic tradition include the provision of liberating slaves after seven years (Ex. 21:2), of freeing all slaves who are maltreated (Ex. 21:26–27), of equality before the law (Ex. 21:20, 23–25), of the prohibition of murder and theft, and of 'the absolute sanctity of human life'—all ideas or concepts logically connected to the idea of monotheism.

Thus does Bauer expound what Hannah Arendt called the "self-deceiving theory" of Jewish historians that "Judaism had always been superior to other religions in that it believed in human equality and tolerance." But while the concept of one God might be taken to mean that all humans are His children and, therefore, are all brothers, it does not necessarily mean that all men are equal. Logically, the idea that two people, or all people, have the same father, or Father, simply does not imply that those people are therefore equal. And as a matter of fact, the idea of one god did not mean to the Israelites that all men were equal. Somewhat more accurately than Bauer, Joan Comay writes, "The concept of the covenant between God and his chosen people implied that all Israelites were equal in God's eyes, and that the human dignity and welfare of each had to be safeguarded."[1] That Israelites (God's chosen people) and non-Israelites were not considered to be equal or

---

1   *The World's Greatest Story*, Holt, Rinehart and Winston, 1978, pp. 220–221.

entitled to equal treatment is easily demonstrated. For one thing, the liberation of slaves after seven years, which Bauer mentions, applied only to Israelite slaves. As Milton Meltzer admits,

> The Hebrew code assigned the full condition of slavery to "the heathen that are round about you, of them shall ye buy bondmen and bondmaids." And for them there was no prospect of liberation: "They shall be your bondmen forever."[2]

The Mosaic code similarly discriminates between Israelite and non-Israelite in prohibiting usury.

> Thou shalt not lend upon usury to thy brother; usury of money, usury of victuals, usury of anything that is lent upon usury.
>
> Unto a stranger thou mayest lend upon usury; but unto thy brother thou shalt not lend upon usury.... (Deuteronomy 23: 19–20.)

And the provision for periodically releasing debtors from indebtedness likewise discriminates between Israelite and non-Israelite.

> At the end of every seven years thou shalt make a release.
>
> And this is the manner of the release: Every creditor that lendeth ought unto his neighbour

---

2 *Slavery: From the Rise of Western Civilization to Today*, Laurel-Leaf Library, 1972, pp. 33–34. Meltzer quoted Leviticus 25:44, 46.

> shall release it; he shall not exact it of his neighbour, or of his brother, because it is called the LORD's release.
>
> Of a foreigner thou mayest exact it again: but that which is thine with thy brother thine hand shall release.... (Deuteronomy 15: 1–3.)

Thus, Yehuda Bauer's claim that monotheism implies egalitarianism is merely pious balderdash.

Bauer also claims (p. 4) that "The laws that bear the imprint of the Mosaic tradition include the provision ... of the prohibition of murder and theft, and of the absolute sanctity of human life...." The absolute sanctity of human life? Because the Mosaic code prohibits murder? But, of course, the Mosaic law also prescribes the death penalty for murder. Is killing a murderer consistent with "the absolute sanctity of human life?" In any case, consider some of the other capital crimes under the Mosaic law: smiting either of one's parents (Exodus 21:15), cursing either of one's parents (Exodus 21:17), bestiality (Exodus 22:19), sacrificing to any god other than "the Lord" (Exodus 22:20), adultery (Leviticus 20:10), incest (Leviticus 20:11–12), homosexual acts (Leviticus 20:13), having a familiar spirit (Leviticus 20:27), blaspheming the name of "the Lord" (Leviticus 24:16), working on "the Sabbath"—at this very moment, I am working on "the Sabbath"—(Numbers 15:32–36), serving gods other than "the Lord" (Deuteronomy 13:12–18), saying "Let us go serve other gods" (Deuteronomy 13:6–10), and being a rebellious or stubborn son (Deuteronomy 21:18–21). If "the laws that bear the imprint of the Mosaic tradition include the provision of ... the absolute sanctity of human life," then Yehuda Bauer is a ham sandwich.[3]

Another manifestation of the "polemical and apologetic bias" of Yehuda Bauer's Jewish historiography is his expurgated version of messianism. According to Bauer (p. 15), "in Jewish belief, the Messiah would come to lead the Jews back to their ancestral home in Israel and thus end their troubles and wanderings." But is this really all there was (is?) to the Messiah myth? Not according to Jewish anthropologist Raphael Patai and the Jewish writings he has brought together in his book *The Messiah Texts*. For example, Patai mentions[4] "the global upheaval and havoc [the Messiah] was expected to wreak among the Gentiles...." Patai also mentions[5] "the time of triumph, in which all the nations of the world recognize him as their spiritual leader and ruler, and he becomes a veritable *pantocrator*, world ruler—always, of course, in his capacity as the faithful servant of God." On page 193, Patai quotes from *Pesikta Rabbati*:

> "In that hour [in which King Messiah reveals himself] the Holy One, blessed be He, lets shine the light of the Messiah and of Israel, and all of the nations of the world will be in darkness and blackness, and all will walk in the light of the

---

[3] Incidentally, a few pages later, on page 10, Bauer asserts that "the Jews" had "elevated the sanctity of human life to a near absolute." Thus, between pages 4 and 10 Bauer reduces "the absolute sanctity of human life" to merely a near absolute. A very slight concession to reality by Yehuda Bauer.

[4] Raphael Patai, *The Messiah Texts*, Avon, 1979, p. xxxvii.

[5] *Op. cit.*, p. 198.

> Messiah and of Israel ... and they will come and lick the dust under the feet of King Messiah... And all will come and fall upon their faces before the Messiah and before Israel, and will say to him: "Let us be servants to you and to Israel!" And each one of Israel will have 2,800 servants....

According to Isaiah 49:22–23, the Gentiles would also lick the dust under the feet of "Israel," that is, the Jews. As Patai explains,[6]

> Living as they did in a state of dispersion among the nations and of oppression by the Gentiles, the Jews nevertheless remained firmly convinced of the centrality of the Jewish people in the divine scheme with all this meant in imaginary privileges and onerous obligations. Thus the Redemption in the End of Days, too, could not but be centered on the Jewish people, whose role, however, was conceived as that of divine instrument in imposing God's rule over the entire world.

Along the same lines, Patai also says,[7]

> For many centuries, in the midst of persecutions, massacres, expulsions, and humiliations, while living the life of hated and despised pariahs, the Jews in their fantasy saw themselves as kings of the World to Come, enjoying great

---

6   *Op. cit.*, p. xxxvii.
7   *Op. cit.*, p. xxvi.

> pleasures of the palate, exquisite luxuries of housing and clothing, wading ankle-deep in floods of diamonds and pearls, studying the new Tora of the Messiah taught to them directly by God, and being entertained by dances performed by God himself to the music of angels and the heavenly spheres.

Yehuda Bauer gives not the slightest hint of the Messiah as "world ruler," of the Jewish people as the "divine instrument in imposing God's rule over the whole world," of all the Gentile nations of the world coming to Jerusalem to lick the dust from the feet of the Messiah and "Israel" (the Jews), or of each Jew having 2,800 Gentile servants. Of course, if Bauer *had* mentioned these amazing ingredients of messianism, then he wouldn't have been able to blithely dismiss the idea of "a Jewish desire to control the world" as nothing but a "false myth". But Bauer is not willing to admit even the possibility that some Jews might desire to control the world. And so he disingenuously attributes the idea of a Jewish desire to control the world to the "Satanic image" of "the Jew" (p. 44): "just as Satan is out to control the world, so the Jew, possessed by the Devil, must be." I do not see "the Jew" as possessed by "the Devil," yet it seems entirely plausible to me that some Jews might well wish to control the world. As Mark Twain said, "The Jews are members of the human race—worse I can say of no man." Jews are human beings. And some human beings desire power over others. And for some human beings, the lust for power is so all-consuming that they actually desire to control the world. For example, Cecil Rhodes.[8] I see no reason for ignoring the evidence to the contrary and assuming that Jews are inherently incapable of such a lust for power.

But in Yehuda Bauer's biased worldview, it is only Gentiles who are capable of lusting for world power. While Bauer dismisses the idea of a Jewish desire to control the world as a "false myth," he approvingly quotes (p. 84) Robert Payne's characterization of *Mein Kampf* as "a blueprint for the total destruction of bourgeois society and the conquest of the world." As a matter of fact, there were a few passages in *Mein Kampf* that envisioned, in the distant future, a world ruled by an "Aryan" master race.[9] But, contrary to the "false myth" perpetuated by Robert Payne and Yehuda Bauer, there was no blueprint, no detailed plan for world conquest.

Bauer finally gets down to the real nitty-gritty in his ninth chapter, "The 'Final Solution.'" He begins by discussing the various conditions which supposedly led to a decision to kill all European Jews (p. 193). But then he says the crucial factor "was the desire to murder the Jews inherent in Nazi antisemitism." Amazingly, however, "Up until early 1941, the Nazis—with the possible exception of Hitler himself—were not conscious of the murderous ingredient of their own ideology because the practical possibilities of implementing it were not apparent." So the Nazis really wanted to kill the Jews all along; they just didn't realize that they wanted to kill

---

8   See Carroll Quigley, *The Anglo-American Establishment*, Books in Focus, Inc., 1981.

9   See pages 383–384 of the Sentry edition, for example.

them until early 1941, when it became possible to do so. Does Yehuda Bauer really expect anyone to take this quasi-Freudian humbuggery seriously?

In any case, like his fellow "authorities on the Holocaust," Bauer does not prove, but merely assumes, that Hitler, at some indefinite date, gave an order to Himmler "to destroy European Jewry." Bauer says (p. 194), "Himmler himself hinted at such an order in various communications." Among such communications which Bauer cites in a footnote on page 362 is Himmler's circular memorandum of 9 October 1942. Here is Bauer's version of that memorandum:

> After executing the less useful Jews, the remaining Jews, who were to become laborers, were to be sent to concentration camps "in the eastern part of the General Governement [German-occupied central Poland], if possible. Even from there, however, the Jews are someday to disappear, in accordance with the Führer's wishes."

But here is the full text of the memorandum, as translated into English by Elizabeth Wiskemann on pages 110–111 of *Anatomy of the SS State* by Helmut Krausnick et al.:[10]

> 1. I have issued instructions that all so-called armament workers employed merely in boot and shoe factories, timber yards and clothing workshops in Warsaw and Lublin will be removed under the direction of SS-Obergruppenführer

---

10 Walker and Company, 1968.

Krueger and SS-Obergruppenführer Pohl to concentration camps. The Wehrmacht should transfer any orders outstanding to us and we will guarantee delivery of the clothing required. I have also ordered that steps be ruthlessly taken against all those who think they can use the interests of the war industry to cloak their real intention to protect the Jews and their own business affairs.

2. Jews who are directly employed in the war industry—that is to say, in armament or vehicle workshops and so forth—are to be released gradually. As a first step they are to be assembled on one floor of the factory. Subsequently all the hands on this floor are to be transferred—on an exchange basis if possible—to a "secure" undertaking, so that all we shall have in the Government General will be a number of "secure" concentration camp undertakings.

3. Our next endeavor will be to replace this Jewish labor force with Poles and to amalgamate the great majority of the Jewish concentration camp enterprises with one or two large, not wholly Jewish, concentration camp undertakings—if possible in the eastern part of the Government General. In due course these will also be cleared of Jews in accordance with the wishes of the Führer.

As you can see, Himmler's memorandum said nothing about "executing the less useful Jews." Nor did it say "the remaining Jews ... were to become laborers." The memorandum dealt exclusively with Jews who already were laborers. As for the final statement of the memorandum, that eventually the concentration camps would be "cleared of Jews in accordance with the wishes of the Führer," this could have been a hint at a Hitler order for the destruction of European Jewry only if there was such an order. But, as I've said, Bauer never proves; he merely assumes there was such an order.

Bauer's chapter on "the Final Solution," like the other chapters of his book, is replete with assertions for which he cites no supporting source(s). For example, after discussing *Einsatzgruppen* massacres in Russia, Bauer asserts (p. 200), "Mass killings also occurred in Odessa in the Crimea, at Rumanian hands, where 144,000 civilians were murdered, largely by drowning." Since this struck me as a bit farfetched, especially the part about drowning, I looked for Bauer's source for this assertion. But Bauer cites no source for it. I then checked but found no confirmation of this assertion in any of the "standard" works on the Holocaust: not in Hilberg's *The Destruction of the European Jews*, not in Reitlinger's *The Final Solution*, not in Dawidowicz's *The War Against the Jews*, not in Levin's *The Holocaust*, not in Poliakov's *Harvest of Hate*, and not in Manvell and Frankel's *The Incomparable Crime*. What I *did* find is that a few of these books claim a massacre of either 19,000 Jews (both Hilberg and Levin—who cites Hilberg) or 26,000 Jews (Reitlinger) in Odessa in October of 1941 as a "reprisal" for the deaths of several dozen Romanian soldiers resulting from the explosion of a delayed-action landmine left behind in what had been NKVD headquarters. These "authorities on the Holocaust" agree that these Jews were shot. Hilberg and Levin (citing Hilberg) also claim that another 40,000 Jews were subsequently taken out of Odessa and shot in anti-tank ditches, bringing the total of Odessa Jews allegedly killed by the Romanians to about 60,000. So where, pray tell, did Yehuda Bauer come up with 144,000 civilians murdered at Odessa "largely by drowning?"

On page 209, Bauer makes the offhand remark that no gassings took place at Mauthausen. He gives no inkling of how he arrived at this revisionist conclusion regarding Mauthausen, but if Bauer is right, the implications are interesting. Consider: In his 1966 book, *The Trial of the Germans*, Eugene Davidson discussed, and dismissed, Ernst Kaltenbrunner's defense at Nuremberg:[11]

> Kaltenbrunner admitted to none of these charges despite all the witnesses and the overwhelming evidence against him. On the stand, under the searching questioning of British prosecutor Colonel Amen, he could only deny the authenticity of his own signature and declare that the witnesses were lying who said they had seen him in Mauthausen when killings were staged in his honor by gas, hanging, and shooting.

Davidson found it inconceivable that witnesses might have lied about Kaltenbrunner attending a

---

11 Eugene Davidson, *The Trial of the Germans*, Macmillan, 1966, p. 323.

gassing at Mauthausen. But Yehuda Bauer implies such witnesses *were* lying when he asserts that "no gassings took place at Mauthausen." In fact, Bauer's statement implies that all the testimonies about gassings at Mauthausen are false, including those of ex-inmate Johann Kanduth, ex-SS guard Alois Hoellriegel, and camp commandant Franz Ziereis. For the deposition of Hoellriegel, which implicated Kaltenbrunner, see *The Case Against Adolf Eichmann*, edited by Henry A. Zeiger.[1] This book also contains excerpts from the interrogation of Kanduth, also implicating Kaltenbrunner.[2] Regarding "the deathbed confession" of Ziereis, see Appendix 2 of Germaine Tillion's *Ravensbrueck*.[3] And see page 8 of Simon Wiesenthal's memoirs, *The Murderers Among Us*[4] for a passing reference to "the horrors of the gas chambers" of Mauthausen. Yehuda Bauer did not mention these testimonies, let alone explain why he rejects them as incredible. Perhaps he feared that had he done so, some of his readers might have wondered why he accepts as credible the similar testimonies about gassings at Polish "extermination camps."

In any case, it certainly is possible to raise questions about the credibility of Bauer's star witnesses about gassing, Kurt Gerstein, Rudolf Höss, and Filip Müller. On pages 210–211, Bauer quotes excerpts from the Gerstein "report" on a mass gassing of Jews at Belzec. Bauer,

---

1 *The Case Against Adolf Eichmann*, edited by Henry A. Zeiger, Signet, 1960, pp. 141–143.
2 *Op. cit.*, 143-145.
3 Anchor Books, 1975.
4 Bantam, 1973.

however, has omitted most of the blatant absurdities of the Gerstein "report," such as the claim that the Nazis gassed a total of 25 million people. And Bauer gives a calculatedly misleading account of the adventures of Jan Karski, another self-proclaimed Belzec eyewitness whose testimony raises questions about Gerstein's story of mass gassings of Jews at Belzec. According to Bauer (p. 300),

> To see for himself what was happening, Jan Karski (a pseudonym), a Polish patriot and a Catholic humanitarian, visited the Warsaw ghetto after the summer 1942 deportation. Disguised as a guard, he then managed to enter Belzec death camp for one day where he witnessed mass murder.

So Jan Karski (a pseudonym) witnessed "mass murder" at Belzec. Bauer does not elaborate on Karski's witnessing of "mass murder," allowing naïve readers to incorrectly assume that Karski witnessed the operation of the infamous "gas chambers" of Belzec described by Gerstein. But, assuming Karski accurately recounted real experiences at Belzec, the only mass murder he saw was the killing of perhaps "a few score" Jews in the process of brutally herding more than 5,000 Jews into the cars of a train which then left the Belzec camp.[5] Karski, who supposedly was at Belzec not quite two months after Kurt Gerstein supposedly witnessed a gassing at Belzec, did not even see any gas chambers, let alone witness a gassing.

---

5   See Karski's 1944 book, *The Story of a Secret State*, Houghton Mifflin, 1944, Chapter 30.

It is true that Karski claimed that Jews were herded into railroad cars at Belzec as part of a process of mass extermination. According to Karski,

> The floors of the car had been covered with a thick, white powder. It was quicklime. Quicklime is simply unslaked lime or calcium oxide that has been dehydrated. Anyone who has seen cement being mixed knows what occurs when water is poured on lime. The mixture bubbles and steams as the powder combines with the water, generating a large amount of heat.
>
> ...The moist flesh coming in contact with the lime is rapidly dehydrated and burned. The occupants of the cars would be literally burned to death before long, the flesh eaten from their bones.[6]

Karski, however, did not claim to have seen the occupants of the cars being "literally burned to death ... the flesh eaten from their bones." And Karski's assumptions about this are implicitly challenged by Bergen Evans in his book *The Natural History of Nonsense*.[7] According to Evans,

> That quicklime will "eat" a dead body is an old delusion that has brought several murderers to the noose, for, actually, it is a preservative that instead of removing the evidence keeps it fresh for the coroner's eye... Oscar Wilde, who

---

6   *Op. cit.*, 349–350.
7   Bergan Evans, *The Natural History of Nonsense*, Vintage, 1958.

> poetically asserted that quicklime ate the flesh by day and the bones by night, served to refute his own assertion, for he was himself buried in quicklime, and on his exhumation two years later was found to be well preserved.[8]

If, as Evans said, quicklime does not "eat" the flesh of a dead body, then would it have "eaten" the flesh from the bones of the living Jews shipped out of Belzec as Karski said it would?

In any case, it so happens that Karski was not alone in "proving" Nazi atrocities by exploiting the supposed power of quicklime to "eat" flesh. According to Bergen Evans,

> when the resourceful Mr. W.A.S. Douglas, of the Paris Bureau of the *Chicago Sun*, was confronted with an empty internment camp, Fort de Romainville, deserted by the retreating Germans, he was quick to perceive that it was actually a "death factory" for "the martyred heroines of France." No heroines or fragments of heroines were found, but that only added to the horror of it all: they had obviously been "buried in quicklime."[9]

Whatever the truth may be about the alleged mass extermination of Jews with quicklime, Yehuda Bauer was clearly delinquent in asserting—without explaining and justifying the assertion—that Jan Karski witnessed

---

8   *Op. cit.*, 349–350.
9   *Op. cit.*, p. 133.

"mass murder" at Belzec. And he was also delinquent in not even attempting to reconcile Karski's testimony with that of Kurt Gerstein.

Another of Bauer's star witnesses to mass extermination of Jews by gassing is Rudolf Höss, who gave a number of confessions to his various postwar captors and interrogators. Bauer cites only one of these confessions, the autobiography written in prison in Communist Poland and published in an English translation as *Commandant of Auschwitz*. Robert Faurisson, however, has identified some significant anomalies in that confession.[10] And Arthur Butz has pointed out numerous anomalies in another Höss confession, an affidavit of 5 April 1946.[11] Rather than repeat the criticisms of Faurisson and Butz, I will simply point out a few additional anomalies to be found in Höss' various confessions.

In a portion of the autobiography quoted by Yehuda Bauer (p. 214), Höss described an experimental gassing.

> Protected by a gas-mask I watched the killing myself. In the crowded cells death came instantaneously the moment the Zyklon B was thrown in. A short, almost smothered cry, and it was all over...

But is Zyklon B capable of killing "instantaneously?" To do so, Zyklon B crystals, when exposed to open air,

---

[10] See "The Gas Chambers of Auschwitz Appear to be Physically Inconceivable" and "The Gas Chambers: Truth or Lie?," *The Journal of Historical Review*, Winter 1981.

[11] See *The Hoax of the Twentieth Century*, Chapter IV.

would have to release lethal quantities of hydrogen cyanide gas instantaneously. Is that possible? I don't know for certain, but it seems unlikely. In any case, it seems pretty certain that hydrogen cyanide gas, once released, does not kill instantaneously. According to page 53 of *Treatment of War Injuries*, a booklet published in 1942 by Merck & Co., manufacturing chemists, "The poison inhibits oxidation in the body and may cause extremely rapid death by paralysis of the respiratory center." The booklet then describes the symptoms of hydrogen cyanide poisoning. "There may be rapid development of vertigo, headache, palpitation and dyspnea [i.e., labored breathing], followed by coma, convulsions and death." Thus, although inhalation of air containing sufficient hydrogen cyanide gas may cause "extremely rapid death," it apparently does not cause *instantaneous* death. (If it caused death instantaneously, how would there be time for the development of the various symptoms described above?)

In "The Gas Chambers: Truth or Lie?," Robert Faurisson has summarized the procedure of gassing condemned prisoners by hydrogen cyanide gas in American prisons. According to Faurisson, "Within approximately 40 seconds [after the release of the gas], the prisoner dozes off, and in a few minutes he dies." Although Bauer, on page 214, uncritically quotes Höss' story about instantaneous death caused by Zyklon B, on the very next page he describes the standard gassing procedure at Auschwitz and says, "After a few minutes of intense suffering, the victims died." Thus, Bauer agrees with Faurisson that gassing by hydrogen cyanide causes death after a few minutes. So why does Bauer approvingly quote Höss' tale about a gassing in which the victims died instantaneously?

In any case, if Faurisson is right that the victim of a hydrogen cyanide gassing "dozes off" after about 40 seconds, then Bauer is presumably wrong about the victim dying after a few minutes "of intense suffering." Although it doesn't say when, the Merck & Co. booklet does say that the victim of hydrogen cyanide goes into a coma before dying. This is at least a partial confirmation of Faurisson's assertion. At any rate, the information that the victim of hydrogen cyanide gas goes into a coma before dying renders quite dubious another statement from Höss' 5 April 1946 affidavit, to wit, "We knew when the people were dead because their screaming stopped." Can someone in a coma scream?

In addition to Höss' autobiography, *Commandant of Auschwitz* includes a statement on "the Final Solution" made by Höss in Cracow, Poland, in November of 1946. Yehuda Bauer does not quote these passages from that statement:

> When I went to Budapest in the summer of 1943 and called on Eichmann, he told me about the further actions which had been planned in connection with the Jews.
>
> At that period there were more than 200,000 Jews from the Carpatho-Ukraine, who were detained there and housed in some brickworks, while awaiting transport to Auschwitz.
>
> Eichmann expected to receive from Hungary, according to the estimate of the

Hungarian police, who had carried out the arrests, about 3,000,000 Jews.

The arrests and transportation should have been completed by 1943, but because of the Hungarian government's political difficulties, the date was always being postponed.

In particular the Hungarian army, or rather the senior officers, were opposed to the extradition of these people and gave most of the male Jews a refuge in the labor companies of the front-line divisions, thus keeping them out of the clutches of the police. When in the autumn of 1944, an action was started in Budapest itself, the only male Jews left were the old and the sick.

Altogether there were probably not more than half a million Jews transported out of Hungary.

The next country on the list was Romania. According to the reports from his representative in Bucharest, Eichmann expected to get about 4,000,000 Jews from there.

...In the meantime Bulgaria was to follow with an estimated two and a half million Jews. The authorities there were agreeable to the transport, but wanted to await the result of the negotiations with Romania.

...The course taken by the war destroyed these plans and saved the lives of millions of Jews.[12]

---

12 *Commandant of Auschwitz*, Popular Library, 1959, pp. 189–190.

Indeed, if the estimates supposedly given to Höss by Eichmann were accurate, then "the course taken by the war" saved the fives of about nine million Jews in Hungary, Romania, and Bulgaria! Since, according to Bauer (p. 334), there were only nine million Jews in all of Europe before the war, it's no wonder he doesn't mention this inconvenient testimony from one of his star witnesses. You don't become "one of the world's top authorities on the Holocaust" by dwelling on the absurdities of Rudolf Höss' confessions.

On page 215, Yehuda Bauer quotes from Höss' testimony regarding cremations at Birkenau: "The two large crematoria I and II ... had five three-retort ovens and could cremate about 2,000 bodies in less than 24 hours." Höss never explained how such numbers of cremations were possible, nor does Bauer explain this. However, another of Bauer's star witnesses is Filip Müller, supposedly a member of the Auschwitz-Birkenau *Sonderkommando*, who has said of Crematorium I at Birkenau, "Its fifteen huge ovens, working non-stop, could cremate more than 3,000 corpses daily."[13] How was it possible to cremate such numbers? According to Müller, three bodies were cremated simultaneously in each oven, and each cremation took only 20 minutes.

To judge from a recent *Los Angeles Times* article by Carol McGraw,[14] Müller's claim about cremating three corpses simultaneously in each oven is within the realm

---

13 *Eyewitness Auschwitz: Three Years in the Gas Chambers*, Stein and Day, 1979, p. 59.

14 "Cremation: Boom Brings Controversy," 13 April 1983.

of possibility. McGraw quotes the head of a cremation company:

> You can tell in 30 seconds if a crematory is legitimate, he said. They [i.e., consumers] should look at the product—ashes should be pure white. If several bodies are cremated together, they won't burn uniformly and the ashes come out very dark.

But to judge from the same article, Müller's claim about cremating three corpses together in 20 minutes is not within the realm of possibility. As McGraw reported, "In the cremation process, a body is placed in a furnace and subjected to temperatures of up to 2,000 degrees for two or three hours." If it takes 2 or 3 hours to cremate a body in a present-day crematory, is it possible that the crematoria of Birkenau could have done so in 20 minutes? As Müller himself says,[15] "These were, of course, not modern or technically advanced crematoria." If one assumes that cremations at Birkenau took two hours, then, even if three bodies were cremated simultaneously in each oven, Crematorium I's 15 ovens, working non-stop, could have cremated no more than 540 bodies in 24 hours. That's a far cry from Höss' "2,000 bodies in less than 24 hours" or Müller's "3,000 corpses daily." And, of course, if cremations at Birkenau took longer than two hours, as seems quite possible if three bodies were being cremated simultaneously in each oven, then Crematorium I at Birkenau could not have

---

15 *Eyewitness*, p. 61.

cremated even as many as 540 bodies in 24 hours. Thus, it appears that Rudolf Höss and Filip Müller have grossly exaggerated the capacity of the Birkenau crematoria. However, Yehuda Bauer, "one of the world's top authorities on the Holocaust," swallows their gross exaggerations as eagerly as if they were lox and cream cheese.

According to Bauer (p. 215), "Between 1.5 and 3.5 million Jews died at Auschwitz." Bauer cites no source for these figures, nor does he provide any explanation of how they were arrived at or of how they could possibly be true. And, strangely, although he can't be any more precise than this about Auschwitz, nevertheless, on page 334, he states that "During the Holocaust, 5.8 million Jewish people died...." Thus, according to Bauer, 5.8 million Jews died in the Holocaust regardless of how many Jews died at Auschwitz. For Bauer, whether 1.5 million Jews died at Auschwitz or 3.5 million Jews died at Auschwitz, in either case 5.8 million Jews died during the Holocaust. Could it be that Yehuda Bauer wants to believe, no matter what, that 5.8 million Jews, i.e., about six million, died during the Holocaust?

In a chapter on "The Last Years of the Holocaust, 1943–1945," Yehuda Bauer reports (p. 326), "When Majdanek was liberated in July 1944, the Russian reports on what they found there were viewed with disbelief in the West." Indeed, Richard E. Lauterbach, one of the journalists who parroted those "Russian reports" in the Western press, complained about such disbelief in his 1945 book, *These Are the Russians*: "The story of Majdanek was printed in American newspapers and magazines. But millions of Americans have never heard

220 | Outlaw History

of it, and many who have do not believe it."[16] But *what* did the "Russian [i.e., Soviet] reports" on Majdanek say? Yehuda Bauer does not spell out for his readers the actual contents of those "reports," perhaps because he does not want his readers to realize that he himself does not completely believe them. The Soviet "reports" on Majdanek included the allegation that "one and a half million people were in one way or another put to death in this camp, about half of them Jews."[17] But according to Bauer (p. 209), "[Majdanek] accommodated 50,000 inmates, and in the course of its history, 200,000 died there." Thus Yehuda Bauer implies that the Soviet "reports" exaggerated the number of deaths at Majdanek by 1,300,000! Thereby, Bauer himself vindicates those who, as Lauterbach complained in 1945, were already saying, "these reports are untrue or exaggerated."

Interestingly enough, Lauterbach also complained about disbelief of other Soviet atrocity "reports," including the "report" that "At Tremblyanka [sic] in Poland, an estimated 2,764,000 Jews were annihilated." By comparison, Bauer claims (p. 209) that 840,000 Jews were killed at Treblinka. Of course, even Bauer's (unsupported) claim may be a gross exaggeration.

Before concluding this review, I want to mention a few miscellaneous items of interest in *A History of the Holocaust*.

On page 18, Bauer says, "Jewish tribes for a time controlled the Yemen...." It would be interesting to

---

16 Richard E. Lauterbach, *These Are the Russians*, Book Find Club, 1945, p. 326.
17 See *Newsweek*, 11 September 1944, page 64.

know more about this historical episode, but Bauer does not elaborate.

On page 61, Bauer makes the following assertion: "Against a background of economic crisis which hit everyone, not only the Jews, one-third of Polish Jewry in the thirties was on the verge of starvation or beyond it." Bauer returns to this theme on pages 143–144, quoting Sholem Asch, who wrote in October of 1936 that the Polish Jews seemed to be "buried alive. Every second person was undernourished, skeletons of skin and bones, crippled, candidates for the grave." But if, as Bauer says, one-third of Polish Jews, about a million Polish Jews, were already "on the verge of starvation or beyond it" *before* the war, then is it really surprising that many Jews (perhaps even hundreds of thousands) would have died of starvation and starvation-related diseases during nearly six years of war and military occupation? Is the explanation for such deaths Nazi diabolism or rather the deleterious effects of a prolonged war on the situation of about one million already impoverished Polish Jews?

In this regard, it is interesting to note the contents of Chapter Four of Reb Moshe Schonfeld's book *The Holocaust Victims Accuse*.[18] According to Schonfeld, the Committee to Boycott Germany of the World Jewish Congress in 1941 demanded, in the name of Zionist bigwig Stephen Wise, that Zeirei Agudas Israel stop sending food parcels to Polish Jewry, because this was a breach of Britain's boycott regulations against Germany. When the demand was rejected, another Zionist honcho,

---

18   Neturei Karta of USA, 1971.

Joseph Tennenbaum, organized the picketing of Zeirei Agudas Israel's office. According to Schonfeld, Zeirei Agudas Israel did not yield to this pressure, but "a majority of naïve New York Jews became confused and the sending of packages sharply declined." If Schonfeld's account is accurate, then it would appear that the Zionists were actually prepared to starve Polish Jewry as a means of starving Nazi Germany.

In a section on "Jewish–Gentile Relations in Eastern Europe," Bauer relates the following (pp. 284–285):

> The accusation of Jewish-Soviet cooperation in Eastern Polish areas occupied by the Soviets in 1939 was leveled by the Poles throughout the war. There was some truth to this. Soviet occupation was better than Nazi rule, and the Soviets abolished the restrictions that had prevented Jews in Poland from entering universities, the administration, and some trades. However, the fact that Jewish attitudes changed as the Soviets restricted religious life, abolished all Jewish institutions, and confiscated property, was ignored by Polish public opinion. According to Polish figures, 264,000 Jews were deported into Soviet exile or Soviet camps, or between 17 and 20 percent of the Jews in Soviet-occupied Eastern Poland. During the war itself, in the absence of any substantial help extended by Poles or Ukrainians, the Soviet army and the return of the Soviet regime were seen by the Jews as the only hope for rescue. Jewish forest and ghetto

> fighters sought aid from the Soviets. The Poles, who feared Soviet rule no less than they hated the Nazi conquerors, could not identify with the Jewish attitude.

Another item of interest is an appendix in which Bauer gives the text of Himmler's 28 May 1940 secret memorandum, "Reflections on the Treatment of Peoples of Alien Races in the East." Some revisionists have cited this memorandum's reference to "the Bolshevist method of physical extermination of a people" as "un-German and impossible." But it is useful to have the full text of the memorandum.

In an interview given to *Conspiracy Digest* and reprinted in his book *The Illuminati Papers*, Robert Anton Wilson opined,

> Those who make a career out of spreading unproven accusations against other humans can only be forgiven if they really are so ignorant and stupid that they don't know the difference between an assertion and an evidential demonstration.[19]

Yehuda Bauer, professor of Holocaust studies and author of seven books, seems to be making just such a career out of spreading unproven accusations against other humans, specifically unproven accusations against Hitler and his henchmen. I doubt that Bauer is really so ignorant and stupid that he doesn't know the difference between an assertion and an evidential demonstration.

---

19   *The Illuminati Papers*, And/Or Press, 1980, p. 43.

But on second thought, maybe he is that ignorant and stupid. After all, he is "one of the world's top authorities on the Holocaust."

> A slightly different version of this essay was originally published in *The Journal of Historical Review*, Fall 1983. (Vol. 4, No. 3).

AZRIEL EISENBERG PRESENTS: THE GREATEST SOB STORY EVER TOLD (WITH A CAST OF MILLIONS)

The Lost Generation: Children in the Holocaust
Azriel Eisenberg
The Pilgrim Press, 1982

AZRIEL EISENBERG STRIKES AGAIN! In *The Journal of Historical Review*, Spring 1983, I reviewed Eisenberg's *Witness to the Holocaust*. Now Eisenberg, Holocaustomaniac *par excellence*, has produced a companion volume to that egregious opus. So here I am, writing a companion review to my earlier one.

Like *Witness to the Holocaust*, *The Lost Generation: Children in the Holocaust* purports to be a collection of eyewitness accounts of "the Holocaust." But this time, these accounts are either by or about those who were 14 years of age or younger during "the Nazi carnage." According to Eisenberg, 1,200,000 of the Nazis' six million Jewish victims were children. And this killing of children is supposed to be the most shocking and terrible part of the Nazis' "bloody work." Thus, a volume devoted entirely to children in "the Holocaust."

In *Witness to the Holocaust*, Eisenberg said (p. 5), "the heart of this book is a compilation of authentic, first-hand, personal, and eyewitness accounts," Similarly, in the introduction to *The Lost Generation*, he says (p. xvii), "The accounts included in this book were chosen from books written by eyewitnesses.... Only authentic personal and eyewitness experiences were selected." Eisenberg emphasizes "authentic, first-hand, personal, and eyewitness accounts" because of the emotional impact they presumably will have on his more reverent readers. In *Witness to the Holocaust*, he explained (p. 5),

> The Sho'ah [the Holocaust] cannot be intellectualized. To validate this contention, readers are invited to test their emotional reactions to the introductions of the chapters in this book as compared to the first-hand accounts that follow them. To establish any meaningful tie with Auschwitz, the Warsaw Ghetto, the partisans, the martyrs, and the survivors, we must share in their experiences. For this reason, the heart of this book is a compilation of authentic, first-hand, personal, and eyewitness accounts. They will affect your innermost being.

In the introduction to *The Lost Generation*, Eisenberg says of the "authentic personal and eyewitness experiences" that he's selected (p. xvii), "They will enable the reader to share the agony, the physical, emotional and spiritual torment of the martyred children."

Well, reading Eisenberg's "eyewitness" accounts may be a good way for devout Holocaustomaniacs to experience agony and torment. But, being the cold-hearted nitpicker that I am, I wonder if reading them is a good way to find out what really happened to Jewish children under Nazi rule.

For one thing, a number of scientific investigators of eyewitness testimony have concluded that most such testimony is to some degree unreliable. In his anthology *The Historian as Detective: Essays on Evidence*, Robin W. Winks included (pp. 182–191) an excerpt, concerning the credibility of testimony, from Thomas Spencer Jerome's *Aspects of the Study of Roman History*. Jerome described experiments conducted by Alfred Binet, William Stern, and others. For example, here is Jerome's account of an experiment by Stern:

> He had three simple pictures in black and white, which he exhibited for forty-five seconds each to about thirty cultivated adults who immediately wrote down what they had seen in each picture, and thereafter at certain intervals of time again submitted written statements. Such parts of their depositions as they were willing to take oath upon were indicated by underlining. Without going into details, it may be said that the results were not of a nature calculated to give one great confidence in the value of testimony. Error was not the exception, but the rule. Out of two hundred and eighty-two depositions only seventeen were entirely correct; and of these seventeen, fifteen were among statements written down

immediately. By the fifth day even, the proportion of misstatements reached about a quarter of all the details submitted. In the depositions containing indications of matters on which the observer was willing to take an oath, only thirteen out of sixty-three failed to contain false statements, to all of which however the witnesses were prepared to swear. Many of these were cases of the introduction of elements which were absolutely absent from the picture. So one student wrote three weeks after the event: "The picture shows an old man seated on a wooden bench. A small boy is standing at his left. *He is looking at the old man who is feeding a pigeon. On the roof is perched another pigeon which is preparing to fly to the ground to get its share of food.*" The italicized statements were wholly incorrect: there were no pigeons in the picture. Perhaps the figure of a cat in the scene may have suggested the idea of a bird to the observer.

Jerome explained the significance of such experiments thusly:

It will appear from these and similar experiments that erroneous testimony was given in simple matters of direct, personal observation by witnesses who were not influenced by any conscious pre-existing emotion or prepossession, and who were actuated by a desire to give an exact and truthful narrative. Yet the

> results were not encouraging. It is evident, as scholars who have conducted or studied such experiments have shown, that good faith, the desire to tell the truth, and the certainty that the testimony is true, as well as the opportunity to secure correct information, and the absence of prepossessions, are far from affording adequate guarantees that the truth will be told. The most honest witness may misstate; the worst may tell the truth. Entirely faithful testimony is not the rule but rather a rare exception....

As reported by French psychiatrist Marcel Eck,[1] Michel Cenac, after studying similar experiments, drew the following similar conclusions about eyewitness testimony:

> 1. Entirely accurate testimony is the exception,
>
> 2. The witness offers false information with the same assurance that he gives true information,
>
> 3. Witnesses are inclined to perceive the facts and reconstruct their memory of them in terms of what seems likely to them rather than what they really saw.

Knowing how fallible my own memory is, these conclusions strike me as being entirely plausible. But if eyewitness testimony is commonly unreliable, then it seems fair to assume that eyewitness testimony about

---

1   *Lies and Truth*, Macmillan, 1970, p. 147

"the Holocaust" is commonly unreliable too. For that matter, eyewitness testimony about "the Holocaust" might even tend to be more unreliable than other eyewitness testimony. According to Gordon Allport and Leo Postman,[2] eyewitness testimony is highly unreliable, "especially in conditions where excitement existed during the original perception or in the process of narration. Normal defects of perception, retention, and verbal report are serious enough, but emotional states greatly magnify them." This is certainly a factor influencing some testimony about "the Holocaust."

Regarding the effect of emotional states, Alexander Leighton, writing about the wartime "internment" of the Japanese,[3] made some interesting and suggestive comments:

> Psychiatrists observing patients who are emotionally unwell have long known that when they go into a state of panic they misinterpret ordinary events as horrible threats. The whistle of a distant train becomes a death scream, or two people seen talking together are instantly assumed to be plotting. More than this, it has been seen that patients in panic can become hallucinated and see people coming to attack them who are not there at all, or may smell smoke and gas where none exists. It is more than probable that this happens to

---

2   *The Psychology of Rumor*, Henry Holt, 1947, p. 53
3   *The Governing of Men*, Princeton University Press, 1946, p. 268

> otherwise normal individuals when in a state of intense fear, and it may be that those persons in the [Colorado River War Relocation] Center [at Poston, Arizona] who saw non-existent machine guns and their crews during the strike were suffering from such distortions of their senses. In the Detroit riots the police were bothered by people calling up and giving specific details of murders and violence, sometimes said to be going on before their "very eyes," but which actually never occurred. There are similar instances in reports on the behavior of people under stress in war zones....

According to Leighton, when psychiatric patients "go into a state of panic, they misinterpret ordinary events as horrible threats. The whistle of a distant train becomes a death scream." But it just so happens that numerous survivors of Auschwitz-Birkenau have given eyewitness (or should I say "earwitness"?) testimony about hearing the screams of people in "the gas chambers." For example, the testimony of Zvi Goldberg, one of Azriel Eisenberg's witnesses in *The Lost Generation*, includes the following (p. 207): "Suddenly the stillness of the night was shattered by the heartrending cries of the victims being forced into the death chambers." But considering how much train traffic there was in the vicinity of Auschwitz-Birkenau, the question arises: Did fearful camp inmates sometimes misinterpret the sound of train whistles as the death screams of people being gassed?

232 | Outlaw History

There are other possibilities. Camp inmates may have sometimes heard real screams and mistakenly assumed that they were the screams of people being killed. For example, consider Sarah Cender's eyewitness account of her arrival at Auschwitz, as quoted by Martin Gilbert:

> Upon arrival we were separated from the males and brought in front of a building where heaps of clothing were lying on the ground. We were ordered to undress quickly and naked we were pushed into a pitch dark chamber (what we naïvely and hopefully thought to be a bath facility—although no soap or towel were given to us).
>
> The doors closed behind us. Anxious seconds and minutes passed. Nothing seemed to happen—for a while. Only cries and laments and hysterical screams we heard from every corner of the chamber. Some of the women started to cough incoherently, believing being choked by gas. The situation became unbearable....[4]

Eventually, after a bombing raid, the doors were opened, and Cender and her companions were ordered out of "the chamber." But how many camp inmates heard their "hysterical screams" and assumed that they were being gassed?

In any case, even some devout Holocaustomaniacs

---

4   *Auschwitz and the Allies*, Holt, Rinehart and Winston, 1981, p. 309

have acknowledged the inaccuracy of some survivor testimony. In a footnote in *The Holocaust and the Historians*, Lucy Dawidowicz writes,[5]

> Many thousands of oral histories by survivors recounting their experiences exist in libraries and archives around the world. Their quality and usefulness vary significantly according to the informant's memory, grasp of events, insights, and of course accuracy.... The transcribed testimonies I have examined have been full of errors in dates, names of participants, and places, and there are evident misunderstandings of the events themselves.

In his foreword to *Voices from the Holocaust*, a collection of such transcribed oral testimonies, edited by Sylvia Rothchild, Elie Wiesel admits,[6]

> here and there you will come up against some errors of fact or perception. For example, the revolt of the Birkenau *Sonderkommando* seems to have been undertaken in cooperation with the Royal Air Force. That's what we read in this book. But, this doesn't agree with the findings of historians... The witness remembers a plan that involved the RAF because he undoubtedly heard rumors: every camp was an inexhaustible source of rumors.

---

5   Harvard University Press, 1981, pp. 176-177.
6   New American Library, 1981, p. 4.

234 | Outlaw History

Yes, indeed—"every camp was an inexhaustible source of rumors." And as Allport and Postman pointed out, "Even firsthand reports are so faulty that they seldom can be trusted in detail. Rumor, being once, twice, or a thousand times removed from eyewitness testimony, is just so much more invalid."[7] This is a point worth emphasizing because, despite Azriel Eisenberg's claims, *The Lost Generation* contains much that is not eyewitness testimony but is merely hearsay, rumor, inference, etc. For example, Eisenberg includes (pp. 108–110) a "document... written in Polish by a nameless thirteen-year-old boy in April 1944." Eisenberg's nameless "eyewitness," a resident of Warsaw, wrote, "On the very first day that the 'resettlement' program was instituted, my mother, father, sister, and little brother were deported and killed at Treblinka." But this nameless witness was not deported to Treblinka and did not see his family members killed there, so this is not eyewitness testimony.

Eisenberg also includes (pp. 138–139) a brief excerpt from Philip Friedman's *This Was Oswiecim*. Among Friedman's revelations is this: "The children were not always liquidated by gas. Dr. Jacob Wollman of Lodz declares that the SS clubbed about five hundred children to death with their rifle butts." Ouch! Of course, this is not eyewitness testimony, since Friedman didn't claim to have seen this particular atrocity. (He didn't even tell us if Dr. Wollman himself claimed to have seen it.) Titling it "THE GAS CHAMBER," Eisenberg has also included (pp. 139–141) an excerpt "From a Memorandum by Mr. Lieberman, September 27, 1945." Mr. Lieberman

---

7   *Op. cit.*, p. 54.

described in some detail the operations of "the crematorium and the gas chamber" of Birkenau. But as he himself explained, "We were separated in quarantine but housed together with another working party, which was serving the crematorium and the gas chamber. It is due to this fact that I know how things occurred." Or as he also wrote, "I have never seen the trolleys for the transport of corpses personally, nor have I seen the ovens operating; but as I have already mentioned, several of the working party, which was serving the gas chambers and ovens, lived with us and have given me all the details." Thus, Mr. Lieberman's account of "the gas chambers and ovens" is hearsay at best. Mr. Lieberman said, "A certain Jacob Weinschein of Paris, who is a survivor of this commando [*Sonderkommando*], is personally known to me." Didn't Jacob Weinschein ever write an eyewitness account of "the gas chambers and ovens" of Birkenau? In any case, Azriel Eisenberg has not given us eyewitness testimony from Jacob Weinschein. Instead, he has given us a heap of hearsay from Mr. Lieberman.

Here is some of that hearsay:

> The men and women entered the so-called bathroom and undressed separately to avoid panic. Once they were undressed they entered by separate doors in the central chamber. This chamber could take 3,000 people. The gas was released through sprays of the showers and from bombs which were thrown through apertures designed to allow for that procedure. Death occurred within five minutes.

> On certain days, when enormous transports arrived at the station of Birkenau, 42,000 people were gassed. Once the gassing process had been completed, the floor of the chamber opened automatically and the corpses fell into the subterranean chamber, where prisoners in charge of extracting the teeth or cutting hair of a certain length, took over... Once the gold teeth had been recovered, the corpses were loaded on to a moving belt and transported to cremation ovens, through subterranean gangways. There were four ovens, a big one and three small ones, which were capable of burning 400 corpses in five minutes. Later on, when the number of corpses exceeded the capacity of the ovens, trenches were dug and the corpses thrown in saturated with petrol.

And the cow in the nursery rhyme really did jump over the moon, which is made of green cheese.

Mr. Lieberman's hearsay account of gassings and cremation at Birkenau is a dilly. For one thing, he said that "Once the gassing process had been completed, the floor of the chamber opened automatically and, the corpses fell into the subterranean chamber...." But Birkenau crematoria IV and V had no subterranean chambers. Crematoria II and III each had two subterranean "chambers," one of which allegedly was a gas chamber, the other allegedly an undressing room. But these two subterranean "chambers" were on the same level, at right angles to each other. There were no subterranean chambers underneath the alleged subterranean gas chambers. So this part of Mr. Lieberman's tale just doesn't fit the facts.

Neither does his statement that "There were four ovens, a big one and three small ones, which were capable of burning 400 corpses in five minutes." There were four crematoria at Birkenau, two larger ones and two smaller ones. The larger ones, II and III, each had 15 ovens, or, as some people put it, five ovens with three openings each. The two smaller crematoria, IV and V, each had eight ovens, or two ovens with four openings each. No matter how you slice it, Mr. Lieberman's testimony about four ovens, a big one and three small ones, is baloney.

As for his claim that those four ovens could cremate 400 corpses in five minutes, that's beyond baloney. According to *Los Angeles Times* staff writer Carol McGraw, "In the cremation process, a body is placed in a furnace and subjected to temperatures of up to 2,000 degrees for two or three hours."[8] At that rate, four ovens might be able to cremate 400 corpses in 50 hours, not in five minutes.

If four ovens at Birkenau could cremate 400 corpses in five minutes, then, by extrapolation, they could cremate 192,000 corpses in 24 hours! This is preposterous in its own right, and it renders absurd Mr. Lieberman's claim that "Later on, when the number of corpses exceeded the capacity of the ovens, trenches were dug and the corpses thrown in saturated with petrol." If the

---

8 See *Los Angeles Times*, "Cremation: Boom Brings Controversy," 13 April 1983, Part I, page 24.

four ovens could cremate 400 corpses in five minutes and, therefore, 192,000 corpses in 24 hours, then the Nazis would have had to have gassed something like 200,000 or more people a day at Birkenau in order to have exceeded the capacity of the ovens! But even Mr. Lieberman didn't claim that they ever gassed that many people in one day, although his claim that on certain days, 42,000 people were gassed far surpasses in magnitude any other such allegation that I recall having seen. All in all, his story just doesn't "add up."

If Azriel Eisenberg really believes Mr. Lieberman's hearsay hokum, then he probably also believes, along with Steve Martin, that robots from Mars are stealing his luggage, and, for his own safety and the safety of others, he probably should not have access to pointed objects, such as pens and pencils, but should only be allowed to write with crayons.

A recurring theme of *The Lost Generation* is the burning alive of children and others by the Nazi beasts at Auschwitz-Birkenau. Variations on this macabre theme can be found in the testimonies of such survivors as Olga Lengyel, Philip Friedman, Halina Birenbaum, Leon Shlofsky, and especially Gisella Perl. (See pages 39, 41–42, 139, 161–164, 165 and 204.) In most cases, the tellers of these tales do not explain how they know them to be true, nor do they explicitly claim to have seen these horrendous events with their own eyes. For example, after claiming that there was a policy of killing pregnant women, Gisella Perl wrote (pp. 163–164),

> Then, one day, Dr. Mengele came to the

> hospital and gave a new order. From now on Jewish women could have their children. They were not going to be killed because of their pregnancy. The children, of course, had to be taken to the crematory by me, personally, but the women would be allowed to live. I was jubilant....
>
> I had 292 expectant mothers in my ward when Dr. Mengele changed his mind. He came roaring into the hospital, whip and revolver in hand, and had all 292 women loaded on a single truck and tossed, alive, into the flames of the crematory.

I'm sure that tossing 292 women, alive, "into the flames of the crematory" was a helluva lot easier said than done. And Gisella Perl did not say that she saw this improbable deed done.

However, in two cases, Gisella Perl apparently claimed to be an eyewitness to the burning alive of people. For example, she wrote (p. 161),

> When we first arrived at Auschwitz, children under sixteen, whether boys or girls, were permitted to accompany their mothers to the women's camps. Then, as usual, there came a counter-order, and all children of fourteen, fifteen, and sixteen had to come forward because they were going to be put into a separate children's camp and receive double bread rations....
>
> The boys left first. They were kept in a camp near ours and we were able to watch

them exercise from morning till night, tired, weak, and thin—without the double bread rations they were promised. Then one night the most horrible screams woke our camp from its deathlike sleep. We ran to the entrance of the camp and witnessed a sight I shall never forget as long as I live.

Several black trucks were standing before the entrance of the boys' camp, and a detachment of SS men were throwing the naked, crying, screaming little boys [of fourteen, fifteen and sixteen years of age?] on the trucks. Those who tried to escape were dragged back by the hair [which wasn't shaved off as with other prisoners?], beaten with truncheons, and whipped mercilessly. There was no help, no escape. Neither their mothers nor God could reach out a helping hand to save their lives. They were burned alive in those crematories which killed and smoked incessantly, day and night.

But, even if the rest of this "eyewitness" testimony is true, the last sentence, the crucial one, begs some questions. Did Gisella Perl see the trucks take the boys to the crematories? If so, why did she omit to mention that detail? In any case, even assuming the boys were taken to the crematories, did Gisella Perl see them burned alive in the crematories? If so, how did she manage this? Did she follow them into the crematories to see what happened? Or did the crematories have transparent walls, allowing any interested persons to see what happened inside?

In any case, at least one part of Gisella Perl's testimony is demonstrably untrue, to wit, her claim that the crematories "killed and smoked incessantly, day and night." In 1979, the CIA published *The Holocaust Revisited: A Retrospective Analysis of the Auschwitz-Birkenau Extermination Complex*. In this publication, two CIA photo interpreters, Dino A. Brugioni and Robert G. Poirier, analyzed aerial photographs taken of Auschwitz-Birkenau between April 1944 and January 1945. Brugioni and Poirier wrote, "Although survivors recalled that smoke and flame emanated continually from the crematoria chimneys and was visible for miles, the photography we examined gave no positive proof of this."[9] Brugioni and Poirier were being diplomatic. But the fact that none of the aerial photographs of Auschwitz-Birkenau show smoke or flame coming from the crematoria chimneys constitutes positive disproof of the familiar claim that "smoke and flame emanated continually from the crematoria chimneys." And it constitutes positive disproof of Gisella Perl's particular version of that claim.

But what is the explanation of Gisella Perl's demonstrably false testimony that the crematoria of Birkenau "killed and smoked incessantly, day and night?" Is this merely an instance of the sort of unintentional distortion that often occurs in eyewitness testimony? Or is it an instance of outright, conscious deception?

What? Outright, conscious deception by a "Holocaust"

---

9   Central Intelligence Agency, *The Holocaust Revisited: A Retrospective Analysis of the Auschwitz-Birkenau Extermination Complex*, 1979, p. 11.

242 | Outlaw History

survivor? Is that even possible? Aren't all survivors Semitic saints, inherently incapable of lying?

That deception by a "Holocaust" survivor is within the realm of the possible has been admitted even by Holocaustomaniac Gitta Sereny. In *The New Statesman*, 2 November 1979, Sereny wrote,

> Personal accounts, such as the recently-published *Dora* ... are not rubbish in themselves.... The problem with books like this is that they are "ghosted" by professional wordsmiths—the French are especially adept—who have neither interest in nor capacity for conveying truth with restraint. It is less the exaggerations than the false emphases and cheap humor which disqualify them.
>
> Worse again are the partial or complete fakes, such as Jean Francois Steiner's *Treblinka* or Martin Gray's *For Those I Loved*....
>
> Gray's *For Those I Loved* was the work of Max Gallo the ghostwriter, who also produced *Papillon*. During the research for a *Sunday Times* inquiry into Gray's work, M. Gallo informed me coolly that he "needed" a long chapter on Treblinka because the book required something strong for pulling in readers. When I myself told Gray, the "author," that he had manifestly never been to, nor escaped from Treblinka, he finally asked, despairingly, "But does it matter?" Wasn't the only thing that Treblinka did happen, that it should be written

about, and that some Jews should be shown to have been heroic?

But if Martin Gray's "eyewitness" account of the mass extermination of Jews at Treblinka is a fake, then how many other "eyewitness" accounts of "the Holocaust" are fake as well? And, more specifically, how many of the "authentic personal and eyewitness" accounts in *The Lost Generation* are fakes? I would bet that Shaye Gertner's "authentic personal and eyewitness" account of his ten weeks as a member of the Birkenau *Sonderkommando* is a fake. Here is part of that account (pp. 210–211):

> After being interrogated by the SS, I was taken to Birkenau and assigned to the *Sonderkommando* Field D, barracks 32. There were four hundred men, mostly Jews, some Poles, and a few Germans. Some wore red emblems [political prisoners]: others the usual green [criminals].
>
> During the first few days I didn't go to the ovens, but did house-keeping chores, But then the squad leader Muller appeared and said, "Such a sturdy lad ought to be assigned to a shift." And I started to work on the ovens. The first days were very hard, and I began to wonder how to extricate myself. Our Kommando had just plunged into the task. Everyone knew that within three months all of us would be dispensed with and replaced with others.
>
> Our unit consisted of four hundred men,

working in two shifts. One oven belonged to us. We were accompanied by orchestral music on our way to work. The SS leader, Dr. Mengele, was our supervisor. He delivered the inmates to the gas chambers. He was followed in rank by Muller, then the Jewish kapos, Poles, and Germans. We were generally guarded by five SS men. When new transports of human cargo arrived, people were unaware of just what was in store for them. Before entering the building carrying the sign "Baths," the people had to disrobe completely and received a number of their belongings, presumably to be reclaimed later. They got soap and towels for their shower. Then the kapos would dash in to beat the unfortunates, to create confusion. During the ensuing commotion, when people trampled over one another, the door of the gas chamber would be thrown open, the prisoners pushed in, and then the door would bang shut after a cylinder of poison gas was flung into the mass, I worked ten weeks in the *Sonderkommando*. I never entered the gas chamber itself; only kapos were admitted there. After the gassing a door in the other side of the chamber would open; there the kapos would enter to throw out the corpses. All of us wore rubber gloves and wads of cotton in our mouths. The corpses exuded a pungent odor that could asphyxiate one. Small cars, loaded with forty corpses apiece, would ride along rails that extended from the gas chamber to the oven. The cars disgorged their cargo into the oven, where the bodies were reduced to ashes by electric current in ten minutes. A weak current left the bones intact; a strong current left small heaps. There was an apparatus, known as an exhaust, that blew the ashes into an adjoining pit, where they were piled into barrels by workers, then hoisted by an elevator and ultimately dumped into the Sola River.

The corpses I loaded onto the carts were yellow from the gas. Some of the cadavers had open, glazed eyes, hands holding their mouths, or clutching stomachs. None of us in this work could stand it. We often spoke of escape.[10]

According to Gertner, "All of us wore rubber gloves and wads of cotton in our mouths." What excellent safety precautions. A wad of cotton in the mouth beats a gas mask any day. Of course, Gertner and his fellow *Sonderkommando* members simply never inhaled through their noses.

Arthur Butz has written, "The ovens at Birkenau seem to have been coke or coal-fired...."[11] And a surviving German document, a letter of 29 January 1943, concerning the construction of Crematorium II, said, "The fires were started in the ovens in the presence of

---

10   Eisenberg cites *Anthology of Holocaust Literature*, Jewish Publication Society, 1969, pp. 141–147, as his source for Gertner's account.

11   *The Hoax of the Twentieth Century*, Institute for Historical Review, 1976, p. 121.

Senior Engineer Pruefer, representative of the contractors of the firm of Topf and Soehne, Erfurt, and they are working most satisfactorily."[12] But now we know that Butz was wrong and the document forged, because "eyewitness" Shaye Gertner reported that "the bodies were reduced to ashes by electric current."

Gertner's "eyewitness" testimony that the bodies were reduced to ashes "in ten minutes" also discredits the previously mentioned reportage of Carol McGraw, who said that the cremation of a body takes two or three hours, not ten minutes.

Another of Gertner's unique revelations: "There was an apparatus, known as an exhaust, that blew the ashes into an adjoining pit, where they were piled into barrels by workers, then hoisted by an elevator and ultimately dumped into the Sola River." Those German barbarians were mighty ingenious, weren't they? But I wonder why they didn't fully automate the disposal of the ashes. Surely they could have designed and constructed devices for conveying the ashes directly from the crematoria to the river.

In any case, Gertner said, "We often spoke of escape." And he went on to describe (pp. 211–212) how they planned and then carried out an escape from Birkenau in January 1944, "perhaps the eighteenth day." The leader was a Polish officer whose name Gertner couldn't remember.

> At a signal from the Polish officer, we killed one SS man and threw the German squad leader

---

12 *Op. cit.*, p. 116.

into the lime pit. Then we began to throw grenades into the oven. Those on the other side of the gas chamber with the other three SS men, who guarded the new arrivals, shouted that it was an air attack alarm. Hearing the explosions, the SS men believed it and ran for cover. The inmates, standing in front of the gas chamber, were at a loss what to do. Meanwhile we fled individually....

An hour and a half went by before the Germans really got their bearings. Then they opened fire in all directions and began to reconnoiter the surrounding area. I learned later from witnesses that about two hundred men were killed in the wake of that event. The rest escaped; it is hard to determine the number killed among the latter.

I was trudging together with a group of twenty-seven men in the direction of Germany. We were led by a Jew from Berlin familiar with the land. We had plenty of money, so we bought shovels and marched along, singing German songs in the manner of German workers. We had already penetrated deep into Germany when we were taken by the German authorities in some town. We declared that we had escaped from a transport in Dachau; they believed us and sent us to Dachau.

I was back in Dachau in March 1944. I said my name was Casiemierz Dudzinski (though they knew I was Jewish).

Thanks to the incredible stupidity and gullibility of their SS guards, Gertner and some other *Sonderkommando* members escaped from Birkenau. So where did they go? Naturally, they headed right into the heart of Germany. What better place to escape the Nazi terror? I'm only surprised that Gertner didn't persuade his inevitable captors that he was Adolf Hitler himself, out for a stroll with his staff. After all, the Germans were apparently willing to believe anything that Gertner and his pals told them.

Although nobody else on Planet Earth seems to know about this revolt and escape of the Birkenau *Sonderkommando* in January 1944, Gertner's story is reminiscent of the tales that have been told of a revolt and attempted escape by the Birkenau *Sonderkommando* on 7 October 1944. However, in that case, none of the prisoners is supposed to have succeeded in escaping.[13]

Speaking of the 7 October 1944 revolt of the *Sonderkommando*, Garlinski (p. 327) names some of those who supposedly were killed in attempting to escape: "Jozef Deresinski, Zalman Gradowski, Ajzyk Kalniak, Lajb Langfus, Lajb Panusz and Josef Warszawski, the leader." Coincidentally, two of these names are mentioned by Azriel Eisenberg on page 141. He writes, "In 1962, in the area of the Birkenau crematorium no. 3, were found the writings of three martyrs, Leib Langfuss, Zalman Leventhal, and Zalman Gradowski." Perhaps these were some of the manuscripts Robert Faurisson had in mind when he referred to "miraculously rediscovered

---

13   See, for example, Jozef Garlinski, *Fighting Auschwitz*, Fawcett, 1975, pp. 325–327.

manuscripts" in *Le Monde* on 16 January 1979. In any case, Eisenberg does not tell us how or by whom the writings of the three "martyrs" were found in 1962. But he does tell us, "Langfuss's manuscript was found in a glass jar. In it he explained why the revolt of the *Sonderkommando* had failed." Eisenberg then includes (pp. 141–142) an excerpt from "Langfuss's manuscript" recounting an incident at "the end of October 1944" in which the SS drove a group of children into "the gas chamber" with great brutality and indescribable glee. But if Jozef Garlinski was correct in writing that Langfuss was among those killed while attempting to escape on 7 October 1944, then how, pray tell, could "Langfuss's manuscript" have "explained why the revolt of the *Sonderkommando* had failed?" And how could it have described events alleged to have taken place at "the end of October 1944?" (This date is quoted from "Langfuss's manuscript" itself.) We seem to be confronted with a miracle similar to the one that enabled Moses to record his own death in verse 5 of Chapter 34 of Deuteronomy.

Another of Eisenberg's selections may also partake of the miraculous, to wit, his excerpt from "the diary of Anne Frank" (pp. 76–78). According to Al Fredericks,

> A report by the German Federal Criminal Investigation Bureau (BKA) indicates that portions of *The Diary of Anne Frank* had been altered or added after 1951, casting doubt over the authenticity of the entire work, the West German news weekly *Der Spiegel* has disclosed....

250 | Outlaw History

> The results of tests performed at the BKA laboratories show that portions of the work, specifically of the fourth volume, were written with a ball point pen. Since ballpoint pens were not available before 1951, the BKA concluded, those sections must have been added subsequently.[14]

Azriel Eisenberg doesn't mention the BKA's report on "the diary of Anne Frank," let alone try to explain how Anne Frank might have written portions of it posthumously. Instead, he devotes pages 355–364 to rebutting revisionism with an excerpt from *The Murderers Among Us: The Wiesenthal Memoirs*, edited by Joseph Wechsberg. According to Eisenberg, this excerpt "illustrates the efforts now being made to rewrite the history of the tragedy, by such individuals as A.R. Butz of Evanston, Illinois, who published an outrageous book, *The Hoax of the Twentieth Century*, as well as others in the East, who are issuing a series of tracts entitled *Did Six Million Really Die? The Truth at Last.*" Eisenberg is obviously well informed about "Holocaust" revisionism (I'm being sarcastic), but his attempted refutation of revisionism from "the Wiesenthal Memoirs" is an exercise in irrelevancy. Confronted by an Austrian boy who disputed the existence of Anne Frank and the authenticity of the "diary," Wiesenthal proceeded to track down the officer who arrested the Frank family. This may prove that Anne Frank really existed. But it doesn't prove that she wrote "the diary of Anne Frank." Nor does it explain

---

14   *The New York Post*, October 9, 1980

how it would have been possible for her to write portions of it more than six years after her death from typhus at Belsen in 1945.

Eisenberg immediately follows the irrelevant Wiesenthal excerpt with another response to "Holocaust" revisionism, this one emanating from the West German Federal Supreme Court. In a civil suit in which an injunction was sought against the display of an "offending" poster, the court on 18 September 1979 passed judgment "against a German citizen who exhibited posters stating that the murder of millions of Jews in the Third Reich was a 'Zionist swindle' and the gassing of six million Jews a lie."[15] Eisenberg paraphrases the Court's decision as follows (p. 364):

> On October 29, 1979, the Jewish Telegraphic Association released the news of a landmark decision by the West German Supreme Court which stated that the unique fate of Jews give them a claim to regard and respect from all German citizens, that the Holocaust is part of the consciousness of Jews and it is a matter of their personal dignity to be perceived as the group who suffered persecution and to whom other citizens bear a moral responsibility.
>
> The court said that respect for these feelings had to be regarded as a guarantee for the non-repetition of the past and an essential condition making it possible for Jews to live in Germany. Whoever denies the truth of

---

15 I am quoting *Patterns of Prejudice*, January 1980, pp. 32–33.

past events denies to every Jew the respect to which he is entitled, the court declared.

It added that any attempt to justify, to gloss over, or to dispute the facts of the Holocaust shows contempt against every person identified with persecution. Finally, the court affirmed that the evidence of the facts of the Holocaust is overwhelming.

There are a couple of discrepancies between the court's decision, as quoted by *Patterns of Prejudice*, and Eisenberg's paraphrase of it. Eisenberg says, "the court affirmed that the evidence of the facts of the Holocaust is overwhelming." But *Patterns of Prejudice* quoted the court as saying, "The documentary evidence on the extermination of millions of Jews is damning." Similar, but different. Also, Eisenberg says the court spoke of other citizens owing Jews "a moral responsibility." But *Patterns of Prejudice* quoted the court as speaking of "a normal responsibility." Otherwise, though, Eisenberg's paraphrase of the court's ruling is reasonably accurate.

But Eisenberg's invoking of the authority of the West German Federal Supreme Court does not refute "Holocaust" revisionism. As W. Ward Fearnside and William B. Holther have written, "An authority must be qualified as an expert in the field in which he is cited."[16] This means that "The authority is expressing an opinion within the field of his special competence. Einstein may have held very worthy opinions on world peace, but he was not to be regarded as an expert on international

---

16 *Fallacy: The Counterfeit of Argument*, Prentice-Hall, 1959, p. 85.

relations just because of his reputation in physics."[17] By the same token, the West German Federal Supreme Court is not to be regarded as an expert on historical matters just because of its presumed expertise in matters judicial.

Eisenberg's appeal to the authority of the court is an instance of the fallacy sometimes known as "argument from authority." This was one of the fallacies referred to by Fearnside and Holther when they wrote the following:

> The appeals described in the following fallacies often serve to take advantage of the ignorance of the audience rather than overcome it. They play on prejudices and misconceptions instead of meeting them squarely. And one must very often suspect that, unlike some fallacies which are the result of ignorance or carelessness, these appeals are dishonest in intent.[18]

That Eisenberg's appeal to authority probably is dishonest in intent is indicated by his brazen falsehoods in *Witness to the Holocaust*, some of which I pointed out in my review of that book, as well as in *The Lost Generation*.

One rather brazen falsehood in this latter book is on page 127, where he says, "When the Red Army freed Auschwitz, fewer than 450 Jews were among the survivors; not a child was left alive." This really involves two falsehoods. First there is Eisenberg's statement that "fewer than 450 Jews were among the survivors" when

---

17   *Op. cit.*, p. 86.
18   *Op. cit.*, p. 84.

the Red Army captured Auschwitz. While it may be true that there were only 450 Jewish survivors of Auschwitz still in Auschwitz when the Red Army arrived (and I don't know if that figure is accurate), Eisenberg's statement conveniently ignores the fact that there were thousands of Jewish Auschwitz survivors who were no longer at Auschwitz by the time the Red Army reached there in late January 1945. Tens of thousands of Auschwitz inmates at least, including many Jews, were transferred to other camps during 1943 and 1944. For example, Dr. Ada Bimko, a.k.a. Hadassah Bimko-Rosensaft, was transferred from Auschwitz to Belsen in November 1944.[19] Furthermore, tens of thousands more Auschwitz prisoners were marched westward out of Auschwitz shortly before the arrival of the Red Army. Martin Gilbert says, "At the end of the first week of January [1945], as the Red Army drew nearer to Auschwitz, the Gestapo began to organize the evacuation of more than 65,000 Jewish prisoners."[20] Gilbert probably exaggerated the number of Jewish prisoners evacuated by assuming that all Auschwitz inmates were Jewish. Jozef Garlinski wrote, "At the final evening roll-call, on January 17th [1945], the whole complex, comprising the central camp, Birkenau and Monowice with a number of sub-camps, contained 48,340 men and 18,672 women."[21] That adds up to 67,012 prisoners, about the same number Gilbert

---

19 Henry A. Zeiger, ed., *The Case Against Adolf Eichmann*, Signet, 1960, p. 180.

20 *Auschwitz and the Allies*, Holt, Rinehart and Winston, 1981, p. 334.

21 *Fighting Auschwitz*, pp. 341–342.

gave just for Jewish prisoners. But elsewhere in his book (p. 236), Garlinski said that Poles comprised the largest nationality within the camp population, Jews the second largest. In any case, there were thousands of Jews, perhaps ten thousand or more, among those evacuated from Auschwitz shortly before the Red Army arrived. So Eisenberg's reference to a mere 450 Jewish survivors is grossly misleading.

And his other statement, that "not a child was left alive" when the Red Army reached Auschwitz, is just plain false. On page 249 of Gerhard Schoenberner's *The Yellow Star*,[22] there is a photo of some children, prisoners of Auschwitz, who "lived to be liberated by the Red Army." What makes this falsehood particularly brazen is that one of Eisenberg's own witnesses in *The Lost Generation* gives contradictory testimony. On page 205, describing events between the evacuation of Auschwitz by the Germans and the arrival of the Red Army, Leon Shlofsky says, "We decided to proceed to Birkenau to save the women and children who were still living." As I said in my review of *Witness to the Holocaust*, Azriel Eisenberg is not a leading Jewish scholar, as it says on the dust jacket of that book. Rather, he is a *misleading* Jewish scholar.

Getting back to the West German Federal Supreme Court's decision, the court said, "Whoever tries to deny the truth of past events, denies to every Jew the respect to which he is entitled." But is it only Jews who are entitled to respect or to whom such respect is denied by attempts to deny the truth of past events? For example,

---

22 Gerhard Schoenberner, *The Yellow Star*, Bantam, 1973.

if someone accuses Germans of committing atrocities which never took place, are they not attempting to deny the truth of past events and thereby denying Germans the respect to which they are entitled? Consider this whopper from "Nazi-hunter" Tuvia Friedman: "We drove a while in silence, until we approached Dachau. Silently, Yoske and I looked at the extermination camp where millions of innocent people had been executed."[23] Millions of people were executed at Dachau? No, not even according to former Dachau inmate Nerin E. Gun, whose estimate of the number of deaths at Dachau was not a conservative one. Gun has written, "it is with some skepticism that I report here certain statistics compiled after the liberation. First, there are those of Domgala, who figured that 206,204 persons went through Dachau. I would put the figure closer to 450,000."[24] Gun also wrote,

> It is impossible to ascertain the number of deaths in the camp from 1933 to 1940. It was certainly more than 15,000. From 1940 to liberation, a former camp inmate, Domgala, a responsible witness, accounts for 27,830 deaths, but that figure must be a minimum. In fact, more than 100,000 died at Dachau, or approximately one out of four inmates.[25]

When Tuvia Friedman said that millions of people were executed at Dachau, was he not attempting to deny the truth of past events? And was he not thereby

---

23 *The Hunter*, Macfadden, 1961, p. 113.
24 *The Day of the Americans*, Fleet, 1966, p. 128.
25 *Op. cit.*, pp. 128–129

denying to Germans the respect to which they are entitled? Or are Germans less entitled to respect than Jews, less entitled to have the truth told about them?

The court said, "Whoever tries to deny the truth of past events, denies to every Jew the respect to which he is entitled." But what exactly is the truth of past events? Where may one find the truth of past events inscribed in clear, consistent, unquestionable, and undeniable form?

Is it true, for example, that Jews were gassed en masse with Zyklon B at Auschwitz-Birkenau? Apart from a few documents, whose meaning is at best debatable, the evidence for such mass gassings consists entirely of testimony, the most important of which being the "eyewitness" testimony.[26] The "eyewitnesses," however, contradict each other on various points, and some of them contradict themselves. More importantly, the stories of these "eyewitnesses" involve what appear to be various physical impossibilities. To give just one example, "eyewitnesses" have claimed that Zyklon B was capable of killing instantaneously, or within a few minutes, or in five minutes, or within three or fifteen minutes. But, citing document NI-9912, Friedrich Berg has written, "the time required for the Zyklon to take effect would range from 6 to 32 hours depending upon the type of vermin and temperature. Since it is well known that cyanide kills very quickly given a sufficient concentration of the

---

26 There is a room (in the crematorium of Auschwitz I) that allegedly was used as a gas chamber before being converted into an air-raid shelter sometime in 1944, but this room constitutes evidence of the alleged Zyklon B gassings only in conjunction with the testimony that it was used for such gassings.

gas, the 6 to 32 hour period must have been essentially the period needed to produce a sufficient concentration by evaporation out of the Zyklon B granules."[27] Would the court insist that the "eyewitness" testimonies about mass gassings with Zyklon B must be true whether or not they involve physical impossibilities? If so, why? After all, a general principle that "eyewitness" testimony must be true would suffice to establish the reality not only of mass gassings with Zyklon B but also of the ritual murder of Christian children by Jews seeking blood for Passover matzohs, witchcraft and everything that involved, werewolves and vampires, the golden tablets from which Joseph Smith translated *The Book of Mormon*, forced conversions in Catholic nunneries, the Angel of Mons, the Miracle of the Sun at Fátima, the "Mad Gasser" of Mattoon, the post-WWII survival of Adolf Hitler, flying saucers and extraterrestrial visitations of Earth, Bigfoot, etc. If, for example, one denies that witches ever flew through the air to sabbats where the Devil appeared as a being half man and half goat and where the flesh of babies was eaten, etc., is one denying the truth of the past and thereby denying to victims of witchcraft the respect to which they are entitled?

In any case, if Robert Faurisson and the revisionists are right, then the Zyklon B gassings, as described by "eyewitnesses," were physically impossible. And if that is

---

27 See the Publisher's Footnote on page 4 of Robert Faurisson's, The "Problem of the 'Gas Chambers'" or "The Rumor of Auschwitz," Revisionist Press, Rochelle Park, New Jersey, 1979. For more on the question of the physical possibility of the alleged Zyklon B gassings, see Robert Faurisson's two contributions to *The Journal of Historical Review*, Vol. 2, No. 4.

the case, then it seems we are again confronted with a miracle—indeed, with a whole series of miracles.

On second thought, perhaps we are confronted not with a series of miracles but rather with a series of lies by "eyewitnesses." As Thomas Paine said, echoing the argument of David Hume,

> If ... we see an account given of such a miracle by the person who said he saw it, it raises a question in the mind very easily decided, which is, is it more probable that nature should go out of her course, or that a man should tell a lie? We have never seen, in our time, nature go out of her course; but we have good reason to believe that millions of lies have been told in the same time; it is, therefore, at least millions to one, that the reporter of a miracle tells a lie.[28]

By the same token, it is at least millions to one that the "eyewitness" reporter of physically impossible Zyklon B gassings has told a lie. (And the same goes for "eyewitness" reporters of any kind of physically impossible "Holocaust" happenings.) According to Robert Conquest, there is a Russian folk saying: "He lies like an eyewitness." Of course, not all eyewitnesses are liars, although even most honest eyewitnesses, for the reasons discussed earlier, give testimony that is to some extent false. But some eyewitnesses are liars. And some liars pretend to be eyewitnesses of places they've never been and things they've never seen (for example, Martin Gray).

---

28 Quoted by George H. Smith in *Atheism: The Case Against God*, Nash, 1974, p. 218.

Azriel Eisenberg's brandishing of the West German Federal Supreme Court's dictum ("Whoever tries to deny the truth of past events, denies to every Jew the respect to which he is entitled.") is both hypocritical and disingenuous. Hypocritical because Eisenberg's regard for the truth of past events is minimal, if not nonexistent. This is demonstrated both by his own falsehoods, in this book and his previous one, and by his selection of "eyewitness" accounts of "the Holocaust" containing palpable falsehoods, the "eyewitness" account of Shaye Gertner and the hearsay testimony of Mr. Lieberman being the most blatant examples.

Eisenberg's invoking of the court's dictum is disingenuous because it is not merely respect that Eisenberg wants for himself and his "eyewitnesses"—it is reverence. As he said of his earlier collection of "eyewitness" accounts of "the Holocaust," "it must be studied with awe and reverence."[29]

Ambrose Bierce wittily defined "reverence" as "The spiritual attitude of a man to a god and a dog to a man." But Eisenberg and his "eyewitnesses" are not gods, nor am I a dog, although I am a Gentile. They are merely human beings, as I am. So I see no reason to revere Eisenberg and his "eyewitnesses," no reason to put them on a pedestal, above skepticism, above criticism. As far as I am concerned, the fact that some or all of Eisenberg's witnesses suffered at the hands of the Nazis does not give them a license to lie.

As Rabbi Richard E. Singer, of the Lakeside Congregation of Highland Park, Illinois, has said,

---

29 *Witness to the Holocaust*, pp. 4–5.

> Jews have suffered, and Christians have suffered. Mankind has suffered. There is no group with a monopoly on suffering, and no human beings which have experienced hate and hostility more than any other. I must say, however, that it is my impression that Jewish history has been taught with a whine and a whimper rather than with a straight-forward acknowledgement that man practices his inhumanity on his fellow human beings ... Out of this peculiar emphasis on suffering there has developed a new attitude of vicarious suffering—a feeling among numbers of Jews today that because other Jews have suffered and died they, the living, are somehow entitled to special consideration.[30]

If only Azriel Eisenberg would take Rabbi Singer's well-chosen words to heart, then *The Last Generation* would be Eisenberg's last compilation of "stories of suffering and death." If only. If only.

A slightly different version of this essay was originally published in The Journal of Historical Review, Volume 6, Issue 4 (1986).

---

[30] Quoted by Alfred M. Lilienthal in *The Zionist Connection*, Dodd, Mead, 1978, p. 401.

THE TERRIBLE SECRET

*The Terrible Secret: Suppression of the
Truth About Hitler's 'Final Solution'*
Walter Laqueur
Little, Brown and Company
Auschwitz and the Allies
Martin Gilbert
Holt, Rinehart and Winston

ACCORDING TO A GERMAN PROVERB recorded for posterity by H.L. Mencken, "It takes a great many shovelfuls to bury the truth." Walter Laqueur, "a distinguished professor of history," whose book *The Terrible Secret* is subtitled "Suppression of the Truth about Hitler's 'Final Solution,'" might find this proverb apt. But, ironically, the question that arises from a critical examination of Laqueur's book is whether, in regard to the burying of the truth about "Hitler's 'Final Solution,'" it is an exposé or an example. Did Laqueur produce this book with a typewriter, or with a shovel?

As I've said, Laqueur's book is subtitled "Suppression of the Truth about Hitler's 'Final Solution,' " which immediately begs the question: What *is* the truth about "Hitler's 'Final Solution' "? In this book, which purports to be a study of when "the information" about "the Final

Solution" became "known," Laqueur reveals himself to be a rather dogmatic exponent of the conventional wisdom about "the Final Solution," to wit, that on Hitler's orders, the Nazi regime during World War II embarked upon a program aimed at killing all the Jews of Nazi-dominated Europe and succeeded in killing millions (five or six million, the figures most often claimed) by shooting and by gassing, mainly the latter.

For example, Laqueur, in line with the conventional wisdom, asserts that Hitler gave orders to Himmler and Heydrich for the extermination of all European Jews soon after he signed the Barbarossa Directive in December 1940 (p. 11). But how Laqueur "knows" this is his (terrible?) secret. He cites no corroborating documentation or testimony; he cites no source of any sort in support of his claim.

This scholarly sin could be forgiven if Laqueur were stating a well-known and indisputable fact. But, in fact, even the exponents of the conventional wisdom cannot agree on when Hitler is supposed to have given his supposed extermination order. According to Helmut Krausnick,[1] "It cannot have been later than March 1941, when [Hitler] openly declared his intention of having the political commissars of the Red Army shot, that he issued his secret decree—which never appeared in writing though it was mentioned verbally on several occasions—that the Jews should be eliminated." But according to Raul Hilberg,[2]

---

1   *Anatomy of the SS State*, Walker & Company, 1968, p. 60.
2   *The Destruction of the European Jews*, Harper Colophon, 1979, p. 177.

we are dealing with two of Hitler's decisions. One order was given in the spring of 1941, during the planning of the invasion of the USSR; it provided that small units of the SS and Police be dispatched to Soviet territory, where they were to move from town to town to kill all Jewish inhabitants on the spot. This method may be called the "mobile killing operations." Shortly after the mobile operations had begun [in June 1941] in the occupied Soviet territories, Hitler handed down his second order. That decision doomed the rest of European Jewry.

Thus, Hilberg does not agree with Krausnick and Laqueur does not agree with either of them about *when* Hitler is supposed to have ordered the extermination of all European Jews. In such a situation, Laqueur's unsupported, dogmatic assertions are worthless, and leave unanswered the question of whether or not Hitler ever actually gave such an order.

Laqueur virtually concedes that Hitler never gave a *written* order for the extermination of European Jewry but then tries to save the day for the conventional wisdom. He says (p. 196) that

witnesses claimed to have seen the order, but it is doubtful whether there ever was a written order. This has given rise to endless speculation and inspired a whole "revisionist" literature—quite needlessly, because

> Hitler, whatever his other vices, was not a bureaucrat. He was not in the habit of giving written orders on all occasions: there were no written orders for the murderous "purge" of June 1934, for the killing of gypsies, the so-called euthanasia action (T-4) and on other such occasions.

But first, *how* does Laqueur know that Hitler ordered the killing of gypsies? Second, regarding the Blood Purge of 1934, David Irving points out[3] that Hitler did give a written order to Sepp Dietrich in the form of a list of seven names of men to be executed. That 82 people were killed resulted, according to Irving, from the exceeding of Hitler's orders, mainly by Himmler and Göring. And third, Hitler's written order for the T-4 "euthanasia" program is well known. Gitta Sereny, journalist and devotee of the conventional wisdom about "the Final Solution," quotes it as follows:[4]

> Reichsleiter Bouhler and Dr. Brandt are charged with the responsibility for expanding the authority of physicians who are to be designated by name, to the end that patients who are considered incurable in the best available human judgment after critical evaluation of their condition can be granted mercy-killing.

---

3   *The War Path*, Viking, 1978, p. 39.
4   *Into That Darkness*, McGraw-Hill, 1974, p. 63.

266 | Outlaw History

Say, Professor Laqueur, just what are you doing with that shovel in your hand? Digging for the truth about "Hitler's 'Final Solution'"? Or *burying* it?

In any case, Laqueur tells his readers (p. 30) that "on 25 October 1941, in a conversation between Hitler, Himmler and Heydrich, rumours among the population about the destruction of the Jews had already been mentioned. ('Public rumours attribute to us a plan to exterminate the Jews.')" But what he doesn't tell his readers is that it was Hitler who was speaking and that this reference to rumors about an extermination plan was made in the following context:[5]

> From the rostrum of the Reichstag I prophesied to Jewry that, in the event of war's proving inevitable, the Jew would disappear from Europe. That race of criminals has on its conscience the two million dead of the first World War, and now already hundreds of thousands more. Let nobody tell me that all the same we can't park them in the marshy parts of Russia! Who's worrying about our troops? It's not a bad idea, by the way, that public rumour attributes to us a plan to exterminate the Jews. Terror is a salutary thing.

If, as Laqueur asserts, Hitler in December 1940 gave Himmler and Heydrich orders to exterminate all

---

5   *Hitler's Secret Conversations 1941-1944*, Signet, 1961, pp. 108-109. See also David Irving, *Hitler's War*, Viking, 1977, p. 331.

European Jews, then why was he making statements implying that his policy was to "park them in the marshy parts of Russia" in a conversation with none other than Himmler and Heydrich almost a year later? Hmmmmm? That is the question that Laqueur seeks to avoid answering by quoting Hitler out of context. Considering how good he is at burying things, perhaps Laqueur should give some thought to a career as a gravedigger.

In the meantime, "distinguished professor of history" Walter Laqueur makes many "factual" assertions about what "could have been known" about "the extermination of the Jews" at various times. Almost invariably, these assertions, like his claim regarding a Hitler order for genocide, are unsupported by the citation of any source. But even when he does cite a source, his interpretations can be misleading.

For example, regarding what "could have been known" by 1 January 1943, Laqueur writes (p. 14) that "According to an official SS report, 2.5 million Jews had been 'deported' by the end of 1942 and were no longer alive." A footnote reveals that the SS report in question is the report of the statistician Korherr, submitted to Himmler on 23 March 1943. But it was not according to the Korherr report that those 2.5 million deported Jews were no longer alive at the end of 1942. Rather, it is according to Laqueur that they were no longer alive then. And by equating deportation with killing, Laqueur is exaggerating the number of Jews killed by the Nazis by the end of 1942. As Laqueur knows, some of those deportees were not only still alive at the end of 1942 but managed to survive to bear witness to "the truth" later on. For example, Vrba (*nee* Rosenberg) and Wetzler, whose escape from Auschwitz in 1944 Laqueur mentions, were among the Slovakian Jews deported during 1942 who according to Laqueur's interpretation of the Korherr report were all dead by the end of that year!

The Terrible Secret is supposed to be a study of when "the truth" about "the extermination of the Jews" became "known" in various quarters. But Laqueur is determined to demonstrate, by fair means or foul, that "knowledge" of "the truth" was widespread by the end of 1942. To that end, he has gathered together a motley collection of wartime rumors (some travelling through diplomatic channels), "reports" of resistance groups, accounts of self-proclaimed eyewitnesses, newspaper articles, radio broadcasts, letters, diaries, etc., as well as way too many postwar recollections, unsupported assertions, specious inferences, and unproven assumptions.

AUSCHWITZ AND THE ALLIES, BY MARTIN GILBERT, a fellow of Merton College, Oxford, and the official Churchill biographer since 1968, covers some of the same ground as *The Terrible Secret* from a similar point of view. The book purports to be "an account of the facts of the extermination as they filtered out of Nazi-dominated Europe, and the Allied reaction to these facts...." But regarding the matter of the Allied reaction to "the facts," Gilbert is concerned not just with the question of belief or disbelief, as Laqueur, but also with what was done, or not done, to save the lives of European Jews. There are other differences in the scopes of these two volumes. Laqueur has focused mainly on the period from July

1941 to December 1942, while Gilbert carries his account through to early 1945. Gilbert is only concerned with when the Allies, especially Britain and the US, "learned" about "Hitler's mass murder," while Laqueur also poses this question in relation to Germany and her allies, the neutral European nations, and the Jews both inside and outside of Nazi-ruled Europe. Finally, Gilbert gives special attention to the story of one particular "extermination camp," Auschwitz.

Like Laqueur, Gilbert repeatedly makes "factual" statements about what was "really" happening to European Jews during the war. And Gilbert is not much better than Laqueur at citing supporting sources for these statements. For example, after alleging a Nazi plan for the extermination of millions of Jews "using the most efficient and modern methods," Gilbert writes (p. 8) that "The first step in carrying out this new plan was taken on 8 December 1941, when several hundred Jews from small Polish towns were taken to a wood outside the village of Chelmno, and gassed in a specially designed building." It's bad enough that this unsupported assertion is contradicted by the conventional wisdom about Chelmno, according to which Jews were gassed there in specially designed motor vehicles of some sort, not in a specially designed building, but, what's worse, the claim is contradicted by the official Churchill biographer himself! On page 40, Gilbert quotes a "report" sent to London in May 1942 by the underground Jewish Socialist Bund of Poland. Regarding the gassing of the Jews at Chelmno, the "report" said, "'A special automobile (a gas chamber) was used.'" And, comments Gilbert, "the details given in the Bund Report were precise, and, as we now know, accurate." So why did Gilbert contradict it on page 18? Who knows? It seems that the mind of the official Churchill biographer, like God, works in mysterious ways, its wonders of scholarship to perform.

It also seems that the official Churchill biographer does not know the meaning of the word "eyewitness," which my dictionary defines thusly: "One who has seen something happen and can give testimony about it." Chapter 10 of *Auschwitz and the Allies*, titled "Eyewitness," is concerned primarily with a group of Palestinian Jews (women children and a few elderly men, according to Laqueur) who, in an exchange for German internees, had reached "the Holy Land" from Europe on 16 November 1942. Writes Gilbert (p. 88),

> All had been eyewitnesses to Nazi brutality. Each one had horrific tales to tell of deportation, brutality, or mass murder.
>
> Among the facts reported were "Harrowing details recounted by eyewitnesses of people thrown into flames, specially constructed crematorium, locked up in poison gas chambers, and other forms of torture." [Gilbert is quoting Moshe Shertok's summary of these "eyewitness" accounts.]

But later in the chapter (p. 92), we find out that "what the eyewitnesses did report ... was 'all sorts of rumours' which told 'of large concrete buildings on the Russian–Polish border where people are killed by gas and burned.'" Thus, on this crucial point in these "eyewitness" reports, the "eyewitnesses" were not eyewitnesses at all. They had not seen anything; they had merely heard some things, some rumors.

Laqueur also discusses the stories of this group of Palestinian Jewish repatriates, since it was their "evidence" which supposedly convinced the leaders of Palestinian Jewry of the "reality" of a program to exterminate all European Jews. Laqueur at least, does not call these people "eyewitnesses"; he merely calls them "witnesses." But he seems to take their "evidence" just as seriously as Gilbert. He writes (p. 191),

> So often before, simple-minded (and even not so simple-minded) people had simply repeated rumours, often baseless in character. But the new arrivals could not be so easily dismissed: among them was a scientific researcher at the Hebrew University, two members of Kibbutz Degania B—members of the Palestinian elite—a Zionist leader of long standing from Piotrkow and other such witnesses. ("People on whose judgment and discernment one could rely," E. Dobkin was later to say.)

But was there really such a big difference between these people and earlier repatriates who "simply repeated rumours, often baseless in character"? Laqueur himself tells us that "what emerged from these accounts was firstly that a German government commission had been set up earlier that summer (*Sander-* or *Vernichtungskommission*) under a certain commissar Feu or Foy to destroy Polish Jewry. (This information was, in fact, wrong or at least inaccurate ....)" (p. 191). Apparently, these people "on whose judgment and discernment one could rely" were simply repeating a baseless rumor. Futhermore, as I've already pointed out, on the crucial question of the fate of Jewish deportees, these "witnesses" reported "all sorts of rumors" about "large concrete buildings on the Russian–Polish border where people are killed by gas and burned." Laqueur says (p. 192) that these rumors "were apparently correct," presumably meaning that they appeared to be correct to those to whom they were repeated in Palestine in November of 1942.

But what was there about *these* rumors that made them appear more correct than any of the other rumors circulating about the fate of Jewish deportees? According to Vladka Meed,[6] "One rumor" regarding the deportees from Warsaw "was that they had been dispatched to the city of Smolensk, close to the Russo–German front, to dig trenches." And in addition to the rumors about gassing, there were rumors about mass extermination by various other methods, including rumors about killing by live burial, rumors about thousands of Jews being run over by heavy motor lorries, rumors about throwing Jews into lime kilns, rumors about mass electrocutions at Belzec and Auschwitz, rumors about killing people with air pressure at Auschwitz, and rumors about mass executions by hot steam chambers

---

6   *On Both Sides of the Wall*, Holocaust Library, 1993, p. 43.

at Treblinka. (*The Black Book of Polish Jewry*, published in 1943, contains an "Official Report submitted to the Polish Government," which includes "the report of an eyewitness" describing in detail the steam chambers of Treblinka [See pages 141-147]. This was asserted to be "irrefutable proof of the atrocious horror wielded over their victims by the Germans.") So why, in November 1942, were the rumors about gassing "apparently correct"? Laqueur does not explain this, though he does give a possible explanation of why rumors about mass extermination (not necessarily by gassing) may have appeared correct. He says of the deportees (p. 192) that "there was not news from them, no letters, no personal regards conveyed." But there *were* letters, and Laqueur knows that. According to Vladka Meed,[7] "Some letters from deportees were received in the [Warsaw] ghetto which gave credence to the German assurances that those forced to leave had been given employment elsewhere." And Laqueur himself writes (p. 153) that

> When ... the Slovak leaders, slightly perturbed, mentioned to the Germans the "fantastic rumours" about the fate of the evacuated Jews, pretending they had no idea about what was happening to them in Poland, Eichmann referred to more than one thousand letters and postcards which had been received in Slovakia from evacuated Jews within the previous two months.

---

7   *Op. cit.*, p. 31.

Laqueur also mentions letters received from deportees in other countries, although he usually emphasizes that the number of letters received was small in relation to the number of deportees. In any case, letters *were* received from some deportees. So if the rumors about the mass extermination of the deportees "were apparently correct" because of the claim that there were no letters from them, then the rumors about mass extermination "were apparently correct" because of what Laqueur knows to be a falsehood! Ironic, isn't it, that people could have learned "the truth" about "the Final Solution" by means of such falsehoods?

Immediately following his mistitled chapter, "Eyewitness," Martin Gilbert discusses the case of another "eyewitness," further demonstrating his incompetence as a historian. Gilbert writes (p. 93),

> On November 25, at the very moment when the half-million Jews in Palestine were learning of the mass murder of their fellow Jews in Europe, yet another report had reached the Jewish leadership in London. This new report described "the liquidation" of the Warsaw ghetto, and the gassings at Belzec. It had been brought from Poland to the Polish Government-in-Exile in London by an eyewitness, Jan Karski, a non-Jew.

A naïve reader would most likely conclude from this passage that Jan Karski, the non-Jew, was an eyewitness to "the gassings at Belzec." But strangely enough, in the course of detailing the contents of "Karski's report," Gilbert says (p. 94), "There followed an account of the different methods of 'mass extermination': execution by firing squads, electrocution, and 'lethal gas-chambers,' and the report continued with an account of the 'electrocuting station' at Belzec camp...." Here is that account:

> Transports of "settlers" arrive at a siding, on the spot where the execution is to take place. The camp is policed by Ukrainians. The victims are ordered to strip naked—to have a bath, ostensibly—and are then led to a barrack with a metal plate for floor. The door is then locked, electric current passes through the victims and their death is almost instantaneous. The bodies are loaded on to wagons and taken to a mass grave some distance from the camp.

The question that all this raises is this: Did the "eyewitness, Jan Karski," see "the gassings at Belzec," or did he see the operation of the "electrocuting station" at Belzec? Or did he, perhaps, see both? Gilbert sees no need to clear up the confusion he has created and moves on to other things. But according to Karski's account of his experience at Belzec,[8] he saw *neither*!

Karski, a Polish diplomat before the war and a lieutenant of the Mounted Artillery in 1939, was a member of the Polish underground. He engaged in some

---

8 Jan Karski, *The Story of a Secret State*, Houghton Mifflin, 1944, Chapter 30.

"black propaganda" operations, such as the printing and posting of fake German decrees, as well as serving as a courier for the underground. According to his book, Karski had a meeting with two leaders of the Jewish underground, one a Zionist and the other a member of the Bund, who, so he says, arranged for him to visit the Warsaw ghetto and then to infiltrate "the Jewish death camp" near Belzec disguised as an Estonian camp guard. Here is Walter Laqueur's synopsis of what Karski said he saw at Belzec (p. 231):

> There he saw "bedlam"—the ground littered with weakened bodies, hundreds of Jews packed into railway cars covered with a layer of quicklime. The cars were closed and moved outside the camp; after some time they were opened, the corpses were burned and the cars returned to the camp to fetch new cargo.

Actually, Karski did not claim to have seen where the train went or what happened to the Jews inside the railway cars after they left the camp. In his book, he wrote,[9] "As I listened to the dwindling outcries from the train, I thought of the destination toward which it was speeding. My informants had minutely described the journey." His informants were the Jewish underground leaders who had arranged his visit to Belzec, in particular, "the Bund leader." According to Karski,[10] "The Bund

---

9   *Op. cit.*, p. 350.
10   *Op. cit.*, p. 339.

leader had never been in it [i.e., "the Jewish death camp" near Belzec] but he had the most detailed information in [sic] its operations." Thus, Karski was *told* by "the Bund leader" (it was Leon Feiner) that, after leaving Belzec,

> The train would travel about eighty miles and finally come to a halt in an empty, barren field. Then nothing at all would happen. The train would stand stock still, patiently waiting while death penetrated into every corner of its interior. This would take from two to four days.[11]

Thus, what Karski saw at the Belzec "death camp" was Jews being herded into railroad cars which then left the "death camp."

Nowhere in his book did Karski mention gassings or electrocution. So why does Gilbert say (p. 93) that Karski's report "described ... the gassings at Belzec" and (p. 94) that it included "an account of the 'electrocution station' at Belzec camp..."? It may be of interest to know that the "account of the 'electrocuting station' at Belzec camp," which Gilbert attributes to Karski, can be found on page 131 of the 1943 publication *The Black Book of Polish Jewry* (Jacob Apenszlak, ed.), where it is quoted as part of a 15 November 1942 "report" of Dr. Ignacy Schwarzbart, a member of the Polish National Council in London. In fact, other parts of what Gilbert calls "Karski's report" can be found in *The Black Book of Polish Jewry*, all attributed to sources other than Karski.

---

11   *Op. cit.*, p. 350.

278 | Outlaw History

Ironically, *The Black Book of Polish Jewry* also contains two descriptions of the Belzec camp, both of them obviously based on Karski's account, though each of them contradicts Karski's book regarding some details as well as contradicting each other.[12] One of these accounts of Belzec, after "reporting" the killing of Jews by their being left in railway cars "from two to eight days," then asserts that "Because there are not enough cars to kill the Jews in this relatively inexpensive manner many of them are taken to nearby Belzec where they are murdered by poison gasses or by the application of electric currents." It would be very interesting to know who actually wrote this statement. Was it Karski, who did not see fit to mention either gassing or electrocution in his own 1944 book? Or was it somebody else, who took Karski's report and, for propaganda purposes, interpolated these references to gassing and electrocution? In any case, Karski, now a professor in the Department of Government at Georgetown University, has not answered my inquiries about these matters.

Laqueur, unlike Gilbert, gives a fairly accurate account of Karski's observations at Belzec, observations which, at the very least, raise questions about the conventional wisdom that Jews were killed by gassing at Belzec. But Laqueur tries to save the day for conventional wisdom thusly:

> Karski says that he learned only in later years that Belzec was not a transit but a death camp and that most of the victims

---

12 See pp.135-138 and 329-332.

were killed in gas chambers. He had not actually seen the gas chambers during his visit, apparently because these were walled in and could be approached only with a special permit (p. 231).

But if Karski "learned only in later years that Belzec was not a transit but a death camp and that most of the victims were killed in gas chambers," then why did he, in his 1944 book, refer to the camp as "the Jewish death camp" while saying nary a word about gassing? As I've already pointed out, Karski's story about the Jews who were shipped out of the Belzec camp being left in railway cars until they died was based on what he was told by Jewish Bund leader Leon Feiner, who supposedly "had the most detailed information" about the operations of the Belzec camp. But if Feiner "had the most detailed information" about Belzec and if "most of the victims were killed in gas chambers," then wouldn't Feiner have known about that? And if so, then wouldn't he have told Karski about that too? In any case, Laqueur suggests that Karski "had not actually seen the gas chambers during his visit, apparently because these were walled in and could be approached only with a special permit...." "Apparently," the gas chambers were walled in, eh? *Apparently*, Laqueur has conjured up an ad hoc hypothesis, based on no actual evidence, in an attempt to reconcile Karski's story with the conventional wisdom about gas chambers at Belzec. But one could read Karski's story and conclude that "apparently," Jews were not gassed at Belzec.

280 | Outlaw History

> Martin Gilbert laments (p. 170) that,
>
>> As 1943 came to an end, and 1944 began, the stories of German atrocities were still not fully believed. One of those concerned by this fact was a Hungarian Jewish refugee, Arthur Koestler, then working as a journalist and lecturer in Britain. "At present," he wrote in an article which was published in the *New York Times Magazine* in January 1944, "we have the mania of trying to tell you about the killing, by hot steam, mass-electrocution and live burial, of the total Jewish population of Europe."
>>
>> Koestler's own "emotion and bitterness" arose, he wrote, because he had in his desk in front of him photographs of the killings, photographs which had been smuggled out of Poland. "People died to smuggle them out," he commented, and added caustically, "They thought it worth while."

But if Koestler had "photographs of the killings," then, pray tell, Mr. Gilbert, were they photographs of the killings by hot steam, or of the killings by mass electrocution, or of the killings by live burial? Hmmmmm? I think it is significant that what Koestler actually wrote was this: "I have photographs before me on the desk while I am writing this, and this accounts for my emotion and bitterness."[13] Koestler did not say that he had photographs "of the killings." He did not say what he

---

13 See "On Disbelieving Atrocities," reprinted in *The Yogi and the Commissar*, Macmillan, 1945, p. 89.

had photographs of. He just said he had photographs. Quite possibly, Koestler wanted his readers to assume, as Gilbert has assumed, that he had photographs "of the killings." but if that was the case, wouldn't he have made that point quite explicit in order to make his appeal for belief in German atrocities that much more persuasive?

In any case, on the two pages preceding his account of Koestler's article (pp. 168-169), Gilbert discusses "the second Soviet trial of German war criminals, at Kharkov," by means of which, he says, "[f]urther evidence of the scale of the slaughter of Warsaw Jewry reached the Allies and western Jewry":

> During the Kharkov trial a twenty-four-year-old SS Lieutentant, Hans Ritz, was questioned about the use of gas vans in Kharkov. On first hearing the words "gas van" mentioned in Kharkov, Ritz told the prosecutor, "I remember the vehicle from my stay in Warsaw, when I witnessed the evacuation in it of the unreliable sections of the Warsaw population." While in Warsaw, Ritz added, "I got to know that part of the Warsaw population was evacuated by railway and another part were loaded into the 'gas vans' and exterminated."
>
> Hans Ritz also gave evidence of the mass shooting, in sand pits and stone quarries, of tens of thousands of people in the Soviet cities of Krasnodar, Vitebsk and Taganrog. During the shooting of some three hundred

> people at a village near Kharkov, Ritz recalled, a woman, trying to save her child, "covered it with her body. But this did not help her, because the bullet went through her and the child."

Although Gilbert seems to take all of Ritz's "confessions" quite seriously, it is interesting to note that Ritz "confessed" to a crime that none of the other postwar exponents of the conventional wisdom have ever accused the Germans of, that is, the killing of Warsaw residents in gas vans. Ironically, a likely explanation of Ritz's "confessions" is suggested by our old friend Arthur Koestler in this passage from "Soviet Myth and Reality" in *The Yogi and the Commissar*:

> The method of gross over-simplifications in Soviet home-propaganda led to the tradition that the accused in a political trial must confess lustily and voluntarily his alleged crimes; and once this tradition became established there was no going back. Hence the curious phenomenon that during the Kharkov trial of German war-criminals in December, 1943, the accused German officers and N.C.O.'s were made to behave like characters from Dostoevsky. One of them at the trail told of his own accord how during a mass-execution of Russians he took a tommy gun from a soldier and shot a mother with a child in her arms. For the foreign observer the Kharkov

trial (which was filmed and publicly shown in London) gave the same impression of unreality as the Moscow trials, the accused reciting their parts in stilted phrases which they had obviously learned by heart, sometimes taking the wrong cue from the State-Prosecutor and then coming back to the same part again. There is no doubt that the Germans committed bestialities in Russia which surpass the imagination of the Western mind; but that those particular Germans committed those crimes was proved by no other evidence than their own confession.[14]

That the official Churchill biographer should take the "confessions" of the Kharkov trial seriously merely demonstrates his gross credulity. No doubt he would also take seriously the "confession" referred to in the following:

the last culprit burned at Paris for heresy suffered in 1663, when a certain Simon Morin, a native of Aumale in Normandy, was sent to the stake. Morin preached that he was Christ Incarnate, that to him all power had been given by God, and that his followers, those who possessed the true light, were incapable of sinning. These Illuminati practiced the most infamous debaucheries under the pretext of religious assemblies, and it was

---

14 *Op. cit.*, p. 143.

shown that Morin was insatiable in his lusts and corruptions. A wealthy widow, named Malherbe, who had joined the sect, confessed the usual catalogue of filth and folly. She had had sexual connexion with the Devil, had attended the Sabbat, banqueted with demons, entertained imps and familiars. The Parliament ordered her to be branded with the *fleur-de-lys* and banished from the city.[15]

The "confessions" of a Soviet show trail are about as credible as the "confessions" of a "witch" trail. That the official Churchill biographer takes such "confessions" seriously is further evidence of his incompetence as a historian. But perhaps he can find work with Walter Laqueur, as an assistant gravedigger.

Gilbert devotes much attention to the story of Auschwitz escapees Vrba and Wetzler and their "report" on Auschwitz-Birkenau. According to Gilbert (p. 236), "The Vrba–Wetzler Report, although based entirely on the power of two men's memories, was remarkably accurate in its details." But what were those details? Gilbert does not quote any substantial portion of the "report" itself, but he does quote (pp. 262-264) a good chunk of an eight-page summary of "the report" that reached the British Foreign Office on 4 July 1944. Here are the details concerning the crematoria of Birkenau:

At the end of February, 1943, four new

---

15 Montague Summers, *The Geography of Witchcraft*, Citadel, 1973, p. 430.

crematoria were built, two large and two small, in the camp of Birkenau itself. The crematorium contains a large hall, a gas chamber and a furnace. People are assembled in the hall which holds 2,000 and gives the impression of a swimming-bath. They have to undress and are given a piece of soap and a towel as if they were going to the baths. Then they are crowded into the gas chamber which is hermetically sealed.

Several SS men in gas-masks then pour into the gas chamber through three openings in the ceiling a preparation of the poison gas megacyklon, which is made in Hamburg. At the end of three minutes all the persons are dead. The dead bodies are then taken away in carts to the furnace to be burnt. The furnace has nine chambers, each of them with four openings. Each opening will take three bodies at once. They are completely burnt after 1½ hours. Thus each crematorium can burn 1,500 bodies daily.

The question that naturally arises (though, naturally, not in the mind of the official Churchill biographer) is, How did Vrba and Wetzler "know" all this? According to a deposition made by Vrba for submission at the Eichmann trail, Vrba's source of information was Filip Müller, "who worked in the Gas Chamber Department."[16]

---

16 See *I Cannot Forgive*, Rudolph Vrba and Alan Bestic, Bantam, 1964, p. 270.

In his own book, *Eyewitness Auschwitz*, Filip Müller expounds (expands?) upon his role as informant to Vrba and Wetzler.[17] However, Müller's "descriptions" of the Birkenau crematoria do not jibe very well with those Gilbert quotes from the summary of the Vrba–Wetzler "report." For one thing, the Vrba–Wetzler summary says the four new crematoria at Birkenau were built at the end of February 1943, while Müller says[18] that hey were ready "[b]y mid-July 1943." According to the Vrba–Wetzler summary, several SS men would pour "a preparation of the poison gas" into the gas chamber. But according to Müller,[19] only "two SS men took the so-called disinfectants, several canisters of Zyklon B and poured their contents into the openings of the gas chamber." An apparently minor discrepancy is the Vrba–Wetzler summary's identification of the poison gas as "megacyklon," while Müller identifies it as Zyklon B. However, this discrepancy becomes more significant in the light of Müller's claim[20] that he gave Vrba and Wetzler "one of those labels which were stuck on the tins containing Zyklon B poison gas." If Müller is telling the truth, how did Vrba and Wetzler manage to get the name wrong? In any case, another discrepancy is that the Vrba–Wetzler summary says, regarding the gassings, that at the end of three minutes, everyone was dead, while Müller says[21] that it usually took more than ten minutes before

---

17 *Eyewitness Auschwitz*, Stein and Day, 1979, pp. 121–122.
18 *Op. cit.*, p. 51.
19 *Op. cit.*, p. 81.
20 *Op. cit.*, p. 122.
21 *Op. cit.*, p. 116.

everybody was dead. The Vrba–Wetzler summary says the furnace of the crematoria had nine chambers, each with four openings, while Müller says[22] that one of the larger crematoria had only five ovens, each with only three combustion chambers. The Vrba–Wetzler summary says the bodies were "completely burnt after 1 ½ hours," while Müller says[23] that corpses went into each oven "at intervals of twenty minutes." The Vrba–Wetzler summary calculated that each crematorium could burn 1,500 bodies daily, while Müller says of one of the larger crematoria[24] that "Its fifteen ovens, working non-stop, could cremate more than 3,000 corpses daily."

Clearly, the "facts" about Auschwitz are rather malleable, somewhat like Silly Putty. But despite the fact that, on the crucial matter of the crematoria, most of the details of the Vrba–Wetzler "report" are contradicted by none other than Filip Müller, Vrba and Wetzlers' source of information about the crematoria, the official Churchill biographer calls the "report" of Vrba and Wetzler "remarkably accurate in its details," demonstrating, thereby, his own remarkable will-to-believe.

In his introduction, Gilbert tells the reader that he has "set out the barest facts of the principal deportations, murders and gassings as they happened...." To give one example out of many, Gilbert asserts (p. 169) that "On December 20 [1943] ... a train-load of 849 Jews reached Auschwitz from Paris; more than five hundred were taken away to be gassed." Gilbert makes this

---

22 *Op. cit.*, p. 59.
23 *Op. cit.*, p. 17.
24 *Op. cit.*, p. 59.

sort of assertion again and again throughout the book. Apparently, his source for the "the barest facts" (at least regarding Auschwitz) is Danuta Czech. In a footnote on page 264, he says that "The principal features of the Vrba–Wetzler report, the arrival of deportation trains at Auschwitz between March 1942 and April 1944, the gassing of the majority of the deportees, and the numbers gassed, are fully borne out by the facts and figures in Danuta Czech's, 'Kalendarium der Ereignisse im Konzentrationslager Auschwitz-Birkenau,' published in *Hefte von Auschwitz*...."

But how reliable are Danuta Czech's "facts and figures"? One indication of their reliability is given in this passage from Pierre Vidal-Naquet's "A Paper Eichmann?" in the April 1981 issue of *democracy*:

> [Robert] Faurisson has triumphantly published a photograph of Simone Veil, the current president of the European Parliament, who, although she was reported to be gassed, is alive and well. The mechanism of this mistake is extremely simple, and the information that Faurisson gives ... makes it easy to understand. According to the Polish historian Danuta Czech, the original camp calendar for April 1944 establishes the fact that convoy number 71, which came from Drancy, near Paris, on April 16 was handled in the following manner: 165 men were registered, and the rest of the convoy were gassed (*Hefte von Auschwitz* no. 7, p. 88). The camp

archives, which were incomplete, no longer included the names of women who had been registered. This mistake was corrected by Serge Klarsfeld, in his [*Le*] *Memorial* [*de la deportation des juifs de France*]: "The Auschwitz calendar gives no names of women who were selected [for labor], but this is misleading, since 70 women survivors of this convoy were counted in 1945. There were also 35 male survivors."[25]

Was Danuta Czech's "mistake" about Convoy 71 from France just a fluke? That it was not is suggested by the one case in which I have been able to compare Czech's "facts and figures," as parroted by Gilbert, with the testimony of a survivor of the convoy in question. According to Gilbert (p. 210),

> On May 21 [1944] the railway sidings, gas chambers and crematoria at Birkenau were more active than they had ever been before. For on that day three trains arrived from Hungary, two from Holland, and one from Belgium.... From the three Hungarian trains, only eleven men and six women were sent to the barracks, and more than 12,000 gassed. This was the largest number to be gassed in a single day in the history of Auschwitz up to that moment. But it was a number that was

---

25 Pierre Vidal-Naquet, "A Paper Eichman," *democracy*, April 1981, p. 83.

now to be repeated day after day.

But, praise Yahweh, who should have been on one of the trains that arrived at Auschwitz from Hungary on 21 May 1944? None other than our litigious old friend, Mel Mermelstein![26] And according to Mermelstein's account of his arrival at Auschwitz, "hundreds of men"[27] from the train he arrived in, including himself, his father, his brother, and four acquaintances named Lajas, Tibi, Bram, and Joey, were selected for labor and sent to the barracks. (He says nothing about how many women were selected for labor, since, according to his account, the men and women were separated before the selections for labor were made.) Mel Mermelstein says that hundreds of men were selected for labor from just one of the three Hungarian trains, yet Gilbert says that only eleven men from all three Hungarian trains were sent to the barracks and that all the rest were gassed. A bit of a discrepancy, eh, Mr. Gilbert? Perhaps Pierre Vidal-Naquet will be so kind as to explain how Danuta Czech and, thereby, Martin Gilbert made this "mistake." In any case, in Gilbert's usage, "the barest facts" turn out to mean something other than the naked truth. One might even suspect that Gilbert's "barest facts" are really the baldest fictions.

The question of what was done, or not done, to save the lives of European Jews is a major theme of *Auschwitz and the Allies*. I'm not going to discuss the matter in any detail. However, I want to make one observation.

---

26 See Mermelstein's *By Bread Alone*, Crescent Publications, 1979.
27 *Op. cit.*, p. 115.

Apparently, none of the people who, in Gilbert's account, were so concerned about saving European Jews ever suggested that this end might have been achieved by trying to bring the war to a more rapid conclusion through a negotiated peace, as opposed to prolonging the war by insisting on Germany's "unconditional surrender." Apparently, saving the lives of European Jews was of less importance than destroying Nazi Germany. "Victory at all costs" was the ruling idea, and one of the costs, it so happened, was the death of many European Jews as a direct or indirect consequence of the war.

The Terrible Secret and *Auschwitz and the Allies*, despite all their flaws, are each, to some extent, interesting and informative. Each contains some new material on the various rumors, "reports," etc. that were circulating during World War II about the fate of European Jewry. They also contain some new information about the skepticism with which those rumors, "reports," etc. were received, at least initially, by various parties, including Jews. And there are tidbits of new information about other matters as well. But each of these books, taken as a whole, is a mishmash of information and misinformation, of fact and fiction, of truth and falsehood. Readers of either book would be well advised to take its author's assertions about "the Final Solution" with not just a grain, but more like a pillar, of salt.

Also available from
THE PORTABLE L.A. ROLLINS

The Myth of Natural Rights *Introduction by TGGP*
In one compact work, L.A. Rollins shatters the myth of natural rights while exposing the "bleeding-heart libertarians" that promote it. With careful research and ample documentation, he shows that thinkers like Ayn Rand, Murray Rothbard, Tibor Machan, and Samuel Konkin not only violate reason and logic in their defense of natural rights but also violate the standards they set for themselves.

Lucifer's Lexicon *Introduction by MRDA*
Inspired by Ambrose Bierce's *The Devil's Dictionary*, L.A. Rollins first unsheathed his lexicographer's lance in the pages of marginal political periodicals during the mid-1980s. At a time when Objectivist orthodoxy and Cold War political theater dominated libertarian discourse, Rollins' distinctive brand of irreverent irony stood out. He skewered shibboleths and dethroned dogmas from all quarters, and his trenchant *jeu de mots* made a lasting impression in the minds of many readers.

www.ingramcontent.com/pod-product-compliance
Lightning Source LLC
Chambersburg PA
CBHW071957110526
44592CB00012B/1114